NOSTRADAMVS

THE NEW
MILLENNIUM

NOSTRADAMVS

THE NEW MILLENNIUM

ST REMY DE PROVENCE
THE BIRTHPLACE OF NOSTRADAMUS

JOHN HOGUE

ELEMENT

© Element/HarperCollins*Publishers* 2002
Text © John Hogue 1994, 2001

First published in Great Britain in 1994 by
ELEMENT BOOKS LIMITED

First paperback edition of
Nostradamus: The New Revelations published 1995
Reprinted 1997

This revised and updated edition of
Nostradamus: The New Millennium first published in 2002

Element
An Imprint of HarperCollins*Publishers*
77–85 Fulham Palace Road
Hammersmith, London W6 8JB

Designed and created by
THE BRIDGEWATER BOOK COMPANY

Printed and bound in Hong Kong by Printing Express

British Library Cataloguing in Publication data available

ISBN 0-00-7140924

TO BUD HOGUE
Father and Friend

OTHER BOOKS PUBLISHED BY JOHN HOGUE:

Messiahs: The Visions and Prophecies for the Second Coming
1000 for 2000: Startling Predictions for the New Millennium
The Last Pope: The Decline and Fall of the Church of Rome
Nostradamus: The Complete Prophecies
The Millennium Book of Prophecy
The Nostradamus Datebook: 1990
Nostradamus: The New Revelations
Nostradamus: The New Revelations (Abridge Audio)
Nostradamus and the Millennium

John Hogue can be contacted at www.HogueProphecy.com

CONTENTS

INTRODUCTION

THE NEW MILLENNIUM EDITION

NEW YORK'S WORLD TRADE CENTER MINUTES PRIOR TO ITS COLLAPSE ON 11 SEPTEMBER 2001

In 1993, Nostradamus scholar, John Hogue, wrote this warning: "The sky ignites into flames on the latitude of New York city."[1] Later in 1996 he added: "Twentieth-century interpreters have pinned this [prophecy] on a future attack on New York City... New Jersey is known as the Garden State (Garden of the world). This would make neighboring New York City the new city. The hollow mountains are Nostradamus' description of the two cavernous skyscrapers of the World Trade Center."[2]

6

※

Throughout history there have been gifted individuals with great powers of prophecy. Foremost among these was Michel de Nostradame, better known to us by his Latinized pseudonym, Nostradamus. Nostradamus lived in Southern France over 435 years ago and has gained tremendous fame in the 20th and 21st century.

The life and work of this 16th-century Renaissance man was an enigma even to his contemporaries and has fascinated generations in the centuries since his death. Today, Nostradamus – "Celestial Scientist," seer, doctor of medicine, herbalist and creator of cosmetics and fruit preservatives – still attracts both praise and blame and provokes controversy.

His ten volume history of the future, *Les Propheties* (The Prophecies)[3], containing the greater part of his 1,104 prophecies contained in four-line stanzas called "quatrains," is one of the few works to remain constantly in print for over 400 years. Efforts to unravel its obscure verses have gathered their own momentum and, in these pivotal times as we enter the new millennium, current interest in his predictions has now reached a new level of worldwide interest never before seen.

The skeptics who believed Nostradamus' popularity would not survive a peaceful passing into the new millennium saw their forecast go up in the smoke and debris of the World Trade Center's collapse. The long acknowledged

The sky will burn at forty-five degrees. Fire approaches the great new city. Immediately a huge, scattered flame leaps up when they want verification from the French.

C6 Q97

Garden of the world near the new city, in the path of the hollow mountains: It will be seized and plunged into the boiling cauldron...

C10 Q49

For this third edition of his milestone first book on the prophet Nostradamus, Hogue reveals new revelations uncovered after the terrible events of 11 September, 2001: "...The new city is New York. It is relatively young as cities go and there are no cities exactly on or near latitude 45 that one could call "new" and significant enough to alert Nostradamus' attention. [He describes] the flaming engines of two jet airliners approaching the great new city. They crash into the World Trade Center towers. Huge fireballs of scattered flame erupt while intelligence sources in the US seek verification from their French opposites about rumors of an imminent attack on America... A day before the attack on New York, on 10 September, French intelligence began looking into troubling indications that al-Qaeda operatives were about to attack American assets in Europe, primarily the American Embassy in Paris. French officials did contact their American counterparts who waited for verification too late to stop the fire falling out of the skies over New York with the roar of jet engines...The hollow mountains are "seized and plunged" into the boiling "vat" or *cuve* as Nostradamus describes it in Renaissance French. The *cuve* is a fermenting cauldron wherein Nostradamus, a physician and cosmetic manufacturer by profession, would plunge materials for the mixing of his medicines and cosmetics. The cauldron would emit boiling clouds as objects were seized and thrown into it. I believe his use of *cuve* is a poetic attempt to capture the vision of vast, mountainous buildings being pushed down by gravity. It describes the hollow mountains crumbling and melting away in the ferment of boiling clouds made of their own pulverized debris." [4]

7

[1] *Nostradamus: The New Revelations*, p. 210
[2] *Nostradamus: The Complete Prophecies*, p. 784
[3] also known as *The Centuries*
[4] *Nostradamus and The New Millenium*, Chapter 13

interpretations of his prophecies about a "great new city" made of "hollow mountains" near the "garden" state of the world (New Jersey) under attack from a "terror from the skies" have captured the attention of the whole world. The terrorist attacks on New York, and the subsequent terror in response coming out of the skies of Afghanistan from US missiles and ordinance have led to a Renaissance of renewed debate and dissemination of the prophet's foreboding about what will happen next. Has the destruction of the "hollow mountains" shown the bloody hand of Nostradamus' third and final Antichrist? Is he a Near Eastern, "dark" and angry man of evil, codenamed "Mabus?" Will his hoped-for rapid annihilation in the response from those people of "the land of the evening star," or, as Nostradamus also may call their nation, the "New Land" of "Americh" trigger a 27-year calamitous world war of terrorism, rather than bring peace to the new millennium?

It is time to answer these, and many other prescient questions in a new millennial edition of my bestselling and fully illustrated overview of Nostradamus' most famous past, present and future prophecies. *Nostradamus & the New Millennium* expands and updates my previous two editions of Nostradamus[1], his home, his family and his times. We review his childhood, youth and studies and meet the people who developed his gift for prophecy. Later, we witness how he cured thousands of plague victims with his medical and herbal skills, but was unable to save those closest to him from the pestilence. In despair after the death of his wife and children, he plunged ever deeper into the prophetic arts until, by his mastery

Nostradamus

of their mysteries, he acquired a legendary reputation.

Hailed as a genius by the royal house of France, the nobility and intellectuals of his age, Nostradamus incurred the wrath of the Catholic Inquisition and was feared by the ignorant and superstitious.

When some of Nostradamus' prophecies were fulfiled in his own lifetime he became the fashionable talking point of the European courts. But opinions were divided – for critics he was a heretic, for believers he became "the voice of God." We take a comprehensive look at the character and personality of the man and examine his attitudes to religious belief and philosophy.

Nostradamus died in 1566, exactly in the manner he had predicted. We trace the stories of his death and of the macabre exhumation of his body some 225 years later, before focusing on his uncannily accurate predictions for the centuries after his death. In this progress through his future and our past, we examine the sections of *Les Propheties* concerning Henry of Navarre, the French Revolution, Napoleon, Hitler, Hiroshima, the Kennedy assassinations, conquest of the moon, the Challenger Space Shuttle disaster and the Gulf Wars. We also see how Nostradamus foresaw the Chernobyl nuclear disaster as the precursor of the fall of communism. We look at Nostradamus' visions of a future that is also our own, a future far beyond the 21st century.

However, *Nostradamus & the New Millennium* focuses on our own time – the latter-days of mankind's most inspiring and horrifying century from which will be born the new millennium's future potentials of terror and hope. Nostradamus devoted much energy

8
✳

---

[1] *Nostradamus & the Millennium*, John Hogue, Doubleday/Dolphin, 1987 and *Nostradamus: The New Revelations*, Element/Thorsons, 1994. The previous editions are translated into nine languages with over a million in print.

to forecasting events set around the important axis of time between an old and new era. He has not laid down his pen after seeing the events leading up to the year 2000. His history of the future continues for at least another 1,797 years. It is a future of travails and transcendence. It is a future chronicle of the unprecedented challenges humanity will face in the first half of the 21st century. By the 2020s the sustainability of civilization itself may be in the balance. His auguries reveal a litany of global crises, social strife, disease, a global civil war, 27 years of terrorism, ecological disasters, a worldwide agricultural breakdown, global famine and change on a scale never known before. The prophet also gives us hope that the end of the 20th century will not only be followed by a 30-year postscript that ends history. Rather, they are the darkest hours before the golden dawn of a new age of peace.

9

*

Over four centuries ago, a man in the grip of a psychic trance peered into a brass bowl full of water and may have conjured up the shadowy images of fantastic and mountainous structures, flying machines, and the horrors of their destruction from the sudden eruption of a huge and scattered flame.

HOW TO USE THIS BOOK

NOSTRADAMUS' PROPHECIES are written in an artful, baffling mixture of old French, Provençal and Latin. They are also wilfully obscured in a miasma of puns and wordplay, allusions and elisions, grammatical trickery and cryptic anagrams. The prophecies are contained in four-line verses called quatrains.

Most of the prophecies are contained in the ten volumes called *The Centuries*. Nostradamus began writing these in 1554. He published the first three *Centuries* in 1555. *Centuries* 4 through 7 were published by 1556. Except for a few special editions, the final three *Centuries* were scheduled for publication posthumously. Nostradamus did not confine his predictive muse to these volumes alone. The first three *Centuries* were dedicated to his new-born son César, and when they were published, he introduced them with a *Preface* written for César. Later, when Nostradamus sent a special copy of the final three *Centuries* to the French king, Henry II, he sent with them a long letter, *The Epistle to Henry II,* outlining the future history of the world seen through the prism of his prophetic trance. Some forecasts were also noted in what Nostradamus scholars call the *Presages*, a collection of disparate quatrains scattered through the prophet's almanacs published between 1554–1567.

To make Nostradamus and his prophecies easily accessible to the modern reader, this book presents the predictions in translation. Whenever a quatrain from *The Centuries* is cited, it is referred to by its own quatrain (Q) and Century (C) volume number. Prophecies foretold in the *Preface to César, The Epistle to Henry II* or the *Presages* are accordingly labeled Preface, Epistle or P for Presages. In some cases a date is added to the quatrain reference. This indicates that the year the prediction will be fulfilled is given by rearranging the numbers of the quatrain and Century in some way. Dates with a question mark after them indicate the author's guess at Nostradamus' intended timing.

CHAPTER ONE

DOCTOR
AND DIVINER

Michel de Nostradame (1503-1566), doctor of medicine,
herbalist, astrologer and prophet, at the age of 59.

MICHEL DE NOSTREDAME was born on 14 December, 1503 into a family of recently Christianized Jews in the small town of St Rémy in Provence. His father Jacques, a prosperous notary, provided a comfortable home for his wife and son and was a generous host to his many friends and business associates. Growing up in a lively household full of warmth, conversation and the rich aromas of Provençal cooking, young Michel was introduced early to the delights of good food, local gossip and the stimulating discussion of ideas. These early impressions laid the foundations for his lifelong passions for intellectual gymnastics and for the culinary arts but, as his grandfathers Jean de St Rémy and Pierre de Nostredame first noticed, he also displayed at a very young age a remarkable talent for prophecy. For a time Michel lived with grandfather Jean, where he was taught Greek, Latin and Hebrew. An enthusiastic student, he displayed exceptional mathematical ability and a great love and mastery of astrology, known then as the "celestial science."

EARLY LEARNING

Both Michel's grandfathers were men of learning and were close friends long before the marriage of Jean's daughter Renée to Pierre's son Jacques. Both had served as personal physicians to the royal house of Provence and had travelled extensively throughout southern Europe with the traveling court of King René and his son, the Duke of Calabria and Lorraine.

The two doctors eventually settled in Provence and their two families became linked by marriage. When their grandson Michel was born both men took a great interest in his development and were to exert a profound influence over his life and education. In his teens, Michel was taught daily by both his grandfathers on a wide range of subjects including classical literature, history, medicine, astrology and herbal folk medicine. The boy was also introduced to "forbidden" arts and sciences such as the Jewish Kabbalah[1] and the enigmatic discipline of alchemy.

After grandfather Jean's death Michel returned home to live with his parents and brothers but his education continued under the supervision of his grandfather Pierre.

At the age of 14 Michel was sent to study in the city of Avignon, a great center of Renaissance learning and the capital of the papal enclave in Provence. Here he was taught philosophy, grammar and rhetoric by Catholic priests but, in his free time, he studied the occult and astrological books in Avignon's renowned papal library, earning from his fellow students the nickname "little astrologer" because of his devotion to the study of the celestial sciences.

When Michel's parents back in St Rémy heard about his open defense of astrology and the astrologer Copernicus they were alarmed, afraid that Michel's outspokenness and his ex-Jewish family background might draw him to the attention of either Protestants or Catholics, between whom there was growing religious tension. He returned to St Rémy to be greeted with a stern lecture from his grandfather on the virtues of holding his tongue.

In the 15th and 16th centuries religious feeling against Jews was strong. Devout Christians condemned them as Christ-murderers and throughout Europe, especially in Spain, they were persecuted and killed. Many Jews, from Spain and from other ghettos throughout Europe, flocked to Provence to find sanctuary. But in 1501 when Charles of Maine, heir to the Provençal throne, died, the region was acquired by France and the new French king, Louis XII, summarily ordered that all Jews should be baptized as Christians or suffer banishment.

Nostradamus' family were baptized and, by the time he was born, were accepted in St Rémy as model Christians although, in private, they followed the Jewish faith and preserved their religious and cultural traditions.

With this backgound of secrecy and persecution Jacques de Nostredame was alarmed at his son's desire to become an astrologer. Knowing that astrologers were generally more accepted if they were also accredited physicians, Michel's grandfather suggested a career in medicine and, in 1522, Michel enrolled as a medical student at the University of Montpellier.

The young student, already remarkably well educated by his learned grandfathers, quickly became dissatisfied with the ignorance and dogma of his professors. With medical science still in the Dark Ages, Michel's observations about cleanliness and the potential hazards of bleeding and physicking patients fell on deaf ears.

For three years Nostradamus endured Montpellier, resolved to gather what valuable knowledge he could. In 1525 he successfully passed the oral and written examinations for

---

[1] Jewish Kabbalah or Cabala, a mystical element of Judaism which sought to reveal hidden symbolic meanings in every word and letter of the Hebrew bible.

his baccalaureate degree but, once in posses-
sion of his medical licence, he determined to
leave the town. In the countryside, away from
the watchful eyes of his professors, he would
be able to test and develop his own methods.
With his astrolabe, and medical and astrological books, Nostradamus took to the road to
follow the plague.

Bubonic plague[1], in a form popularly
known as "Le Charbon" for the ugly black

*As waves of pestilence swept through
16th-century France, physicians were
powerless to cure their stricken
patients. Ignorant, superstitious and
in terror of falling victim to the
plague, doctors visited afflicted
households clad in leather "armor,"
said to ward off the invisible arrows
of plague demons. Their eyes were
protected by goggles, ears and nostrils
stuffed with sponge to keep out "evil
humors," and their mouths filled with
raw garlic to protect against the
plague's invisible armies. The
ludicrous leather suit shown left,
worn by plague doctors in the town of
Lyons, even offers complete head
protection, in the form of a macabre
mask embellished with crystal eyes
and a long nose soaked with perfume.
At the University of Montpellier the
young student Nostradamus quickly
became disillusioned with his medical
colleagues and had to defend his
unique, advanced medical
understanding against their
ignorance, superstition and fear.*

13

✳

A PLAGUE DOCTOR IN HIS PROTECTIVE LEATHER "ARMOR."

[1] Bubonic plague. Severe infectious fever transmitted by rat fleas and characterized by painful swellings (buboes) and dark patches caused by
bleeding in the skin. The dark patches gave the disease its nicknames: Black Death, Charbon etc. Waves of plague swept over Europe between
1349 and 1665, killing almost half the population.

BUBONIC PESTILENCE RAVAGES EUROPE

pustules it inflicted on its victims, was the curse of 16th-century France. Little medical help was available to stricken households until the arrival of Nostradamus - a serious intelligent young man of just under medium height with a dusky beard, rosy cheeks and confident, fearless gray eyes.

This young doctor worked tirelessly among the sick with a new approach to the disease; instead of bleeding, he prescribed fresh, unpolluted water and air, and administered herbal cures. In Narbonne, Carcassonne (where he became personal physician to Bishop Amenien de Fays), in Toulouse and Bordeaux, his healing skills saved thousands from certain death.

LEFT *Saint Charles Borromeo administers communion to dying victims of the plague.*

NOSTRADAMUS' REMEDIES

✳

IT MAY have been through his visions of the future that Nostradamus understood about the importance of sanitation and the existence of germs. Louis Pasteur, the great 19th-century medical pioneer of microbiology and vaccination, is named in Nostradamus' writings four centuries before his birth.

Contemporary reports on how Nostradamus worked with plague victims in the city of Aix give us a good outline of his strategy for fighting against "Le Charbon."

First, he would have all the corpses removed and the streets thoroughly cleaned. Before sunrise he could be found in the fields surrounding the town, overseeing the harvest of rose petals. These would be carried back to his makeshift pharmacy where they would be dried and crushed into a fine powder, then made into rose pills.

ROSE-PILLS
✳ *Sawdust from green cyprus - 1 oz.*
✳ *Iris of Florence - 6 oz.*
✳ *Cloves - 3 oz.*
✳ *Odorated calamus - 3 drams*
✳ *Lign-aloes - 6 drams*

The rose petal powder was mixed with the ingredients above. This odoriferous mixture was shaped into lozenges which Nostradamus called "rose pills." His patients were told to keep these pills under their tongues at all times without swallowing them. Uncontaminated water, clean bedding, and fresh air helped most of his patients to respond. Psychologically speaking it cannot be denied that Nostradamus' legendary health and fearlessness when facing disease, may have done more to cure his patients than the rose pills themselves.

15
✳

PROPHET
AND POLYMATH

Nostradamus is best known now for his prophetic gifts but he was much more than a successful clairvoyant. A famous doctor who had cured whole cities of the plague, he was also a consummate gourmet and creator of fruit preservatives.

A master astrologer, Nostradamus was avidly sought out by Europe's wealthy and noble citizens to draw up their horoscopes, and by their wives for his advice on cosmetics. He was also a noted translator of classics into French and wrote a comprehensive book called *Trakte des Fardemens* on the doctors and pharmacists he met on his travels in southern Europe. When traveling he often stayed with doctors and pharmacists he respected, many of them also from ex-Jewish families, by day working with them to cure the sick, by night studying the occult under their guidance. These men participated in an underground network of alchemists and Kabbalists who sought answers to mysteries beyond the certainties preached by mainstream Christianity.

In 1529 Nostradamus returned to Montpellier to take his doctorate degree. His oral examination, held in the university's great hall before the entire faculty, attracted a large crowd, drawn by news of his healing powers. Expertly countering arguments against his unorthodox practices and citing his successes in his defense, the young Nostradamus gave an impressive performance and was awarded the cap and ring of a doctor of medicine and a place in the faculty of Montpellier. For three years he was a professor at the university, until restrictions imposed on his liberal departures from accepted text resolved him once more to take to the road.

After revisiting the cities he had saved from the plague, Nostradamus set up a permanent practice in Toulouse where, in 1534, he received an invitation from the great scholar and philosopher Julius-César Scaliger[1] to visit

Agen. Scaliger's reputation was second only to that of Erasmus and Nostradamus delighted in pitting his wits against the famous scholar's sharp mind.

Scholar and doctor became fast friends and Nostradamus settled in Agen, where his flourishing medical practice and respected position quickly made him the town's most eligible bachelor. He married a young woman of great charm and beauty who bore him two children and, for the next three years, had a loving happy home and, at the house of his friend Scaliger, enjoyed the company of some of Europe's greatest scholars.

When plague struck Agen in 1537 Nostradamus confidently sprang into action against his old enemy. But, despite his success in curing his fellow citizens, he was powerless to prevent his own family falling victim to "Le Charbon." When the telltale black boils appeared on the burning faces of his wife and children all his knowledge and skill could not cure them.

Once the townspeople of Agen learned of Nostradamus' failure to save his own family his reputation as a doctor was destroyed. His wife's family took legal action against him when he refused to return her dowry and Scaliger, whom he thought his closest ally, provoked a bitter quarrel which shattered the friendship completely.

But fate had not finished with the grief-stricken doctor. More trouble loomed in the shape of a chance remark he had made three years before to a workman casting a bronze statue of the Virgin Mary - he had joked that the workman was "casting demons." With the doctor's reputation now in ruins, the workman seized his chance for revenge and alerted the Church authorities to Nostradamus' long-forgotten comment. Called to defend himself on a charge of heresy, Nostradamus explained that his comment had been meant only as a light-

---

[1] Julius-César Scaliger (1484-1558). Italian born doctor of medicine who became a French citizen in 1528 and settled in Agen. He wrote learned books on Latin grammar, philosophy and medicine.

THE INQUISITION

hearted description of mediocre workmanship. Unconvinced, the Church authorities ordered him to stand trial before the terrifying Inquisitors at Toulouse.

Nostradamus escaped from Agen under cover of darkness, heading for Italy. For the next six years he wandered through Europe on a journey of self-discovery, avoiding the Church Inquisitors and trying to piece together the fragments of his ruined life. It was during these wanderings that his prophetic powers awakened.

Nostradamus showed excellent judgment in fleeing Agen to escape the clutches of the Inquisition. Those suspected of witchcraft were mercilessly tortured to extract their confessions and death by burning awaited those convicted.

A FUTURE POPE

A GROUP of Franciscan monks traveling one day along a muddy road near the Italian town of Ancona suddenly saw the solitary doctor walking towards them. As they approached he stood aside to let them pass but, on seeing Brother Felice Peretti, he immediately bowed, then knelt in the mud before him. The friars, knowing that Peretti had previously been a swineherd and of lowly birth, were puzzled by this homage and asked Nostradamus to explain. He replied: "I must yield myself and bend a knee before his Holiness."

The friars were highly amused at the explanation but, 40 years after this chance meeting, Brother Peretti became Pope Sixtus V, 19 years after the death of Nostradamus.

Torrential rains in Provence in the year 1544 heralded one of the century's worst periods of pestilence. For several years hysteria and death stalked most of southern France and, when Nostradamus arrived in the Provençal capital of Aix, the town was a living hell. Large areas lay abandoned to the dead and the air was laden with the stench of corpses and wails of grief. The town's leaders, powerless to help their fellow citizens, were hopeless and broken men; the doctors had either died or fled in fear, unwittingly spreading the contagion to other towns.

For the next 270 days Nostradamus worked day and night, administering hundreds of rose pills and exhorting his patients to follow his proven strategies for fighting the horrors of the plague.

Once again he triumphed and the city parliament showed their gratitude by giving him a pension for life. The grateful citizens of Aix showered him with gifts, many of which he distributed to the families of those he had not been able to save.

After Aix, Nostradamus was called by the city fathers to help the plague-stricken citizens of Salon. From there he was summoned urgently to Lyons where it is claimed he eradicated a whooping cough epidemic through mass prescriptions filled by the pharmacist René Hepiliervard.

In 1547, ten years after the death of his wife and children, Nostradamus settled in Salon. Now 45 years of age he longed once more for the love and stability of family life. He married Anne Posart Gemelle, a rich widow, and took up residence in a fine house in the rue de la Poissonerie in the Farrieroux quarter of the city.

After many long years of wandering Nostradamus once more had a secure outer world. In Salon's agreeable climate his professional life was more relaxed and he was able to set up a highly successful cosmetic business. At the top of the house in the rue de la Poissonerie he had a floor remodelled into a private study and there he installed his treasured collection of forbidden magical devices - astrolabes, divining rods, magic mirrors, and a brass bowl and tripod designed after that used by the classical oracle Branchus.

Widely respected as one of Salon's chief citizens and most devout Catholics, Nostradamus was zealous in his fasts and prayers and generous to the poor. But this reputation began to be called into question when the townspeople noticed the light burning in Nostradamus' upstairs study throughout the night. Speculation grew at what the doctor could be up to in the dead of night while good Christians slept, and in ignorance and fear the people of Salon began to shun him.

If they could have seen behind the heavy study window the worthy citizens of Salon would have seen Nostradamus consulting his ephemeris, plotting the night's course on a horoscope. If the aspects were auspicious, they would have seen him sitting on a brass tripod set over a brass bowl filled with steaming water and pungent herbs. Staring into a thin candle flame, he would empty his mind and slip into a trance. In this ecstatic state he saw visions projected in the rising mist before the candle light; the strongest images were always of impending religious war in France, sparked off by a shattered lance piercing the golden visor of the French king ...

Should Nostradamus share this vision with his countrymen and risk persecution for it? His lengthy struggle with this dilemma resulted in the publication of his first almanac of prophecies in 1550. Immediately acclaimed, the almanac owed its popularity primarily to the section of 12 four-line poems called "quatrains," each poem giving a general prophecy for a month of the coming year. The success of this first almanac encouraged Nostradamus to continue and he produced an almanac every year for the rest of his life.

Visitors came from all over France to seek counsel from the now famous prophet, among them a young man called Jean-Aymes de Chavigny who joined Nostradamus' household as secretary and disciple. He had abandoned a

UN-KOSHER WAGERS

NOSTRADAMUS once stayed at the château of Lord de Florinville where, on a stroll with his host around the grounds, the conversation turned to prophecy. Florinville wanted to put the prophet's powers to the test. They had stopped before a corral containing two suckling pigs, one black, one white. When Florinville asked Nostradamus which pig would provide dinner that night, he replied without hesitation, "We will eat the black pig, but a wolf will eat the white."

Florinville secretly ordered his cook to slaughter the white pig. The cook dressed the pig for the spit and left the kitchen on some errand, forgetting to close the door. On his return, he found Florinville's pet wolf cub happily devouring the white pig. The horrified man shooed it away and ran to the corral to fetch the black pig.

At dinner that night all mouths watered as the cook set the roasted pig before Lord Florinville who smiled at Nostradamus across the table.

"We are not eating the black pig as you have predicted. And no wolf will touch it here."

Nostradamus was so adamant that this was the black pig that Lord Florinville eventually summoned the cook. Florinville was stunned, and his guests entertained, when the cook admitted everything before the penetrating eyes of Nostradamus.

promising career in politics and law to study judicial astrology and prophecy with his new master and was destined to become editor of Nostradamus' prophecies and one of his chief biographers and defenders.

It was to Chavigny that Nostradamus first revealed his idea for a book of prophecy that would predict the future of mankind until the end of time. The book, to be called *The Centuries*, would be set in 10 volumes, each containing 100 quatrains; the completed work would offer 1,000 predictions.

Work on *The Centuries* began on the night of Good Friday, 1554 and Chavigny records how, after each night's work, his master descended from the study with eyes and voice still glowing from a prophetic trance. Century 1 through part of 4 were published in Lyons in 1555; the rest of Century 4 through 7 appeared later that year. *The Centuries* were received enthusiastically by the upper classes and the nobility, a readership already well established by the almanacs.

Not all reaction to *The Centuries* was so favourable, however. The quatrains, written in a medley of French, Provençal, Greek, Latin, and Italian, contained riddles and epigrams of bewildering complexity. To ignorant peasants Nostradamus was a creature of the devil, his dark cryptic verses hellish babble; from philosophers he drew praise and curses, and poets were perplexed by the meaning of his wild crabbed verses.

But for high society and the Parisian court of Queen Catherine de Medici, Nostradamus was a genius and his greatest admirer was the queen herself. Queen Catherine, a ruthless and ambitious head of state, had to appear in public as a devout Catholic. In private, however, she practiced pagan religious rites, consulting her gods beyond the magic mirror and using forbidden arts to help her look into the future and plot her political intrigues.

But at the time of Nostradamus' publication of *The Centuries*, Catherine was troubled by signs and portents which threatened her husband, King Henry II. If they were right, the future fortunes of their four sons and three daughters would also be in danger. Like the great Medicis before her, Catherine was driven by an ambitious plan to rule Europe through marrying her children into the most powerful royal families.

When she read *The Centuries* the queen was convinced, as were her courtiers, that the older lion mentioned in Quatrain 35 Century 1 was King Henry II. When she showed her husband the quatrain, Henry, who did not share Catherine's preoccupation with the occult, shivered. Nostradamus' words mirrored exactly a prophecy made by the court astrologer Luc Gauric some months before. In both prophecies the king was warned not to participate in any tournament or ritualized combat during his 41st year because the stars predicted he would suffer a dangerous head wound which, left unheeded, would result in blindness and death. The fearful Henry immediately summoned Nostradamus from Salon to explain his prophecy.

Nostradamus accomplished the harrowing eight week journey to Paris in half the usual time thanks to the fact that the queen had personally arranged for fresh horses from the royal post to be waiting for him at each stop. Arriving late on 15 August 1556 he was escorted early the next morning by the Grand Constable of France, Anne de Montmorency, to an urgent meeting with the king and queen at their country residence in Saint-Germain-en-Laye, just outside Paris.

The entire French court had assembled to see Nostradamus arrive; he was led to the royal apartments through a pressing throng of elaborately dressed nobles and ladies, assailed from all sides by questions and the scented aroma of strong perfumes. Nostradamus was polite but maintained his silence.

The queen received him excitedly but Henry showed little interest and left the chamber once Nostradamus had diplomatically explained Quatrain 35 of Century 1 to his satisfaction. Catherine and the prophet then spent several hours in deep conversation, finally discussing astrology and prophecy. Nostradamus made a deep and lasting impression on the ambitious queen.

She arranged for Nostradamus to lodge in Paris at the magnificent palace of the Archbishop of Sens and the king sent him a velvet purse of 100 crowns, plus 30 more from Queen Catherine. Nostradamus was angered by what he considered a paltry reward since the trip to Paris alone had cost him 100 crowns, but his financial fortunes soon recovered when numbers of courtiers began to visit him, all willing to pay for his specialist advice and horoscopes.

THE VISIONARY AND THE VALOIS

In August 1556 Nostradamus was summoned to a private audience with Henry II of France and his queen Catherine de Medici at their country residence near Paris. Nothing was recorded of the interview, but Nostradamus may have predicted two destinies for the king and for the Valois royal line[1], as we will see here and in Chapter Three. Either Henry would become a second Charlemagne, unifying the divided French Catholics and Huguenots in a new French empire, or he would die from wounds sustained in a jousting accident, throwing the burden of kingship on his young sons. The latter course was fulfilled, bringing about the extinction of the House of Valois in a legacy of treachery and religious war.

CATHERINE DE MEDICI (1519-1589)

21
✳

HENRY II OF FRANCE (1519-1559)

---

[1] Valois. Family name of the dynasty of French kings that ended with the death of Henry III in 1589.

NOSTRADAMUS AND THE LOST DOG

During Nostradamus' stay at the archbishop's palace his rest was disturbed one night by a loud knocking at the door. A young page of the eminent Beauveau family had been vainly searching the nearby streets for a lost dog. This was not just any dog, however, but his lord's prized hunting dog and, in desperation, the boy sought the prophet's help.

"What troubles you, king's page?" exclaimed an angry voice behind the door. "You are making a lot of noise over a lost dog. Go along the road of Orléans. There you will find the dog led on a leash."

The boy sped to the road of Orléans and there, just as predicted, he found the dog being led back to Paris by a servant on a leash. Once this story spread through Paris the prophet's reputation rose to legendary proportions.

When Nostradamus had recovered from his attack of gout Queen Catherine sent him to the royal château of Blois, where he met her seven children and was asked to draw up their horoscopes. Apparently, the Queen was satisfied with his prediction that all her sons would become kings but for Nostradamus this must have been a difficult interview since he had already written prophecies foretelling a tragic fate for each royal child.

On his return to Paris Nostradamus was greeted by a waiting visitor whom he describes as a very honest, kind woman of noble birth. She warned him that the Justices of Paris wished to interrogate him about his magical secrets; sensing the Inquisition behind this sinister development Nostradamus determined to return to the safety of Salon with all speed.

On his return he found himself a hero in Salon and his fame had spread throughout the country. Soon he was receiving visits from members of the most affluent and influential

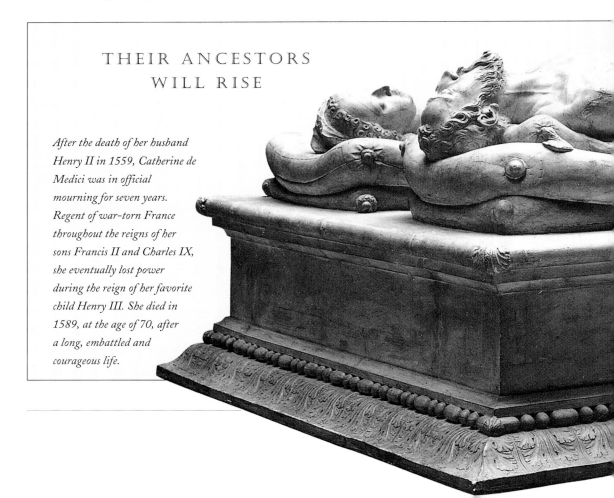

THEIR ANCESTORS WILL RISE

After the death of her husband Henry II in 1559, Catherine de Medici was in official mourning for seven years. Regent of war-torn France throughout the reigns of her sons Francis II and Charles IX, she eventually lost power during the reign of her favorite child Henry III. She died in 1589, at the age of 70, after a long, embattled and courageous life.

The coffin is put in a vault of iron
Where seven children of the King are held
Their ancestors will rise from the
depths of hell
Lamenting to see the fruits of their line dead.

C1 Q10

The lady left alone in the realm
Her unique (husband) first
extinguished on the bed of honor:
For seven years she will weep with grief
Then a long life and good fortune for
the kingdom.

C6 Q63

families of France. But his nightly vigils continued and, by the start of 1558, he had completed his work on *The Centuries*.

Although a few copies of the last three *Centuries* were printed in 1558 Nostradamus decided not to publish them widely while he was alive. This was probably due to a sense of foreboding about the king who in 1559 would be in his 41st and, according to the prophecy,

his most perilous year. But at least one copy was sent to the royal couple, with a long dedication letter to Henry II. This "Epistle" is a most ambitious outline of future history, chronicling events from 1557 to possibly beyond the year AD 8000.

TOMB OF HENRY II AND CATHERINE DE MEDICI

✳

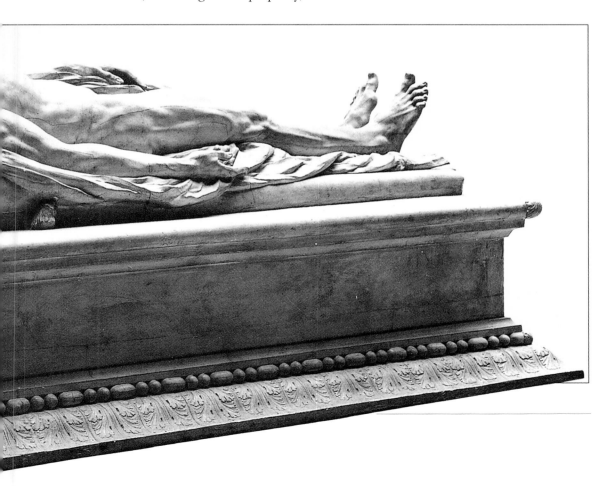

A ROYAL TRAGEDY

HENRY II FATALLY WOUNDED IN 1559 TOURNAMENT

The young lion will overcome the older one
On the field of combat in single battle
He will pierce his eyes through a golden cage
Two wounds made one, then he dies a
cruel death.

C1 Q35

Nostradamus' reputation as one of history's greatest prophets began with a royal tragedy. In 1559, ignoring all warnings against ritual combat, Henry II celebrated the dual marriage of his sister Marguerite to the Duke of Savoy, and his daughter by proxy to King Philip II of Spain, with a three-day tournament. On 28 June, thousands gathered from all over France to watch the jousts on the rue St Antoine outside Paris. Their king, mounted on a splendid charger, was resplendent in full armor and bore a great lion-decorated shield. After each victorious bout he rode fiercely up and down the lane, his golden visor raised to show his face, to receive the homage of the roaring crowd.

But on that happy day Queen Catherine remembered Nostradamus' warning, written three years before.

At sunset on the third day Henry prepared for his final bout against the young captain of the King's Scottish Guards, the formidable Count Montgomery. When the bout ended in a draw Henry called for a second match but his worthy opponent, aware of the prophecy, tried to excuse himself. Henry insisted and, as the second charge began, the crowd fell silent. Suddenly, there was a loud crack of shattered lances and a cry of horror rose from the crowd as a splinter from Montgomery's broken lance pierced the king's golden visor, lodging behind his left eye, blinding him and penetrating deep into the brain. After ten days of suffering in agony King Henry II died and Nostradamus' prophecy was fulfilled.

It is reported that, on the night of the king's death, an angry mob gathered in a Paris suburb, ceremonially burnt an effigy of Nostradamus and called upon the Church Inquisitors to burn him as a heretic.

After Henry's death courtiers began to take *The Centuries* even more seriously, especially Quatrain 39 of Century 10. The first line, they believed, told of Henry's heir, the timid, sickly boy king Francis II, and of his unhappy marriage to the Scottish princess, Mary Stuart[1]. The widow was Catherine de Medici, now queen regent.

As the health of Francis deteriorated, the ambassador to Tuscany wrote to inform the

The first son, a widow, an unfortunate marriage
Without any children.
Two islands plunged into discord:
Before eighteen years, still a minor,
For the other one betrothal happens
while even younger.

C10 Q39

> ✳
> *"Cursed be the divine who predicted so evilly and so well."*
>
> **Comte de Montgomery, commenting on news of Henry II's death**
> ✳

Duke of Florence that Nostradamus had predicted the king's death before the new year. By the 5 December, three days after the letter was posted and just before his 18th birthday, Francis was dead.

At this second fulfillment of prophecy Chantonnay, the Spanish ambassador, was moved to complain in a letter to Philip II, "These catastrophes have struck the court with stupor, together with the warning of Nostradamus, who it would be better to punish than to allow to sell his prophecies, which lead to vain and superstitious beliefs."

In the ensuing years more of Quatrain 39 was revealed. Mary Stuart, "childless," returned to Scotland and became queen. This threw the two island kingdoms (England and Scotland) into "turmoil" over a power struggle between Mary and the "childless" Queen Elizabeth I of England. Charles IX, the heir to the French throne and betrothed at the age of 11 to Elizabeth of Austria, is the "other" mentioned in line four.

The fulfillment of Quatrain 35's prophecy of Henry's death made Nostradamus famous throughout the courts of Europe but a year later admiration turned to suspicion. The

25

✳

---

[1] Mary Stuart (1542-87). Daughter of James V of Scotland and Mary of Guise. Betrothed to Francis II and married him in 1558. On the death of her husband in 1560, she returned to Scotland to take over the throne as Mary, Queen of Scots.

The great queen will see herself conquered...
She will pass over the river pursued by the sword
She will have outraged her faith.

C1 Q86

Mary Stuart had thoroughly outraged her Catholic subjects by her affair with the notorious Bothwell. She escaped prison only to see her army defeated at the Battle of Langside. Mary fled across the Solway River to England to seek refuge in Queen Elizabeth's court. She became the English queen's prisoner and eventually met her death at Fotheringay in 1587. The quatrain numbered "86" may be a near-miss attempt at predicting the year of her beheading.

26

MARY QUEEN OF SCOTS AGED 16-18 YEARS

author of so many tragic predictions was apparently expected to be sad and stern, so visitors to Salon were surprised to find instead the positive, good-tempered doctor. The contradiction engendered suspicion and books condemning Nostradamus as a charlatan and heretic began to appear.

Nostradamus wrote in his own defense that the potential for human cruelty he foresaw in the future made the need for positive living in the present more important than ever. At this time he began writing quatrains for an extra Century 11 and 12, which he never finished. His house was frequently stoned by mobs of young Catholic peasants called Cabans. The threats of violence became so extreme that, for a time, he and his family were forced to seek voluntary imprisonment.

In 1564, the queen regent decided to calm the growing religious unrest in France by making a "Royal Progression" through the realm, taking with her the adolescent King Charles IX, the whole royal family and a reduced court of 800. The two-year tour was to end on the Spanish border where Catherine planned to discuss with her daughter, the Spanish queen, and her advisers, plans to unify Catholics against the Huguenot threat.

A visit to Nostradamus in Salon was to be an important part of the royal progress; the royal misfortunes so accurately predicted by the prophet had only increased Catherine's respect for him and perhaps she hoped that he could foresee solutions to her present troubles.

In October, a crimson-clad King Charles led his entourage into Salon to summon Nostradamus to a private audience with his mother. At the papal mansion Nostradamus entertained his royal patrons for several hours and drew up a horoscope for Catherine's favorite child, Edward of Anjou, reaffirming his promise that the boy would become a king (the infamous Henry III).

THE PEASANT MAID'S STORY

ALTHOUGH many stories about Nostradamus concern grave matters there are also some amusing tales of how he trained his prophetic eye on more everyday events. One summer afternoon as he sat outside his front door enjoying the first cool breeze of a stifling day, his neighbor's pretty young daughter passed by on her way to the woods to gather firewood.

"Good day, Monsieur de Nostredame," she said with a curtsey.

"Good day, little girl," he nodded.

An hour later she returned, balancing the firewood on her shoulder.

"Good day, Monsieur de Nostredame," she said.

"Good day...little woman" came the response.

Before leaving Salon, the young king honored Nostradamus with the title of Counselor and Physician in Ordinary, together with the privileges and salary pertaining to the title. In addition, Nostradamus received gifts of 200 crowns from the king and 100 crowns from the queen regent.

27

A CHILD'S MOLES PROCLAIM
A FUTURE "HERETIC" KING

A TEN YEAR old prince in Queen Catherine de Medici's traveling court intrigued Nostradamus and he wished to read his moles and divine the child's future. The prophet asked permission for such a reading from the prince's tutor but, once the boy realized that he would be required to undress, he stubbornly refused and ran away. On waking the next morning he found the tutor and Nostradamus waiting by his bedside and this time the prophet had the chance to explain the reason for his persistance. Gradually the boy was gently coaxed out from the bedclothes to stand naked on the floor.

With a hand on the boy's head he slowly turned the prince around so that he could study the complete pattern of moles on his body. Then, turning to the tutor, he declared that the boy would grow up to be not only King of Navarre but a great King of France. When news of this prediction spread through the royal camp even his most fervent admirers probably thought Nostradamus was crazy. His prediction meant that the French throne would be occupied by a Huguenot prince - an unthinkable suggestion in the political circumstances.

But in 1572 the boy became King of Navarre and, 25 years after the "crazy" prophecy, he ascended the throne of France in 1589. The new King Henry IV[1] put an end to decades of religious wars, brought wealth and security to the country. He became France's most beloved monarch.

L. Denis Valverane's fanciful rendition of Nostradamus reading the moles of the young Prince Henry of Navarre and predicting that he would become a future king. History records only the prophet and his tutor being present at the actual reading. However word of Nostradamus' radical prediction was well documented. As a grown man the prince did indeed become Henry IV. He often joked about running away from France's greatest Oracle. He admitted to being a mischievous boy and thought his tutor had brought the intense old man with the long white beard to give him a whipping.

PRINCE HENRY OF NAVARRE

[1] Henry IV (1553-1610). King of Navarre and France, son of Antoine de Bourbon and Jeanne d'Albret, a Calvinist. He married Margaret of Valois. Henry IV converted to Catholicism but in 1598 signed the treaty of Nantes which guaranteed Protestants the right to practise their religion without persecution.

NOSTRADAMUS THE SCHOLAR　　　NOSTRADAMUS IN HIS THIRTIES　　　NOSTRADAMUS THE ASTROLOGER

This royal acclaim marked the peak of Nostradamus' prophetic career. A year and eight months later he visited the embassy at Arles as the king's representative from Salon but on his return in June 1556 suffered a severe attack of gout. On 17 June, sensing that death was near, he made a last will and testament. His fortune, a substantial 3,444 crowns, was to be distributed among his wife Anne, who was pregnant at the time of his death, his three sons and three daughters. The will made contingencies for the possibility of Anne giving birth to twins and also made arrangements for the death of any daughter before marriage.

For his last days Nostradamus moved to his beloved study. His bed was moved there and a special bench built so that he could maneuver his disabled body around the room. His gout deteriorated into dropsy and on 1 July Father Vidal, the Superior of Salon's Franciscan monastery, was called to hear his last confession and perform the final rites.

According to contemporary witnesses Nostradamus stayed alert and calm to the end, despite his acute pain. He wished to spend his last night alone and when his secretary Chavigny rose from the bedside and asked hopefully, "Until tomorrow, Master?"

Nostradamus replied, "You will not find me alive by sunrise."

The final prophecy in Nostradamus' last almanac foretells his own death:

"On his return from the Embassy, the King's gift put in place. He will do nothing more. He will be gone to God. Close relatives, friends, brothers by blood (will find him) completely dead near the bed and the bench."

The next morning at sunrise Chavigny led family and friends to the top floor study. They found Nostradamus's body lying on the floor between his bed and the makeshift bench.

Anne carried out her husband's final request that his coffin should be enclosed, standing upright, within a wall inside the Church of the Cordeliers of Salon. On his tomb these words were inscribed in Latin:

"Here rest the bones of the illustrious Michel Nostradamus, alone of all mortals, judged worthy to record with his near divine pen, under the influence of the stars, the future events of the entire world. He lived sixty-two years, six months and seventeen days. He died at Salon in the year 1566. Let not posterity disturb his rest. Anne Posart Gemelle wishes her husband true happiness."

29
✳

CHAPTER TWO

THE SEER
AND THE STARS

THE ALCHEMIST IN HIS LABORATORY

WE ALL PERCEIVE the phenome-
nal and metaphysical worlds through
our own judgement, emotions, fears and
hopes. Any gift, therefore, and especially the
gift of "sight," is filtered though our individual
mental and emotional identifications – rather
like water strained through tea leaves.

Nostradamus believed his gift of sight –
his oracle – had a divine source. So it is important for us to understand both his religious
beliefs and the environment which shaped his
early years, in order to appreciate how they
may have colored his vision of the future.

From early childhood Nostradamus' spiritual development was guided by his two
grandfathers. They steered his interest towards
the occult but also taught him Greek and
introduced him to the work of early Greek
philosophers. It was in his reading of Plato's
Symposium that Nostradamus first encountered
the teachings of Socrates, considered to be the
father of Western mystical thought.

Socrates[1] taught that life should be experienced at first hand, that the individual should be a participant, not an observer. Understanding was not to be gained by living vicariously through other men's learning nor in the intellectual life only. The seeker after truth must strive to experience and achieve union with absolute love, first by understanding the beauty of the body, then the beauty of the soul and finally, the ideal but impersonal beauty of the universe around and within him.

In his philosophical studies Nostradamus was also introduced to the work of Plotinus who believed that the seeker's path was a "flight from the alone to the alone," and to the amoral, or transmoral, view of life taught by the Greek mystic Heraclitus. In Heraclitus' philosophy, the cycles of existence have no beginning and no end and the universe functions on a hidden harmony of opposites in which the truth, or God, is a play of darkness and light, war and peace, hunger and satiety.

From his grandfathers and from his philosophy studies Nostradamus came to an understanding of man as an holistic play of body, mind and soul, falling in and out of harmony with himself and nature.

The repeated use of occult language of Nostradamus' prophecies indicate that he was strongly attracted to Hermetic magic and philosophy. Hermetic mysticism, the oldest mystic tradition in the West, has many parallels with the Eastern school of Tantra and Shivaic Hinduism and its world view is similar to that of Heraclitus who maintained that, "As above so below, all is divine."

During his long travels Nostradamus studied many occult disciplines and was particularly interested in the Jewish Kabbalah. This teaches that although Adam and Eve, representing mankind, had fallen from union with God into a state of amnesia, reunion was possible through a study of the Tree of Life, a mystic path with ten levels of consciousness (similar to the eastern kundalini chakras). All Kabbalists must understand this mystic path if they are to return to the crown of God.

Nostradamus the mystic guided Nostradamus the physician. He saw medicine and alchemy as a two-edged occult sword which could be used to penetrate the secrets of healing the body and the soul. It is known that he studied *On Nature and the Healing Power of the Universe* by Alberto Magnus (1200-1280), and that he applied the discoveries of the legendary alchemists Paracelsus (Theophrastus Bombastus von Hohenheim, 1493-1541) and Cornelius Agrippa (1486-1535).

Paracelsus believed that a doctor must first heal the soul and that the source of all good cures and evil disease is the mind. Like Paracelsus, Agrippa demonstrated that all man's "conscious" knowledge was useless. He believed people were conditioned from early childhood to believe that they were separate from the power of nature and that an alchemist must be aware of this conditioning before exploring magic techniques which would reconnect him to the creative source of the universe.

Many of Nostradamus' progressive views on hygiene and medicine came from Islamic sources. While in Sicily he made contact with Sufi mystics and read *The Elixir of Blissfulness*, by the great Sufi master, al-Ghazzali in which the mystic says, "On the path of human growth from man to God – from man the potential to man the actual, from possibility to reality – there are seven valleys." It was al-Ghazzali's insight that every seeker of mystical truth must pass through those seven valleys, or seven dark nights of the soul, before reaching to God. The Valleys are: (1) knowledge; (2) repentance; (3) stumbling blocks; (4) tribulations; (5) thunders; (6) the abyss; and finally, (7) the valley of hymns and celebration.

31

❋

---

[1] Socrates (c. BC 469-399). Athenian philosopher declared by the oracle at Delphi to be the wisest man in the world. He wrote no books but his pupil Plato (c. BC 427-347) noted his theories and teaching methods in his *Dialogues*.

Al-Ghazzali's map to the superconscious must have intrigued Nostradamus the Kabbalist. But he may also have been aware of mystical Sufi teachings long before his journey to Sicily. His grandfathers had both been members of King René's progressive traveling court which welcomed mystics of Islam as well as Christianity within its ranks; it is, therefore, possible that Nostradamus had learned about Sufi in his boyhood studies.

The 20th-century Indian mystic, Osho (see p. 240), describes the seven valleys on the path from man to God in his book *The Sufis: The People of the Path, Vol II*: (p.9):

"If you understand rightly what to do with a valley you will be able to go beyond it, and you will attain to a peak – because each valley is surrounded by mountains. If you can pass through the valley, if you don't get entangled in the valley, if you don't get lost in the valley, if you don't become too attached to the valley, if you remain aloof, detached, a witness, and if you keep on remembering that this is not your home, that you are a stranger here, and you go on remembering that the peak has to be reached, and you don't forget the peak – you will reach to the peak... Once you have reached the seventh then there are no more [valleys]. Then man has attained to his being, he is no longer paradoxical. There is no tension, no anguish. This is what those of the East have called Buddhahood; this is what Christians call the state of being a Christ."

The metaphor of seven valleys was to have a strong influence on the way Nostradamus interpreted the future peaks and valleys of human history. In some prophecies he refers to "seven millenniums" or to "the great seventh number, completed," perhaps occult allusions to the seven valleys of future history through which mankind must pass to obtain a millennium of peace. As we will see later, the final seven years of the 20th century are indicated by the prophet as the most important years of tribulation (valleys) and revelation (peaks) humanity will yet experience. The many references to "seven" throughout *The Centuries* and his Epistle can be interpreted as another metaphorical seven valleys we must all cross to obtain the god-head of a new humanity.

Nostradamus believed in God, or a divine godliness, and his approach to belief may best be summed up in the words of his favorite philosopher, Meister Eckhart[1]: "The eye, with which I see God, sees me; my eye and God's eye is one eye, one seeing, one realizing and one love."

In the Preface to his first book of prophecies, written in 1555 and dedicated to his new-born son César, Nostradamus confides his feelings about his predictions.

"Although for a long time I have been making predictions of events which have come to pass, naming the particular locality, I wish to acknowledge that all have been accomplished through divine power and inspiration. Predicted events both joyous and sinister have come to pass with increasing promptness throughout the world. I was willing to hold my peace by reason of the injury, not only of the present, but future time as well, and refrain from writing because if the present kingdoms, sects and religions were to see the future kingdoms, sects and religions to come, and see how diametrically opposed they are to their pet fantasies, they would condemn that which future centuries will know to be true... Later, because of foreseeing the advent of the common people (i.e. modern times), (I) decided to relinquish withholding my tongue and pen from paper by declaring in dark and cryptic sentences the causes of the future changes of mankind, especially those of the greatest import as well as those perceived – which would not upset the illusions (of my readers) – by clouding them in obscure but, above all, prophetic language."

(see p. 240)

---

[1] Meister Eckhart. Johannes Eckhart (c. 1260-1327). German mystic and Dominican monk. His mystic pantheism led to charges of heresy and his writings were condemned by Pope John XXII in 1329.

THE PATH TO ENTRANCEMENT

I sit at night alone in secret study
Resting upon the brass tripod:
A thin flame comes forth from the solitude
making successful
that which should not be believed in vain.

C1 Q1

The divining wand in hand is placed in
the middle of the tripod's brass legs
With water he anoints the hem of his
robe and foot:
Fear! A voice is heard. He trembles in his robes:
Divine splendor. The divine one sits nearby.

C1 Q2

CONSULTING THE ORACLE

The ancient Greek oracle at Delphi was Nostradamus' model for his visionary practices. He too would sit erect upon a brass tripod before a bowl of steaming water and pungent oils.

Nostradamus used many magical techniques to conjure visions and it is known that he was acquainted with a volume called *De Mysteriis Aegyptorum* (concerning the mysteries of Egypt), even if he did not possess a copy of it. This book on classical Chaldean and Assyrian magic was written by Jamblinchus, the 4th-century neo-Platonist of the Byzantium Empire and later included text from *De Daemonibus* (concerning demons), a black magic tract by Michael Psellus[1]. Nostradamus also possessed an ancient family book on the Keys of Solomon and the Kabbalah. This he claimed to have burned, along with the writings of men such as Psellus, perhaps to mislead the Church Inquisitors. He said, "...fearing what use might be made of them, I consigned them to the flames. Fire of unusual brightness shot forth, clearer than that of natural flame, suddenly illuminating the house with a conflagration as bright as lightning." (Preface to César, ibid.)

Nostradamus used a variety of magic arts to induce ecstatic trances. Visions came to him through flame or water gazing, sometimes both together. He also followed the practice of

33

*

---

[1] Michael Psellus. An 11th-century politician and teacher, head of the philosophy faculty at the University of Constantinople (now Istanbul).

Branchus, a Delphic prophetess of ancient Greece, requiring him to sit, spine erect, on a brass tripod, the legs of which were angled at the same degree as the Egyptian pyramids. The upright position, and possibly the use of nutmeg[1], stimulated the mind; the angle of the tripod legs was thought to create a bio-electric force which would sharpen psychic powers.

Or the prophet would stand or sit before a tripod that held a brass bowl filled with steaming water and pungent oils. Between deep inhalations of perfumed vapour he would chant magic incantations:

"I emptied my soul, brain and heart of all care and attained a state of tranquillity and stillness of mind which are prerequisites for predicting by means of the brass tripod." (Epistle to Henry II). The first stages of trance begin: "The prophetic heat approaches...like rays of the sun casting influences on bodies both elementary and non-elementary..." (Preface to César, ibid.)

When the moment is auspicious, Nostradamus dips a laurel branch into the steaming bowl and anoints his foot and hem. By so doing he releases a rush of paranormal energy which propels him into another dimension. In fire and water gazing he then sees what he describes as a " clouded vision of great events" (Epistle). Such visions are achieved by a union with what he calls, "the divine one" which may be God, the collective unconscious, or perhaps his own divine self or oversoul.

Carrying out the elaborate magic rituals apparently helped Nostradamus to overcome his fear before surrendering to the full ecstatic trance, of which he says:

"Although the everlasting God alone knows the eternity of light proceeding from himself, I say frankly to all to whom he wishes to reveal his immense magnitude – infinite and unknowable as it is – after long and meditative inspiration, that it is a hidden thing divinely manifested to the prophet by two means: ...One comes by infusion which clarifies the supernatural light in him who predicts by the stars, making possible divine revelation: the other comes by means of participation with the divine eternity; by which means the prophet can judge what is given to him from his own divine spirit through God the Creator and his natural intuition." (Preface, ibid.)

Sublime essence forever visible to the eye
Come to cloud the conscious mind for
reasons of their own:
Body and forehead together, senses
and the overseeing ego become
invisible,
As the sacred prayers diminish.

C4 Q25

The divine word will give to the essence,
(that which) contains heaven and earth
The hidden goal in the mystic deed:
Body, soul and spirit are all powerful.
All existence is beneath his feet as at the feet
of heaven.

C3 Q2

---

[1] nutmeg. The kernel or the fruit from the nutmeg tree *myristica fragrans*. Grated nutmeg has a very mild hallucinogenic effect when consumed in quantity.

AN ASTROLOGER'S HOROSCOPE

For centuries scholars have studied the stars and planets to understand how they may influence the fates both of mankind and of individuals. For Nostradamus, astrology was fundamental to his life and work; he attributes his healing power to knowing the astrological composition of his medicines and his patients, and was careful to administer cures at times when the aspects of planets and constellations were favorable.

A century before Newton, Nostradamus' calculations show that he had an understanding of the laws of gravity and motion. Nostradamus plotted elliptical orbits for the planets in his horoscopes preceding Kepler's Law[1], as well as Kepler himself who would not be born until two years after the prophet's death. So astonishing are Nostradamus' astrological predictions that perhaps it is time to re-evaluate this ancient "intuitive" science.

35

THE COPERNICAN SYSTEM

Nostradamus was 40 years old when the Polish astronomer Nicolas Copernicus published his revolutionary thesis proving that the sun, not the earth, was the center of the universe. Kepler's theories, accurately foreseen by Nostradamus, were based on the Copernican system.

---

[1] Johannes Kepler (1571-1630). German astronomer and mathematician who devised laws to explain the movements of the planets.

14 December, 1503, 12:03 pm

From Pluto, the Evolutionary Journey of
the Soul Volume I, *1986 by Jeff Green. This
chart is calculated according to the Julian
Calendar system.*

ASTROLOGICAL ASPECTS

CHART A AND B

A Conjunctions denote a magnification of energy and expression of the planets involved. The Sun (☉) and Mercury (☿) are conjunct the midheaven in the Earth sign of Capricorn. These indicate a powerful personality, with a strong interest in intellectual pursuits, who works steadily with patience and discipline to achieve goals. This conjunction is common among great astrologers and men and women of genius. Mercury is one of the three planets in retrograde (℞) – a sign of a deep thinker and a persistent, hard-working pupil who reaps the rewards of his efforts only in later life. All this is directly relevant to Nostradamus, whose rise to the top of his profession was not meteoric but steady and painstaking and who, in his 30s, was forced by circumstances to re-evaluate and rebuild his life. A Mercury retrograde conjunct the Sun enables him to achieve his goals according to his own carefully plotted timescales.

B The three other planets in retrograde, Jupiter (♃) Saturn (♄) and Mars (♂), are all together in a conjunction in the water sign of Cancer. They magnify success or failure through the importance of a positive psycho-logical, physical and intuitive environment. Some of Nostradamus' major problems may have stemmed from his need for security or to win praise from superiors. One contemporary comment on the prophet describes him as "...the most diplomatic man in the world and never says anything to displease anyone..." The conjunction blessed Nostradamus with a happy secure childhood. Experience and wisdom learned from his grandfathers were to shape his whole life (Jupiter-retrograde) and his disciplined scholarship finds its best expression in occult studies (Jupiter-Saturn-retrograde). But for Nostradamus nothing was to come easily and it was not until his 50s that his years of application to the prophetic arts brought him the success he deserved.

C The powerful grand water trine of five planets in Nostradamus' chart reveals clearly his gift for prophecy. This aspect denotes harmony, creativity and expansion – in his case toward intuition and clairvoyance (water element). The Moon (☽) in Scorpio anchors the trine in strong, private emotions which make him defensive when attacked. But the strength of the trine balances this vulnerability, making him a born survivor, able to judge when to stand and fight his critics and when to run, as he did from the Inquisition. The Moon in Scorpio also endows him with his intuitive knowledge and his drive to penetrate the mysteries of paranormal phenomena. The Moon, combined with the retrograde conjunction of Jupiter, Saturn and Mars, provides him with the education, courage, persistence, good humor and love of ritual needed for practicing magic and prophecy and the trine is closed by Uranus (♅) in Pisces - the source of awe and wonder.

Uranus, assisted by the other planets, makes Nostradamus receptive to ecstatic visions and gives him a scientific curiosity in the unconscious mind. Uranus in Pisces makes him fascinated by the study and analysis of the mind and the life-long process of self-discovery. The retrogrades,which could have made him a contented homebody, are opposed by Uranus which inspires his years of wandering to enrich his study of the occult sciences. But, after the shock of losing his first family to the plague and the resulting scandal, this life-long desire to "wander" becomes more and more directed toward finding his inner spiritual truth, his real "home." The outward wandering ceased when Nostradamus settled in Salon and, from then on, the home-making instincts of his Jupiter, Saturn, Mars retrograde/conjunction provides for a happy domestic life by day, while at night in his occult study Uranus guides his "travel" instincts toward the internal search for truth and revelation.

D Two oppositions in Nostradamus' chart indicate difficulty in relationships. Neptune (♆), the ruler of spiritual truth and illusions, is in powerful opposition to retrograde Saturn and Mars, influencing the physical and psychological environments. The oppositions played a role in his rare but volcanic explosions of temper, in his quarrel with Scaliger and, at their worst, gave him a martyr complex. This aspect is common in individuals whose secretive, taciturn nature causes them to be distrusted, as Nostradamus discovered in 1537 when the suspicious townspeople of Agen took the opportunity of the tragic death of his wife and children to accuse and defame him. This aspect is, however, tempered by an optimistic streak given by retrograde Jupiter conjunct Saturn and Mars. The intuitive power of the grand water trine plus retrograde Mercury conjunct the Sun, gives Nostradamus insight into the nature of truth and the ability to learn from his mistakes.

Those of a mystical bent are often compassionate sociopaths. They have the intelligence to recognize what is hypocritical about mainstream society and sufficient courage to live apart from society's socially accepted lies. They live among us, hiding their true occult natures with varying degrees of success. Some, like Nostradamus, die peacefully in their beds, others are persecuted and, in the past, were burned as witches. A balance of this eccentricity with practicality was a potential accessed by Nostradamus for the greater part of his later years. Indeed, the fact that he was not condemned to death as a witch testifies to his success in balancing the energies of his Neptune-Saturn/Mars opposition. In other words, he had the courage to teach openly, giving readings to courtiers and queens, but also the practicality to move quickly out of harm's way, as demonstrated in his swift departures from Agen in 1537 and Paris in 1556, and in his decision not to publish more than a few special editions of the second half of *The Centuries* during his lifetime.

In astrological terms it is easy to understand why Nostradamus was successful in accessing the higher potentials of Neptune in

CHART C AND D

38

CHART E AND F

his chart. A man who could accurately foretell the great moral changes of the future must be deeply meditative. He must be adept in witnessing dispassionately that concepts of decency and virtue, including his own, are destined to be lost in tomorrow's world. A man who can envisage his own death must have the necessary spiritual centeredness to accept both the death of his own ego, and of the egos that, in their own times, were proud of creating and defending monarchies, republics, communisms, and near-countless religious faiths. Such a meditative observer, of himself and the future, must be able to countenance even the fade-out of today's popular political icon, democracy, in the lathe of future possibility.

Nostradamus' life was deeply shaken by a personal apocalypse which cast a painfully bright light on the impermanence of earthly love, marriage and social hypocrisies. When all permanence of the external world, and of the mind and emotions, is dashed, the ordinary man either goes mad, drowns in self destruction or grasps hold of some religious or philosophical comfort to enable him to carry on. A potential mystic responds with a journey inward to find that which never changes.

E. Squares in the horoscope denote difficulty and disharmony in attaining goals and cover areas of friction and tension in Nostradamus' life which required great self-awareness to overcome. Uranus squares Pluto, the ruler of forces beyond the individual and into the collective unconscious mind. This aspect, in an era of social and religious upheaval, affects Nostradamus' whole generation and indicates the contradiction of the times, at once fascinated by and intolerant of, radical ideas and eccentric professions such as prophecy and the occult. Where Nostradamus went against popular belief, as in Montpellier when he was prevented from teaching new medical ideas, he encountered fierce opposition.

F. The conjunction of retrograde Mercury, the Midheaven (MC), and the Sun (☉) are squared his ascendant (ASC) and north and south Earth nodes shine a light on Nostradamus' character in relationships. The ascendant denotes public expression of philosophical ideas, the nodes determine his relationship to social customs and trends. The square reveals a continual struggle with understanding and being understood. Indeed, some of his poetic gibberish may have been as much a personal catharsis as a conscious act to hide prophetic insight in the obscure verse. His peculiar writing style and contradictions may explain how social trends forced him to obscure his prophetic messages, or to play the devout Catholic to appease the Church and avoid persecution. If he was genuinely devout it was upon his own secretive terms. The Aries ascendant helps him tackle problems with decisive, intense energy. It could also trip him up with a hasty egoistic judgment, as was the case in 1534 when a careless jocular remark to a workman later gave his enemies the opportunity to have him summoned before the Inquisition. On the positive side, this square

39

shows that, deep down, Nostradamus was at least subconsciously in love with the uphill struggle to prove himself and that he used his mistakes and failures as challenges in his spiritual growth.

G A sextile gives Nostradamus good potential for mastering planets covered by these aspects. The Moon (☽) sextile Neptune (♆) reveals an individual in touch with both his psychic and practical instincts, able to profit from most of his important decisions. The aspect denotes a sharp mind and a deep and powerful imagination, capable of entering into transcendental states of consciousness achieved through disassociation with the mind and the struggles of daily life.

H Venus (♀) sextile Pluto (♇) acts as a counterpoint to the Uranus/Pluto square, endowing Nostradamus with the ability to accept human frailty with humor and a keen sense of the transcendental power of love. It is the sign of a great healer who recognizes that sicknesses of body and soul have their source

CHART G AND H

in an imbalance of energies. In cases of this "dis-ease" he could instinctively feel, and sometimes express, ways to restore harmony and balance. He explored prophecy as a healer trying, through the medicine of awareness, to "cure" the evils of the future. In other words, his brand of prophecy was a dose of prescient preventative medicine.

CRACKING THE CODE

Four centuries of scholarship have uncovered a
number of Nostradamus' decoding techniques.

ORACULAR OPACITY

To the modern reader most of Nostradamus' predictions seem obscure tangles of syntax and jumbled meaning. Of his known 1,082 quatrains over 800 are little more than augury-babble. They may be just his prophetic mistakes, or perhaps they are nonsense to us because their details concern events in our unknown future. But, in my opinion, many of the incomprehensible quatrains are accurate chronicles of events which might have been, if history had taken a different turn – predictions for a parallel universe, in fact. A good example of this is examined in the following chapter.

ANAGRAMS

Words and phrases are scrambled to construct other words and phrases using the same letters; for example: "rapis" becomes "Paris" or "chyren" is "Henryc," Henry II's Latinized name. Phonetics allow for "V's" to become "U's," or "Y's" to become "I's," "S's" to become "C's" or "I" to be "J."

Nostradamus made his own variations for switching or replacing letters. One or two letters can be dropped, for example: "noir" becomes "roi" – king. Letters can be added: "Hister" becomes "Hitler," "Hadrie" becomes "Henrie," finally Henri of Navarre.

So we might translate the anagrams for a future antichrist emerging from the Middle East thus: "Mabus" – mABUs, where the first "M" and the last "S" are dropped. Spell m-a-b-u-s backwards; then turn any letters around that can represent a new letter once reversed, such as "b" turned to a "d." Thus, "Mabus" spelled backwards is "Sudam." Use the law of replacing one letter and you get "Sadam." Phonetic redundancies allow you to spell it with an extra "d" and it becomes "Saddam" Hussein. "Adaluncatif" – "Cadafi," where the "T" is dropped and the word "Luna" stands for the crescent moon, symbolizing Islam. From this you derive the decoded name "Cadafi Luna" = Qaddafi of the Crescent (Islam).

At this point you might wonder whether perhaps a monkey is as capable of throwing significant light on Nostradamus' anagrams as a mystic, given enough time. One primary "rule" of this word play is to keep that question unanswerable.

NAMES, LOCALITIES

Places appear under their historical or classical names. The current names will appear in parenthesis alongside the text when possible: for example, Aquitaine (France), and Boristhenes (Dnieper River region). Similarly, people can be hidden in wordplay: Cimbrians – an ancient Teutonic tribe – stands for the Germans.

ELLIPSIS

Another classical grammar trick excluding words and phrases which are understood. This is a frequent device and the excluded words would be returned to the text in parenthesis, for example:

...Friends, relatives, brothers of the blood (will find him) completely dead between the bed and the bench.

REVERSE IMAGE WORD PLAY

Reading words in reverse in a mirror is also acceptable. For instance, write out the word "Mabus" and hold it against a mirror. The new spelling looks similar to that of "Saddam" for Saddam Hussein of Iraq.

SYNECDOCHE

A grammatical trick in Greek and Latin to make the part represent the whole. For example: Paris stands for France, Boristhenes for the Ukraine or perhaps even Russia.

THE POLITICS OF ANIMAL NAMES

Countries are described as animals after heraldic or mystical symbols associated with a particular country. For example, "Cock" for France, "Bear" for Russia, "Neptune" for England or "Wolf" for Italy .

NO SEQUENCE OF TIME

The prophecies rarely follow any logical sequence. The events they describe are frequently scrambled out of chronological order, requiring the interpreter to find key phrases and words linking quatrains together.

COMMON NAMES IN UNCOMMON PLACES

Common names can be hidden in normal words and phrases. For example, de Gaulle can stand for "of" or "from Gaulle" or the French leader Charles de Gaulle; Pasteur can mean either a church pastor or, more literally, Louis Pasteur. It all depends on corresponding clues in the quatrain. Even verbs can hide a name. "Abas" meaning to put down, can stand for the future Antichrist, Mabus, or even Abbas, a common Arabic name. In line one of Quatrain 63, Century 3, "abas" could stand as a double pun for "putting down," or figuratively stand for Abu Abbas, the Palestinian terrorist who hijacked the Italian ocean liner Achille Lauro in the mid-1980s.

INSIGNIAS AS PORTENTS

A play on words and phrases identifying people and movements through their insignias, coats of arms or other emblems: The crooked cross – the swastika; swarms of bees – perhaps Napoleon whose family coat of arms featured swarms of bees; the eagle – Napoleon's armies carried eagle standards.

GEOGRAPHIC CURRENTS IN "THE SIGHT" AND THEIR FRENCH CONNECTION

Geographically, the predictions applying to France and its neighbors are clearer than those of distant lands. The farther away the land the more foggy the prediction. When a prediction concerning a far-off country is unusually clear, there is often a French connection. Examples of this will be given later, when we examine the formation of the American republic and the notion that Nostradamus may have forewarned America of a plot to assassinate the Kennedy brothers, because the real assassin was a Frenchman.

Nostradamus used the movements of the stars to plot future history.

PUNCTUATIONAL PORTENTS

Nostradamus' obscurity and disregard for punctuation makes translating his prophecies and letters still harder. I have tried to capture the essence in simple language. My intention in writing this book was to introduce Nostradamus and his remarkable prophecies to the widest possible audience and to avoid the dry, academic approach likely to result from an attempt to cover a thousand of the prophecies. The quatrains and volume "Century" numbers will, therefore, be found alongside each prophecy or quote. For example C1 Q25 signifies Century 1, Quatrain 25. This should enable the reader to check the translations against the original French and other available translations.

INDEXING AS PROPHECY?

In hundreds of cases the quatrain numbers appear to correspond to the predicted events in the quatrains themselves. For instance, a prophecy mentioning the forest of the Ardennes in Luxembourg as an attack route bringing down destruction on an empire is numbered C5 Q45. This forest was used twice as an German attack route, once for the fall of France in 1940 and later for the fall of Hitler's Nazi Empire in 1945! Sometimes, the quatrain indexing also seems to represent specific dates corresponding to the subject of the particular quatrain. A clear example is the famous prophecy describing in detail the attempted escape from France of Louis XVI and his family during the French Revolution. The royal party made their escape from Paris on the night of 20 June, 1791. The quatrain is numbered C9 Q20.

THE RULES OF AN OCCULT GAME

Is the quatrain indexing described on page 43 a coincidence or a code? If it is an attempt by the prophet to date his quatrains it is doubtful that a survivalist and magician of his stature would create a comprehensive number code that covered all of his quatrains. Contemporary friends and dangerous enemies were trying to decode his mysteries as soon as they came off the presses. Nostradamus was nearly burned at the stake by the Inquisition even without a code broken.

Contrary to the claims of many imaginative dilettantes and a few sincere theorists, no one has yet found the key to any single all-encompassing code that unlocks his secrets. After 27 years of study I conclude that a magician of his intelligence would not be so stupid as to forge a weak link in the chain of his future legacy. At best there may be random devices, as his laws of anagram and use of Latin devices attest; but, as we will see, even unlocking a random code brings more questions and mysteries than answers. It seems to be Nostradamus' rule to keep them guessing.

Some of the most entertaining of Nostradamus' books boast about unraveling some secret code. One recent attempt boldly claimed that its authors had made a complete scientific decodification of the prophet, from his chapeau of anagrams down to his syllable toes. With such a marketing "hook" I wondered why the "detailed" and scientific instructions were hidden in the back of the book? The back cover boldly declares that one of the authors was foreseen by the prophet as the one who will unlock his secrets. So far this book is only remarkable in its remarkably detailed failures, such as Prince Charles failing to become king of England in 1993, George Bush failing to win a second term as President of the United States, and California failing to sink into the Pacific Ocean at exactly 7 pm on 8 May, 1993.

I would cordially suggest to any future codebusters that they submit their claims to an impartial test. Anyone who believes he or she has decoded Nostradamus' quatrains should: (1) send their selection of decoded quatrains, with down-to-the-day-and-minute declarations for the coming year, to a reputable metaphysical organization such as the American Society For Psychical Research; (2) After one year those interpretations can be unsealed before an audience of debunkers, journalists and true believers to test their veracity. After predictions are verified, then, and only then, should that author publish their book claiming to decode Nostradamus.

Rather than play hide-and-seek for some code to dispel all mystery, Nostradamus may have intended future translators to apply the perspectives of their own era to his prophecies.

By his own very astrological makeup Nostradamus was not an ego wishing to be found out. But he was an alchemist of controversies. His obscurity has worked to keep alive for centuries what may be a practical joke or a true prophetic gift. Debunkers and blind believers alike ought to be aware that attempts to make the prophet fit their own preconceived ideas and prejudices, and then to call it his "real" intention, are futile.

The best way to defeat Nostradamus is to ignore him. The open-minded might use the prophet's psychedelic mutterings as the base metals for a golden insight into existence. I conclude from my own 27-year study of Nostradamus and of the science of meditation, that he was laying down something of far more significance to future generations than the mere prediction of events. The secret will not come cheap. There is no all-encompassing code to break. Nostradamus the Kabbalist, alchemist, and healer is cooking up something else. And so am I. The occult rules of play require that each reader find the secret alone.

CHAPTER THREE

OF CAPTAINS,
KINGS & EMPIRES

FRANCE'S DESTINY SHOWN IN A MAGIC MIRROR AT CHATEAU CHAUMONT

BY PUBLISHING PREDICTIONS of the future, Nostradamus also influenced events. This is particularly true of his predictions relating to the French royal house; after the fulfillment of his first prophecies concerning her family Catherine de Medici looked increasingly to the prophet for guidance.

In 1560, a year after the death of her husband, Catherine was convinced of the veracity of Nostradamus' prophetic gift. She also knew that he had predicted an early death for her son, King Francis II. Determined to discover the truth about the fate of the Valois royal line she summoned Nostradamus to an audience.

At midnight in the château's dark laboratory Nostradamus beckoned the queen into a magic circle traced on the stone floor before a magic mirror and took her hand. On the four corners of the mirror the Hebrew names for God – Yahweh, Elohim, Mitratron and Adonai – were inscribed in pigeon's blood and, to invoke the mirror's power, Nostradamus lilted an incantation to the Angel Anael. Through the dim light queen and prophet saw a vision of a room beyond the laboratory in which walked the young Francis, his eyes fixed on his mother. After one tour of the room the young king vanished, signifying his death.

TWO DESTINIES FOR HENRY II

After Francis came a vision of his brother and heir, the young prince Charles, whose 14 turns around the room were interpreted as signifying that he would only live to reign for 14 years. Catherine's favorite child, the future Henry III, appeared next, circling the room 15 times. As Catherine prepared herself for the fate of her youngest son, the Duke of Alençon, the child's image clouded over and faded into the image of the young Huguenot prince, Henry of Navarre.

It was this last revelation that prompted Catherine to marry her daughter, Marguerite, to Henry of Navarre. Haunted by the vision, she chose this way to ensure the survival of the house of Valois through the female blood line.

Nostradamus' warning to King Henry II not to participate in ritualized combat during his 41st year was echoed in every detail by a vision granted to Catherine de Medici's own astrologer. The prediction, like Jeane Dixon's famous President Kennedy prophecy, became well known years before the event. What has never been attempted until now is an interpretation of a number of quatrains in *The Centuries* which concern the alternative destiny in store for Henry II if he had not been mortally wounded during his 41st year.

The predictions, which might cover this unfulfilled life, are linked by two enigmatic names, "CHYREN" and "SELIN." Most interpeters agree that "CHYREN" is an anagram for "HENRYC," the old French spelling for Henry. "SELIN" stands for "Seline" the Greek word for "moon," which was the device of Henry's mistress, Diane de Poitiers[1]. His heraldic device of the letter "H" combined her family's heraldic crescent.

SWEET DREAMS OF DIVINITY

The great Chyren (Henry II) will be chief of the world,
Beyond 'Plus oultre' (...Carlo Quint – device of Charles V) loved, feared and dreaded.
His fame and praise go beyond the heavens
And he will be greatly satisfied with the sole title of victor.

C6 Q70 *1570?*

If ever there was a quatrain to boost the ego of a king living in fear because of an anti-jousting prediction, this is the one. Nostradamus elevated Henry to the top of the power-mongering kings of Christendom. Even Charles V, the unquestioned master of the 16th-century (European) world, - King of Spain, protector of the Netherlands and the Holy Roman Emperor – is relegated to a complimario part in future record. It is a historical fact that Henry II's weakness for gushing flattery equalled Nostradamus' need to survive the Inquisition.

HENRY II CAPTURES THE SPANISH KING?

Between the two distant monarchs
When the clear Sun is lost by Selin:
Great enmity between two indignant ones,
So that liberty is restored to the Islands and to Siena.

C6 Q58

Here we have the royal feud between Philip II of Spain and Henry II of France set for a climatic resolution. The "clear Sun" implies Philip's heraldic device of the sun of Apollo. The moon is Diana (Greek goddess of the moon) representing Diane de Poitiers "Selin." Had Henry avoided ritual combat he might have defeated the Spanish Hapsburgs and even killed or captured his nemesis, King Philip. The final line promises that Henry would succeed in his conquest of Corsica by using bases in Sienna.

---

[1] Diane de Poitiers (1499-1566). Mistress of Henry II when he was still a prince. When he became king, he made her Duchess of Valentinois.

HENRY II

HENRY II AT THE BATTLE OF LEPANTO?

The man with the curly, black, beard
Will subdue the cruel and proud nation
through skill.
The great Chyren (Henry II) will take from
afar
All those captured by the Turkish banner.

C2 Q79 *1579?*

Christendom's defeat of the Ottoman Turks at the naval battle of Lepanto is exhaustively detailed by Nostradamus in several quatrains examined in the following pages. In this first entry the skillful and bearded commander of the Christian forces could be Henry II, if he had lived past his 41st year. As it turned out, Don Juan of Austria earned the glory of commanding the Christian armada to victory and achieved the honor of freeing thousands of Christian galley slaves from captured Moslem ships.

HENRY II ON HIS DEATHBED 1559

THE KING THAT NEVER WAS

A LIFE OF FULFILLMENT – NOT FAILURE

Selin king, Italy peaceful,
Kingdoms united by the Christian king of
the world.
When he dies, he will want to lie
in Blois territory,
Having chased the pirates from the sea.

C4 Q77 *1577?*

If the king had listened to his Protestant jousting competitor, Comte de Montgomery, and called it a day – if Henry had led the multitude into celebration of the happy double marriage, rather than see himself carried from the field mortally wounded – who could say what course world history might have taken? Northern Italy might today be a part of France. There would have been no ruinous religious wars between French Catholics and Protestants because Henry II would have united Christendom. The Bourbons might never have ruled and the Palace of Versailles would not exist. Instead tourists would flock to the Château de Blois and the tomb of Henry II and Catherine de Medici at Saint-Denis. And interpreters like myself might be praising Nostradamus for so clearly foreseeing Henry II sweeping the Mediterranean clean of Arab corsairs and Turkish navies.

Instead of writing this segment on alternative destinies I might be questioning why the Great Henry II "didn't" die in a prophecy of ritual combat proposed in C1 Q35. This interpreter might be sitting here over four centuries later listing scores of apparently failed quatrains by Nostradamus describing a bloody religious civil war in France, which obviously never took place because Henry had lived until April of 1577 (according to the quatrain's indexing) and was laid to rest at his beloved Château de Blois.

It is an alternative future to rival any that the king might feverishly have dreamt as he lay on his deathbed surrounded by his weeping family and courtiers – a prisoner of a sadder destiny long forewarned and thrust home by a wooden splinter in his brain.

Ignorant envy supported by the great king,
He will propose forbidding the writings.
His wife, not his wife, tempted by another,
No longer will the double dealing couple
protest against it.

C4 Q57

This quatrain betrays Nostradamus' true feelings about the king and his mistress (his wife, not his wife...), Diane de Poitiers. It implies that she was first of a long line of Nostradamus debunkers, whom the prophet condemns as ignorant and envious of his gift. This quatrain may also be the closest we can come to Nostradamus' own account of his first meeting with the King and Queen of France concerning his prophecies; a meeting he may have foreseen years before it happened. Censure of his writings and persecution by those "ignorant" and envious of his prophetic gift always haunted the prophet. The first lines could infer that Nostradamus expected the king's cool reception. In other words, this prediction could be as much a case of common sense as of prescient insight.

There is no documentation to prove whether the king brought up the subject of censuring Nostradamus' prophecies at their meeting. But, since Nostradamus left the meeting a celebrity instead of a candidate for the stake, his power to please had clearly not failed him. Perhaps he countered the dire prediction of C1 Q35 with the alternative prophecies displayed on these pages? Where there is prophetic smoke there is often a burning heretic's fire. The Chyren-Selin predictions could be a seer's literary smokescreen. The "double dealing" king and his mistress would certainly have forbidden his writings, had not a jousting lance ended the king's growing domination by the anti-Nostradamian "wife" who wasn't really his wife – his mistress, Diane de Poitiers.

48

THE KING IS DEAD, LONG LIVE THE HOLY WAR

Henry II's premature death in the rue St Antoine tournament marked the beginning of a long power struggle between Protestant and Catholic and long years of religious wars. The ferocity of these wars is exemplified by the St Bartholomew's Day Massacre of Protestants, masterminded by Charles IX under the regency of Catherine de Medici. The Protestant Henry of Navarre converted to Catholicism and survived the massacre, eventually ascending the French throne and leading the country through the painful process of religious reconciliation.

CATHERINE WITNESSES THE ST BARTHOLOMEW'S DAY MASSACRE

THE WARS OF RELIGION
1559-89

*In the year that France has a
one-eyed king,
The court will be in very great trouble.
The great man from Blois will kill
his friend,
The kingdom put into difficulty and
double doubt.*

C3 Q55

Henry's premature death left the French court in chaos. The tenuous arrangement of Protestant and Catholic princes could not survive for long and four decades of war lie ahead. In the second two lines Nostradamus describes the coming power struggle for the French throne. The dead king's son, Henry III (the great man of Blois), will convene a meeting of the Estates-General at Blois in 1588. There he will assassinate his chief rival, the Duc de Guise, by first feigning reconciliation with his old friend. The assassination splits the Catholic alliance into a three-way civil war between Huguenots, the Catholic Royalists and the Catholic League.

CATHERINE DE MEDICI'S
REVENGE

49

*He who in a struggle with a lance in a
deed of war
Will have carried off the prize from one
greater than he:
At night six will take the grudge to his bed,
Without his armor he will be
suddenly surprised.*

C3 Q30

In a "deed of war" – a joust – Montgomery carried off the prize from Henry II. Montgomery fled Paris after Henry's death to lead Protestant forces in Normandy during the Wars of Religion. In further insult to the king's memory his battle flag bore the device of a broken lance. Catherine de Medici no doubt identified Montgomery in this quatrain and proceeded to take her revenge (grudge) by choosing six hand-picked men to steal the Huguenot prince from his bed (without his armor) and have him executed.

HENRY III ASSASSINATED

That which fire and sword could not accomplish
Will be managed by a sweet speaking
tongue in council:
The king will be made to contemplate the dream
seen while sleeping,
He will see the enemy not in war or
military blood.

C1 Q97

The king king not to be, calamity
for the Clement One...

P58

By 1588, Henry III's position was precarious in the extreme and there were calls for his death from all sides. The instrument of revenge was to be Brother Clément, a Dominican friar, who obtained a private audience in the king's bedchamber at St Cloud on 1 August. Clément's mild manner and gentle speech threw the king off-guard and, as the king moved close to hear a promised secret, the priest stabbed him with a concealed dagger. When loyal bodyguards responded to the king's cries, it is said that Clément met their sword blades with arms outstretched like a crucified Christ.

It was well known that Henry III, king of France and Poland, was morally and physically spent and that, three days before death, he had foreseen his demise in a dream and related to his courtiers and homosexual lovers its nightmare vision of the crown and scepter of France being trampled by a monk-led mob.

50

Henry III meets his death at the hand of assassin Jacques Clément, a Dominican friar, in August 1589.

GREAT "HADRIE" ENTHRONED

*How often will you be captured, O city
of the sun?
Changing the laws that are barbaric
and vain:
Evil times approach you.
No longer will you be enslaved,
The great Hadrie will revive your veins.*

C1 Q8

Paris, the city of the sun, as it would be named a century after the seige, has known many conquests. The "barbaric and vain" laws belong to the Seize Parliamentarians – the first effort in Parisian history to establish a cult republic by commune – a concept the Royalist prophet found horrifying. Nostradamus foretells good fortune coming from Paris and all of France in the double meaning of "revive your veins." Throughout the six-month siege, Henry sent food to the starving citizens. Later, as undisputed king he would "revive" the French people with peace and prosperity.

The civil war ended with an incident foreseen by Nostradamus 40 years before in Quatrain 55 of Century 2:

"In the conflict the great man of little worth Will commit an astonishing deed at his end..." Charles, Duc de Mayenne, fearing that the Seize Parliamentarians would prevent him from taking the crown in the name of the Catholic League, invited the People's Parliament to a banquet and had each representative murdered as they ate. As line four of the quatrain states: "He stabs the proud during a banquet."

The chronological end to the quatrain, however, appears in line three: "While Hadrie sees what is needed." "Hadrie" is an anagram for Henry of Navarre who capitalizes on Mayenne's blunder by becoming a Catholic and declaring "Paris is well worth a Mass."

With this well-timed change of religious party label Henry united France.

By 1594, the mirror prophecy was fulfilled to the letter. All Catherine de Medici's sons were dead and Henry of Navarre was crowned Henry IV.

*The House of Lorraine
will make way for Vendôme.
The high put low and the low exalted,
The son of Hammon will be elected in
Rome
And two great ones will be put at a loss.*

C10 Q18

The Brothers Guise of the House of Lorraine lose all to Henry IV, also known as the Duke of Vendôme. "Hammon" is an anagram for the Egyptian sun god, Amon, who gained respect from the Romans after he was merged with their chief god, Jupiter. Nostradamus plays with anagrams and mythology to compose an accurate parallel with "Romans" of the Vatican who would accept a heretic Huguenot Prince "Hammon" as their own. The two losers are the Duc de Guise and his brother, the Duc de Mayenne.

HENRY IV RALLIES HIS TROOPS AT IVRY 1590

"KING HADRIE FALLS"

VISIONS OF "ARMIES IN THE SKY"

In 1619 the "Mercure Français"
described what may have been some form
of solar light in the Parisian skies as an
army of armed ghosts parading in their
thousands on the eve of Henry IV's
assassination.

Under Henry IV the Huguenots were granted freedom of worship. For the next 16 years, the king dedicated himself to leading France through the painful process of reconciliation and to reconstructing the nation's life. But in 1610, while walking with his retinue on the rue Ferronnière in Paris, he was stabbed to death by a fanatic. Nine years later the "Mercure Français" recorded that hundreds of Parisians could bear witness that, on the day of Henry's assassination, they had seen thousands of heavily armed ghosts marching up and down the sky until sunset. Whether this phenomenon was actually observed or fabricated after the assassination we do not know. But it is with this scene in the heavens that Nostradamus begins his prophecy in Century 3, Quatrain 11: "The weapons fight in the sky for a long time. The tree has fallen in the middle of the city. The sacred branch is cut by a blade opposite Tison, then king Hadrie falls." Henry, the branch of the Bourbon royal house, is the fallen tree. The rue Tison is not far from the place where he fell.

CHRISTENDOM VS TWO "ARAB" EMPIRES

In the 16th century, Christendom was locked in holy combat against the powerful Ottoman Turks[1] and their Arab vassals, the Barbary Corsairs of North Africa. Nostradamus no doubt shared Christianity's prejudice against the Moslems, but he did accurately plot the course of Islam's naval raids and conquests in the Mediterranean which led to their seizure of Christian outpost colonies in Rhodes and Cyprus. He also foresaw with amazing detail how Arab-Turkish forces would be checked by Christian navies led by Don Juan of Austria at the great battle of Lepanto on October 7, 1571. At least 25,000 men of the Ottoman fleet died.

The prophet warns of future threats to Christian believers stemming from a treaty between Turks and Persians in 1727. This will set the stage for a future "Arab" or Barbarian Empire revived by the discovery of "a new source of wealth," although Nostradamus seems to have difficulty in defining exactly what the source of wealth is. Perhaps his 16th-century conditioning did not prepare him for understanding the significance of oil but, as we will see in predictions examined later, Christendom's lust for this new source of wealth may yet bring it to disaster before the new millennium, even as peace seems at hand.

CHRISTENDOM DEFEATS OTTOMAN TURKS AT LEPANTO

[1] Ottoman Turks. Rulers of an Empire which began in 1307 in Turkey and expanded over the following centuries until it stretched from Budapest to Baghdad in 1683.

The remaining blood will not be spilt,
Venice seeks for help to be given:
After having waited for a very long time
The city is handed over at the first call of
the trumpet.

C4 Q1

Venice, the Mediterranean sea power, got little or no help from other Christian allies in their battles with Ottoman forces in Crete (1545-64) and in Cyprus. There the Turks finally overwhelmed the starved defenders of Famagusta, the Cypriot capital, in 1573, after an eleven month seige.

a(Acts of) plunder made upon the sea coast,
In the new city and relations
brought forward;
Several of Malta through the deeds
of Messina,
Will be closely shut up, sweetly rewarded.

C9 Q61

During the Siege of Malta in 1565, several hundred Knights of the Maltese Cross withstood a sustained attack of 40,000 Turks between May and August of 1565. Before the Turks departed three-quarters of the invasion force was killed by combat and disease. Six years later, the Knights of Malta sent four galleys to join the gathering Christian naval forces at Messina for an all-out showdown with the Turkish navy at Lepanto, where the Turks and Barbary corsairs lost over 230 galleys sunk and captured (shut up).

CYPRUS OVERWHELMED (1571)

THE GALLANT KNIGHTS AT THE SEIGE OF MALTA (1565-1571)

From Barcelona (Spain), from Genoa
and Venice
From Sicily, pestilence allied with Monaco.
They will take their aim against the
Barbary fleet
The barbarian driven very far, as far back
as Tunis.

C9 Q42

The fleets of the Papacy and Venice rendezvous at Messina with Spanish galleys (including contingents from Monaco and Genoa) to form the Christian armada commanded by Don Juan of Austria. They crushed the combined Turkish and Algerian Barbary (barbarian) fleet in the Gulf of Lepanto – present day Corinth – ending forever Moslem dominance of the Mediterranean. The quatrain also chronicles the immediate strategic results of Lepanto, Don Juan's invasion and conquest of Tunis in North Africa.

The third climate included under Aries,
In the year 1727, in October,
The Shah of Persia, captured by those
of Egypt
Conflict, death, loss: great shame to the cross.

C3 Q77

Here we have a rare example of a relatively unobscured quatrain, which clearly mentions the correct month and date of a major peace treaty concluded by Shah Ashraf and the Ottoman Sultan. The climate of Aries is War. Egypt is a synecdoche for the Turks and the Ottoman Empire, of which Egypt was a province at that time. Although the Shah of Persia was not captured, many historians agree that the peace arrangement was more advantageous to the Turks. By recognizing Shah Ashraf's dynasty, the lands of Tauris, Emvan, and Hamadan were returned. The Shah recognized the Ottoman Sultan as legitimate successor to the Caliph.

The loss to Christendom reverberates to this day. Two great empires of Islam were strengthened as a result of this peace. The Ottoman Empire survived until this century. And the stage was set for Nostradamus' second "Arab" Empire to feed the addiction of modern Christendom to oil.

SADDAM HUSSEIN

The leader of Nostradamus'
predicted second "Arab" empire
could be Saddam Hussein,
current leader of Iraq.

THE ASCENT OF ALBION

A great empire will be for England
The all powerful one through the sea
for more than three hundred years:
Great forces will pass by land and sea,
The Portuguese will not be satisfied.

C10 Q100

At the time Nostradamus wrote the words of Quatrain 100 in Century 10, England was a minor sea power. It would have seemed impossible then that this small island kingdom would eclipse great 16th-century powers such as Portugal, to become a world empire through its domination of the seas. Yet this is exactly what Nostradamus predicts. But from which date does Nostradamus begin to count his 300 years? We know that the British Empire seriously declined after World War II and that, by the late 1950s, the British had acceded to the American "Empire's" request to position nuclear missiles on British soil. By the early 1960s, the British Empire was almost completely dismantled. If we define this period as the end of the empire, the beginning, according to Nostradamus' timescale, would be towards the end of Oliver Cromwell's time. After the English Civil War, Cromwell's reforms had indeed assisted England to move towards world power status and the English Navigation Act of 1661 prompted the rapid growth of her merchant marine fleet and economic domination of the international shipping lanes.

Skill in seamanship, both in peace and war, established England's long domination of the waves. When Nostradamus wrote the quatrain (right) Spain and England were allies. It refers to an English attack on Spanish treasure galleons to take place 37 years later when, in 1590, 40 Spanish treasure ships, laden with gold from South America, sailed through the narrow mouth of the Bay of Cadiz to lay anchor after a seven-month voyage. The Bay of Cadiz received its name from the Punic word "Gaddir," meaning "enclosed place" – like a "lake." Shortly after midday, the Spanish spotted the sails of English raiders on the horizon. The Spanish were not too concerned. No sane mariner would enter the narrow opening of the bay to engage in battle. The captains of the 13 Spanish man-o-war escorts would not consider setting sail to tackle the English raiders until they had enjoyed a good siesta. That was their mistake.

While the Spanish dozed, the English rode the wind straight into the harbor and attacked the treasure fleet's escort with deadly cannonades. To keep the gold from English hands the Spanish were forced to set fire to the entire fleet.

Nostradamus calls the English "Albions" after the Latin name given the island by the Romans. The quatrain indexing "94" could be a near miss for 1590, the year of the attack.

Before the lake where most of the treasure
was cast
Of seven months, and its host frustrated.
The Spanish will be plundered by
the Albions
By delaying giving battle.

C8 Q94

57

ENGLISH ATTACK SPANISH TREASURE SHIPS AT CADIZ

ROUNDHEADS AND CAVALIERS

More a butcher than a King
of England
Born of obscure rank he will gain
Empire through force.
A coward without faith, without law,
he will bleed the land.
His time approaches so near that I sigh.

C8 Q76

For a man who could look perhaps 7,000 years into the future the birth of Oliver Cromwell[1], the man who made England a republic, might well have seemed very near indeed. Nostradamus, the committed royalist seems to have had little affection for the Puritan leader, describing him as a man who would "butcher" a king and "bleed the land," but he does not begrudge him his key role in making England a world power. Perhaps too, Nostradamus' visions showed him the real Cromwell who, despite his public claims to divine protection, was "A coward without faith," only removing his armor behind the safety of a bolted door and living in daily fear of assassination.

The divine wrath will surprise
the great prince
A short time before he will have married,
Both support and credit will suddenly
diminish:
Counsel, he will die because of the
shaven heads.

C1 Q88

This quatrain pinpoints the beginning of Charles' troubles and their outcome many years later. In 1625, Charles I declared on his wedding day that persecution of Catholics in England should stop. Parliament, already estranged by the king's disregard of its powers, openly refused him (divine "Puritan" wrath) by vetoing his request for subsidies (credit) for his war against Spain. Marrying a Catholic princess further rubbed their Puritan noses in what they condemned as his Papist intrigues (divine wrath, again). Twenty-four years later communication between king and Parliament broke down and Civil War ensued. The day came when the king's own court (counsel) would sentence him to die because of pressure from the victorious Roundheads (shaven heads).

THE CIVIL WAR BATTLE OF MARSTON MOOR 1644

[1]Oliver Cromwell (1599-1658). Soldier, statesman, enthusiastic Puritan and denier of the divine right of kings. Decisive in winning the English Civil War (1642-1651) for the Puritans, he was declared Lord Protector in 1653 and established excellent and beneficial links with Protestant countries in Europe.

The fortress near the Thames will fall
When the king is locked up inside,
He will be seen in his shirt near the bridge,
One confronting death then barred
in the fort.

C8 Q37

Lines one and four bracket the execution with a story of the captured king taken to Windsor Castle (fortress) near the Thames. On January 30, 1649, Charles was led to the scaffold at Westminster, there to be stripped to his shirt for execution by beheading. Later, his blood-stained shirt was hung on a pole from London Bridge two miles from the place of execution (near the bridge).

THE EXECUTION OF CHARLES I

The great plague of the maritime city
Will not cease until there be avenged the death
Of the just blood, seized and condemned
without a crime.
The great lady is outraged by the pretense.

C2 Q53

Many Londoners thought the plague of 1565 was a punishment sent from God for Parliament's murder of Charles I. Whatever the true cause – divine retribution, mass suggestion, or simply bad sanitation – Nostradamus the Royalist describes the plague, which carried off 68,596 Londoners, as a scourge come to avenge an innocent king. The "great lady" is contemporary slang for either a Cathedral or the Catholic Church, which is "outraged" by the rise of English Protestantism which followed the plague.

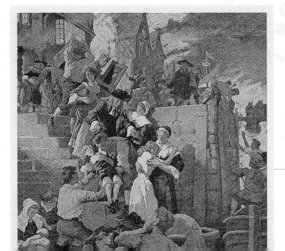

The blood of the just will be demanded
of London,
Burnt by fire in twenty-three the sixes (66)
The ancient lady will fall from her high place.
And many of the same sect will be killed.

C2 Q51

Many interpreters believe that "twenty-three the sixes" is a accurate-though-figurative prediction of the year of the Great Fire of London in September 1666. Six in plural could be "66". The fire took place on 1 September, in the "sixes" which could target the correct decade, the 60's. Nostradamus' love for complex verbal and numerical puns cannot, however, be ruled out and sixes could mean the number of man and sin, "666."

The quatrain supports the date with details of the fire itself and elaborates on the previous quatrain's "great lady" metaphor. This time it is the "ancient lady," personification of St Paul's Cathedral. The Church falling to Protestantism becomes a more graphic warning of the Church roof of St Paul's collapsing from heat onto the faithful who sought shelter within its stone walls from the firestorm devouring their wooden houses.

THE GREAT FIRE OF LONDON

SEVEN TIDES OF ROYAL BLOOD

*The rise and fall of the British Empire
is foretold in four brief lines on the
theme of royal blood.*

*Seven times you will see the British
nation change,
Dyed (or stained) in blood for two
hundred and ninety years.
Not at all free from Germania's influence,
Aries doubts the protector of Poland.*

C3 Q57

ELIZABETH I (1533-1603)

*Elizabeth I was the last Tudor
monarch. On her death the throne
passed to James I of the House of Stuart.*

OLIVER CROMWELL (1599-1658)

*The English Civil War brings
bloody, violent change. The word
"taintz," used by the prophet, can
mean "dyed," describing the famous
British redcoats worn by English
soldiers throughout the days of
empire. The coats were first worn by
Cromwell's New Model Army, the
restructured military force that
brought him victory. The prophet has
a second meaning to the word
"tainz." In a manner of speaking
Charles' defeat destined him to "stain"
the headsman's block with his blood.*

60

CHARLES II (REIGNED 1660-85)

The ascension of Charles II to the throne in 1660 restores the royal House of Stuart.

WILLIAM III (REIGNED 1688-1702)

The Glorious Revolution of 1688 shuffles Stuarts out, in favor of William III of Friesland.

QUEEN ANNE (REIGNED 1702-1714)

The House of Stuart returns with the ascent to the throne of Queen Anne in 1702.

61

GEORGE I (REIGNED 1714-1727)

German blue bloods take the throne warmed by Queen Anne with the arrival of George I and the House of Hanover in 1714.

ADOLF HITLER (DICTATOR 1933-1945)

Line four foresees an end to royal blood-power from a more malevolent German influence. It foretells the bloodbath of World War II set off by Hitler (Aries = God of War) ignoring England's threat of going to war if the Nazis invaded Poland.

FIFTY-SEVEN PEACEFUL YEARS

The walls will change from brick to marble.
Fifty-seven peaceful years:
Joy to humans, the aqueduct renewed,
Health, abundant fruit, mellifluous times.

C10 Q89

In 1656 Jaubert interpreted duplicate Quatrain 100 of Century 10 in these words: "By this quatrain the King of France would appear to be Emperor of the World in 1660. One may indeed hope for this, but it does not seem likely to be accomplished…"

It is thought that a reading of this interpretation may have prompted Louis XIV, then king of France, to visit the prophet's tomb at the beginning of 1660, in the company of the queen and his mentor, Cardinal Mazarin. The quatrain opens with a riddle:

"When the fork will be supported by two columns,
With six half-bodies and six open scissors…"

This should be read in terms of Roman numerals. The fork – V – supported by two columns becomes – M. Six half-bodies – Cs – six open scissors – Xs – spell out MCCCCC-CXXXXXX which gives us the year 1660, when the prophet says:

"…A very powerful lord, heir of the toads,
Will subjugate the whole world to himself."

Louis XIV, the future "Sun King," became sole ruler of France in 1661 after the death of Cardinal Mazarin. He was destined to subjugate his people and prove himself a worthy descendant of the ancient Merovingian kings who bore toads as a heraldic device.

Louis determined to have no internal conflicts in France, even though he might have to fight foreign wars. He kept this promise and throughout his reign France enjoyed domestic peace – a period of stability which Nostradamus had accurately predicted 100 years before in Quatrain 89 of Century 10. The reign of Louis XIV is characterized by innovative building – the Palace of Versailles was constructed at his command and a network of canals (aqueducts), notably the "Midi" connecting the Atlantic to the Mediterranean Sea, was laid.

At the beginning of the 18th century a collapse in the prosperity of France seemed inconceivable. But Nostradamus, who had then been dead for over one and a half centuries, had seen evil times ahead through the astrological dating recorded in C1 Q51 (right). The conjunction of Jupiter and Saturn in Aries mentioned in the first line took place on 13 December, 1702. A century later, in 1802, France lay in the grip of Napoleon Bonaparte and was entering its eighth year of war in Italy. Replacing the chaos of the French Revolution with 13 more years of war Napoleon was to win and lose an empire – 2 million Frenchmen sacrificed their lives to his ambition.

THE BIRTH OF REPUBLICAN EMPIRES

In the second quatrain (below, right), Britain's elder sister is a figurative description of the British Empire's 13 American colonies. With the help (promise) of an alliance with France (her brother), America will defeat Britain and eventually become an even greater republican empire than France as "the kingdom of the Balance." The "Balance" of the last line, with its possible allusion to the scales of Justice, refers to democracy.

Later, France would become America's "brother" in republicanism. Nostradamus accurately foresaw the creation of the First Republic of France, 15 years after America asserted its liberty with the Declaration of Independence in 1776. As we will see, however, the shadow of the blood-stained guillotine loomed over his vision.

Jupiter and Saturn in the head (sign) of Aries
Eternal God what changes!
Then the bad times return after a long century,
What turmoil in France and Italy.

C1 Q51

The elder sister of the British Isles
Will be born fifteen years before her brother,
Because his promise proves to be true,
She will succeed to the kingdom of the Balance.

C4 Q96

63

REPUBLICANISM BRINGS
JUSTICE'S SCALES AND SWORD

CHAPTER FOUR

THE HEADLESS IDIOTS

"MADAME" GUILLOTINE

WHEN NOSTRADAMUS was living in Salon he was pursued one day by a Caban peasant gang who cursed and threatened him. Eventually, Nostradamus turned on them with his cane, roaring at them to be off. As they fled from the prophet he shouted after them "You will never put your filthy feet on my throat while I'm alive or after I'm dead."

Nostradamus made plans to ensure that this prophecy came true. During his last illness he gave his wife instructions concerning his burial. She was to have his body entombed in the wall of the Church of the Cordeliers in Salon and, most important of all, it was to be placed upright. Throughout the centuries that followed stories circulated about Nostradamus' last resting place, including a rumour that the prophet had had buried with him a secret document containing the key to all his prophecies. When in 1700 the city fathers decided to move the body of their illustrious citizen to a more prominent wall of the church they took a quick, careful look inside the coffin.

OPENING THE TOMB

It contained no paper of any kind. But there was one surprise for the city fathers. It is claimed that around the skeleton's neck hung a medallion inscribed with the date 1700 - it would have amused Nostradamus to see how the leading citizens of Salon responded to his practical joke devised some 134 years before. Reverently, the city fathers re-sealed the coffin and installed it, again upright, in its new location; for 91 years it rested in peace.

But in 1791, during the turbulence of the French Revolution, some national guards from Marseilles broke into the church on a drunken looting raid, armed with picks and shovels. They smashed the eight-foot marble slab concealing the prophet's coffin and began to ransack its contents. When the noise of their vandalism and singing aroused the neighborhood, the mayor of Salon hurried to investigate the commotion. He arrived at the church to find a macabre dance of death in progress, with soldiers and townspeople tossing the prophet's bones in the air; in the center of this grisly scene a shaggy guardsman was drinking wine from Nostradamus' skull. The peasants, believing that drinking blood from the skull would give you the prophet's powers, had dared the guardsman to drink. Wine seemed an acceptable substitute for blood and may also have helped the soldiers blot from their minds Nostradamus' warning that a quick and violent death would be visited on anyone who dared to desecrate his grave.

Faced with the prospect of Salon's most illustrious bones being carried off as souvenirs and mindful of the prophet's warning, the mayor had to act quickly. He explained to the soldiers that Nostradamus had predicted the French Revolution and was thus a hero to be revered. He soon had them collecting up the bones they had scattered in their drunken riot and later made sure that the prophet's remains were safely reinterred.

The man who opens the tomb when it is found
And who does not close it immediately,
Evil will come to him that no one will be able to prove...
C9 Q7

By the next morning the guardsmen were on their way back to Marseilles. On the road from Salon they were ambushed by royalist sympathizers and the soldier who had used the prophet's skull for a wine glass suffered a quick and violent death from a sniper's bullet.

On 14 July 1789 the fortress and prison known as the Bastille in the centre of Paris was stormed by an angry mob. For ten days following the "liberation" of the Bastille, hundreds of Parisians touring the fortress filed past a table displaying a copy of *The Centuries*. It lay open at the section containing Nostradamus' prediction of the French Revolution, written 273 years before. He had described it as the "Common Advent of the people."

In his Epistle to King Henry II, Nostradamus had warned of a future time when the powerful Church, its very sanctity and strength, would be called into question and even overthrown by the people of France. "...The Christian Church will be persecuted more fiercely than it had ever been in Africa and this will last to the year 1792, which they will believe marks a renewal of time..."

The Revolution's persecution of the Church had only begun in 1792. But Nostradamus had accurately foreseen the year the revolutionaries were to replace the old calendar with a new one devised to mark the dawn of a new age.

THE FRENCH REVOLUTION

THE MURDER OF MARAT

The "whirlwind" of the revolution claimed victims amongst its most prominent leaders. In 1793 the revolutionary Marat, idol of the sans-culottes, was murdered in his bath by Charlotte Corday.

Coins depreciated by the spirit of the kingdom
People will be stirred up against their king.
New saints make peace, holy laws become worse
Paris was never in such great trouble.

C6 Q23

The leaders of the Revolution, breast-fed on the wit of Voltaire and the sincerity of Rousseau, rode the national wave of dissent over inflation and lack of bread, to overthrow Louis XVI and the aristocracy. These writers became the "saints" of a new religion, the Cult of Reason, and perpetrators of its counterpart, the Reign of Terror.

Many of Nostradamus' finest predictions are those for the period of the French Revolution. In the language and tone of the Revolution quatrains we can feel the prophet's horror, disbelief and struggle for understanding at the vision of chaos and blood which came to him. Twice he refers to it as a "whirlwind," a description which may not just be metaphor but a factual clue to dating the Revolution. On 13 July, 1788, exactly one year before the storming of the Bastille, France was visited by a violent windstorm, one of the worst ever recorded. Named "The Great Tornado of 1788" by contemporary journals, this cyclonic storm rained down hail the size of pebbles and caused fierce tornadoes that cut a swath of destruction from Tours, Chartres and Paris, through Lille and into Belgium.

When the litters are overturned by
a whirlwind
And the faces are covered by cloaks,
The new republic will be troubled
by its people:
At this time whites then reds will
rule wrongly.

C1 Q3

From the enslaved people, songs,
chants and demands,
The Princes and Lords are held captive
in prisons:
In the future by such headless idiots
These (demands) will be taken as
divine utterances.

C1 Q14

Nostradamus foresees the common people overturning the litters of the aristocracy. The irresistible storm of revolution would force them to leave France as refugees, their faces covered by cloaks on the windy passage across the English Channel, or leave life with their heads "covered by cloaks" within a bloody wicker basket carried away from the guillotine. "Whites" are the Bourbons whose cockade was white. They ignored their people's needs bringing disaster upon themselves.

It appears that Nostradamus heard and saw the tattered Paris mob of a distant century marching through the narrow streets yelling popular slogans or singing the Marseillaise. Their contemporary rivals called men like Danton[1] and Robespierre "maniacs." To Nostradamus they are "headless idiots," a pun for their character and their violent fate. Add to this the indexing of the quatrain as "14" which could stand for the date the Bastille was stormed July 14, 1789.

NATIONAL GUARDSMEN DEFEND THE REVOLUTION

---

[1] Georges Jacques Danton (1759-94), revolutionist and lawyer who became Minister for Justice in 1792. Outmaneuvred by Robespierre, he was sentenced to death in 1794 by the Revolutionary Tribunal he had helped to set up.

FLYING BY NIGHT

Although historians attribute the French Revolution to the weakness of Louis XVI, Nostradamus reveals great affection for the hapless king. Opposed to violence, Louis appeared lacking in leadership, an ineffectual ruler of a great nation. But perhaps Nostradamus sensed the humanitarian in him; he wrote one quatrain which may foresee Louis offering equal rights to Jews, an action which would have greatly endeared him to Nostradamus.

Forced by the revolutionaries to surrender his power to the new constitutional monarchy, Louis also had to exchange his royal name, Bourbon, for Capet, the "oldest name of his blood." Virtually imprisoned with his family in the Tuileries, Louis made plans to escape, but the ill-fated venture was doomed to failure.

On the night of 20 June, 1791, the royal family, disguised as servants of the Baroness de Korff, left Paris in a heavy covered carriage to journey north to the border and freedom. Traveling throughout the night and the next day they arrived at the town of Varennes just

When the Bour' is very "bon"
Bearing in himself marks of justice
Then bearing the oldest name of his blood:
Through flight he will unjustly receive
his punishment.

C7 Q44

before midnight in search of rest and refreshment. The town's mayor, a man called Sauce, invited the weary travelers into his grocery store to take a glass of wine and, while they drank, he and his wife asked them about themselves and their journey. Sauce was suspicious of the couple - the nervous man dressed in a monk-like gray hat and cloak and the woman who, although clad simply in a plain white dress, was betrayed by her manner and bearing as a lady of noble birth.

THE ROYAL FAMILY FLEE TO VARENNES

When a visitor to the store recognized the royal couple Sauce sent him to alert the town garrison. In desperation, Marie Antoinette, with tears streaking her face, begged Madame Sauce to let her family continue their journey. She was unmoved by the royal tears. "I love my King, but I love my husband as well and would not have him lose his head." Louis and his family were returned to Paris as prisoners.

Over two centuries before the playing out of this doomed escape attempt and its tragic consequences Nostradamus had foreseen it all.

BELOW LEFT *The royal family flee in disguise from Paris to the north.*

BELOW *While resting at a grocer's store in Varennes, the king and queen were taken prisoner and sent back to Paris.*

THE KING AND QUEEN TAKEN PRISONER

"A MONK KING, IN GRAY, IN VARENNES"

By night he will come by the forest of Reines
A married couple, devious route,
Queen white stone:
A monk-king in gray in Varennes
Elected Cap, causes tempest, fire, and
bloody slicing.

C9 Q20

This quatrain, above, is startlingly accurate in every detail. It is numbered 20 after the date of the attempted escape - 20 June, 1791. The royal family's road to freedom took them past the forest of Reines but the coach was eventually forced, by the poor road and lack of replacement horses, to make a detour. "Devious" thus describes the detour, the secrecy and their disguise. Witnesses who reported seeing the royal pair during their escape described them as "Married couple" and "monk," and the town of "Varennes" was the scene of their discovery. "Queen white stone" gives in just three words a perfect description of Marie Antoinette's appearance and emotional state: she wore a white dress and some said that shock and distress turned her hair white overnight; "white stone" could be a double pun, alluding both to her hardness of heart and lack of personal warmth, and to the notorious Diamond Necklace scandal. "Elected Cap," is Louis Capet, formerly the supreme ruler Louis XVI, now elected monarch of the new constitutional government (causes tempest), whose death will spark off a counter-revolution to be suppressed by the Republicans with the guillotine (bloody slicing).

The second quatrain names the mayor of Varennes and anticipates two violent incidents at the Tuileries – the abuse of the king and the massacre of his Swiss guard. The "husband" links this quatrain to the Varennes prophecy's "married couple." Louis, separated from his family, will face a murderous mob at his Tuileries apartments and be forced to put on the revolutionary cap, described by Nostradamus as a "miter" because it resembled the caps worn by the ancient priests of Mithras[1].

"Le thuille," the word used in *The Centuries* for the Tuileries, means, "place of the tiles." When Nostradamus visited Paris in 1556 the site on which the palace was later to be built was an area of tile kilns. In August 1792, the Tuileries was ransacked in a bloody attack led by the 513 Fédérés, better known as the "Five Hundred Marseillaise" for their song which became the French national anthem.

The enobled "betrayer" of Quatrain 35 is Sauce, spelled with an "L" in the archaic form; Narbon was a moderate revolutionary who tried to persuade the National Assembly to pardon the king. Nostradamus couples the names of Sauce and Narbon to pit radicals and moderates against each other over line four's cryptic play on words: "we have oil for our blades." As a grocery store owner Sauce would also have been an oil merchant. In figurative terms his role in the king's arrest oiled the blade which was to sever not only the king's head but Sauce's own, in the Reign of Terror to come.

The husband, alone, afflicted, will be mitered
Returned, conflict will take place at
the Tuileries:
By the five hundred one betrayer will
be ennobled
Narbon and Saulce we have oil for our blades.

C9 Q35

---

[1]Mithras. Ancient Persian god of light, in the Zoroastrian tradition he wages constant war with the forces of darkness. Mithraism became a highly ritualised religion very popular with soldiers of ancient Rome.

While the royal family languished in the Temple prison, Louis occupied a solitary, gloomy cell in the tower keep. From his tower he could look down on his son playing in the prison gardens under the watchful eyes of the guards. Two hundred years before Nostradamus had shared this view and, almost as if he was peering over Louis' shoulder, had written: "The young son playing outdoors under the arbor...The father king in the Temple is solemn..." C9 Q23.

Taken prisoner by the revolutionary forces and returned to Paris, Louis is forced to don the "cap of liberty," symbol of the revolution.

Gorsan and Narbonne by the salt to warn
Touching pardon the Paris pledge betrayed,
The red city will not wish to consent to it,
By flight gray drape's life is ended.

C8 Q22

Gorsas (Gorsan) was a moderate journalist who with Narbon (Narbonne) tried to send a message to Louis XVI in the Temple prison hidden inside a salt shaker (by the salt to warn). The king had promised never to leave Paris before his flight to Varennes (Paris pledge betrayed). "Red" Paris wanted him dead for his "flight" disguised in a "gray drape," or cloak of a Carmelite monk.

THE KING HUMILIATED BY THE REVOLUTIONARIES

FAMOUS "AND FORESEEN" LAST WORDS

In the early morning chill of 21 January, 1793, Louis, tied and bound, rode in a dung cart to the guillotine: "The white bourbon is driven out...Made a prisoner led to the tumbril (dung cart), his feet tied together like a rogue..." C4 Q85.

As a prophetic postscript to the king's death the royalist Nostradamus had written 236 years earlier "The death conspired will come into full effect, the charge given and the journey to death. Elected, created, received by his own and undone. Blood of the innocent before them in remorse" C8 Q87.

When Louis mounted the scaffold his eyes swept over the jeering mob below. Under his piercing gaze the drums and crowd fell silent and the fallen king began to protest his innocence in clear steady tones. But the drums began to roll again and the executioner Sanson proceeded. As he raised the blade witnesses heard the king reciting the fourth verse of the Third Psalm, "Thou, oh Lord are my Glory, and lifter of my head..." until his voice was silenced by the falling blade. Sanson lifted the king's severed head high in the air before the crowd but was so shaken by the experience and moved by the king's courage that he vowed never to climb the scaffold again.

This remarkable prophecy (right) was written 235 years before the event and, as in other predictions, Nostradamus describes the French Revolution as a "whirlwind" which trembled with the death of Louis XVI, setting into motion the lunacy of the Reign of Terror. Louis had promised to remain in Paris but was caught escaping (broken accord). The prophet describes the executioner displaying the king's severed head to the mob and, in a double pun, records his last words "lifting the head to heaven," echoing the words of the Third Psalm which Louis recited as the blade fell. Line three gives a vivid description of beheading (bloody mouth will swim with blood).

In *Prophecies of World Events By Nostradamus* Stewart Robb gives an ingenious interpretation for the last line which dates the beginning and end of Louis' life as king. Louis had been crowned on the feast day of St Agnes[1] and in honor of that day his face was anointed with milk and honey. The holy offices of St Agnes contain the key words to line four: "Mel (honey) et lac (milk) ex ore ejus (mouth) suscepi, et sanguis (blood) ejus ornavit oras (face)."... Louis was guillotined 19 years after his coronation, on St Agnes Day 1793.

---

[1]St Agnes. Roman Christian martyred when she was only 13. Her feast day is January 21.

On 21 January 1793, Louis XVI
was taken to the guillotine. On the
scaffold before the jeering mob he
protested his innocence, but his voice
was drowned by a drum roll and
then silenced by the swish of the
falling blade. The head of the man
who had been king was lifted high
for the great crowd to see.

*By great discord the whirlwind
will tremble
Broken accord, lifting the head to heaven,
Bloody mouth will swim with blood:
The face once anointed with milk
and honey lays in the soil.*
C1 Q57

73

THE EXECUTION OF LOUIS XVI

DEATH BY CHOSEN LOT

...The queen sent to death by jurors
chosen by lot:
They will deny the queen's son,
And the prostitute shares the fate of the consort.

C9 Q77

Nine months after the death of her husband Marie Antoinette followed him to the guillotine. Her arch rival, Madame du Barry, mistress to the king's father, suffered the same fate and is also mentioned in Quatrain 77 (above).

Nostradamus' prediction concerning the death of Marie Antoinette is uncannily accurate; he even mentions the fact that the jurors for her trial were chosen by lot, a practice which was rarely used. The fate of the son and heir to the royal house, who would have become Louis XVII, is still a mystery but it may be that Nostradamus' visionary powers enabled him to see the truth of what actually happened to the young prince.

Removed from his mother, the 11 year old prince was placed in the care of Simon the Cobbler who was instructed by Stenart, the procurer of the Commune, to "humble" the boy. Stenart hinted that there was no reason to kill him nor to keep him alive. That the cobbler took Stenart at his word and maltreated the prince is confirmed by the report of a Dr Harmand who examined him in December 1794. He noted tumors on his left arm and unsightly swellings on his knees. In June 1795

Imprisoned in Paris, Marie Antoinette's children are roughly torn away from her. She remains alone and abandoned until she follows her husband to the guillotine.

the boy's death was announced to the Committee of General Security by Achille Severstre who stated that the cause of death was complications arising from a severe swelling of his left wrist and knee which, over the past few months, had required frequent dressing and bandaging (hand in a sling and his left leg bandaged). The Commissioners later visited the Temple prison where they viewed a body, claimed to be that of young Louis. It was lying under a sheet stained with blood and was so badly disfigured that positive

MARIE ANTOINETTE IN PRISON

identification of the boy was impossible. The words of Nostradamus, written two centuries earlier, suggest that he bled from a cruel beating during Easter and that his injuries were so bad that they led to his death in the summer of 1795. The real truth of this mysterious incident will probably never be known.

His hand in a sling and his leg bandaged,
Young Louis will leave the palace.
At the word of the watchman his death
will be delayed.
Then he will bleed in the Temple
at Easter.
C8 Q45

BELOW RIGHT *Young Louis is given into the brutal charge of Simon the Cobbler.*

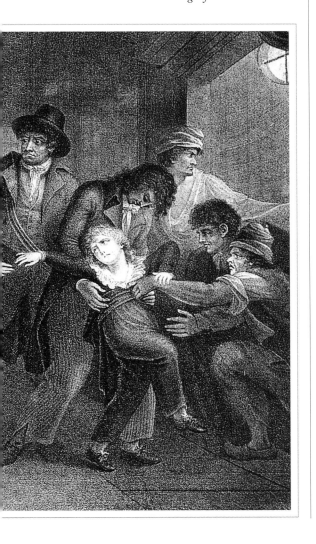

YOUNG LOUIS GUARDED BY SIMON THE COBBLER

COUNTER-REVOLUTION

From Mount(agnard) Aymar the
noble obscured,
The evil will come at the junction
of the Saône and Rhône:
Soldiers hidden in the woods
on St Lucy's Day,
When never was there so horrible a throne.

C9 Q68

The execution of the king and queen trig-gered an orgy of blood-letting known as The Reign of Terror. The men responsible – those of the most "horrible throne" – are most likely the faction in the National Assembly called "the Mountain." The Jacobin-dominated government made Paris "the city of the blade" as Nostradamus describes it in other quatrains. Using the old style of spelling, he names Amar (Aymar) the speaker of the bloodthirsty Committee of Public Safety, whose members were responsible for voting the king's execution (the noble obscured). Amar's fiery words stirred the montagnard delegates into ordering a quick and ruthless reprisal for the pro-royalist city of Lyons which sits on the "junction" of the Rhône and Saône rivers. Sixteen hundred houses owned by counter-revolutionaries were demolished, including the city fortifications and most of Bourgneuf quarter. Many thousands were shot and guillotined. Some citizens of Lyons were tied to a wall and shot point blank by cannons. What mangled mess was still alive was dispatched by sabers.

The royalist guerrilla army in the Vendée was defeated in the battle of Le Mans on 13 December, 1793 (St Lucy's Day). The republican forces shattered the royalists' defensive line drawn along the edge of a wood covering the approach to the town. No quarter was given. At least 15,000 royalists were shot by the sanction of "the Mountain."

The Reign of Terror during the counter
revolution was seen in the stars.

ATROCITIES OF THE TERROR

When the victorious republican forces occupied Nantes, the chief rebel city, General Carrier rounded up all the men of the richest families, including old men and boys, and despatched them in carts to Paris and the arms of "Madame Guillotine" (the men are cut up). The phrase "unhappy mixture" describes the macabre games of "Republican Marriage," played by the soldiers on the river docks. Monks and women were stripped of their clothes, bound together in couples and thrown into the Loire river. The soldiers took turns shooting at the naked screaming targets writhing in the bloodstained water.

Republican soldiers shoot the hapless rebels of Nantes like fish in a barrel.

The premier citizens of the city in revolt
Who will struggle hard to regain their liberty:
The men are cut up, unhappy mixture,
Cries, howlings at Nantes, piteous to see!

C5 Q33

"MONT GAULFIER'S" BALLOON

There will go forth from Mont gaulfier
and the Aventine,
One who through the hole will
warn the army.
The booty will be taken from between
two rocks,
The renown of Sextus the celibate
will fail.

C5 Q57

Nostradamus sometimes scrambles his words and events like a mad cook throwing a seven course meal in a blender. A clue, like a strong spice lost in this mess, can help one piece together the original flavor of meaning. The riddle "from the hole" conjured many imaginative interpretations before 1794. One could assume it stands as a metaphorical hole rather than literal "hole" – more like a peep "hole" in the sky, as it could describe the Montgolfier brothers, the inventors of the hot air balloon, perched in an unsteady wicker gondola beneath the hot air hole of his balloon, signaling the Republican generals of any "holes" to exploit in the enemy lines during the battle of Fleurus. "Aventine" stands for the Holy See in Rome. "Sextus" is Montgolfier's contemporary Pope, Pius "the Sixth" – "Sextus" – who would see the treasures (booty) of the Vatican stolen by victorious Revolutionary armies a few years after their victory at Fleurus.

The Montgolfier brothers, Joseph
Michel and Jacques Etienne,
constructed the first hot air balloon
in 1782. Its first manned flight
was on 21 November 1783. It flew
six miles at a height of 300 feet.

ASCENT OF MONTGOLFIER'S FIRST BALLOON

THE FALL OF ROBESPIERRE

THE DOWNFALL OF ROBESPIERRE

*Robespierre's downfall came in 1794
after his dictatorial excesses proved too
much for the Revolutionary Tribunal.*

79

*The fox will be elected without speaking
a word
Playing the public Saint, living on
barely bread,
Afterwards he will suddenly become
a tyrant
Placing his foot on the throats of
the greatest.*

C8 Q41

To his revolutionary contemporaries Robespierre[1] was known as the fox for his ruthless and cunning methods of ensnaring and exterminating his enemies. Two centuries before he was born Nostradamus too chose to describe him as a fox. By 1793, having eliminated most of his opposition in the Assembly, Robespierre was virtual dictator of France. As the high priest of the new "Republic" religion, The Cult of Reason, he played the "public Saint" at a celebration to mark its birth held before a crowd of uneasy spectators in the Champs de Mars. The words "barely bread" may describe more than his austere and puritanical character.

Robespierre[1] tried to avoid the guillotine by shooting himself but succeeded only in shattering his jaw. At his trial in the offices of Public Safety, the dictator, his self-inflicted wounds bandaged and bleeding, was seated on a box of army bread supplies.

At the height of his power Robespierre had decreed that "Any individual who usurps the nation's sovereignty will be immediately put to death by free men." The legal machinery he had perfected led to his execution in 1794. His death ended the Reign of Terror.

---

[1] Maximilien Marie Isidore Robespierre (1758-94), revolutionist who dominated Paris for three months between April and July 1794. His escalating power was considered too dangerous and he was guillotined on 28 July 1794.

CHAPTER FIVE

"NAPAULON" THE FIRST ANTICHRIST

NAPOLEON DISTRIBUTES THE "EAGLES" OF THE GRANDE ARMÉE

I N *THE CENTURIES* Nostradamus foresaw the future coming of three tyrants whom he called "Antichrist." These men, he warns, could move mankind towards total world destruction by the year 2000. The first of these, the subject of Century 1, Quatrain 60, concerns a man who would set the military and political course of modern European history - Napoleon Bonaparte, born near Italy on the island of Corsica.

Nostradamus' vision of the bloody "common advent of the people" for 1792, would give birth to the reign of a commoner dictator destined to force the crowned heads of Europe to adopt his laws and strategies to defeat his revolutionary empire. As a consequence, the united Europe that defeated Napoleon became ever more "Napoleonic." Moreover, the first Antichrist succeeded in steering European history towards the demise of monarchies, a development which set the geopolitical stage for the two future Antichrists. Nostradamus predicted that they would emerge in the 1940s and the 1990s.

Setting out on his glittering career, Napoleon crossed the Alps in 1796 to subdue Italy.

An Emperor will be born near Italy.
He will cost his Empire very dearly;
They will say that from the sort of
people that surround him
He is less a prince than a butcher.
C1 Q60

THE 18TH BRUMAIRE

By Mars contrary to the Monarchy
Of the great fisherman will be in trouble
The young red king will take over
the government.
The traitors will act on a misty day.
C6 Q25

Each line takes us a step closer to dating the month Napoleon seized power: "Mars," the color of war and revolution, i.e., "red," overthrows the Bourbon monarchy thereby establishing that this quatrain concerns itself with the 18th century. Line two brings us to the late 1790's. The "great fisherman" is Pope Pius VI, already troubled by young Bonaparte's successful campaigns in Italy. Pius will soon suffer imprisonment and death on the year of the attempted coup, 1799. The "young red king," of line three is Napoleon. He leads his fellow conspirators in the coup d'état in the month of November, which was known in the revolutionary calendar as Brumaire – "the month of mists."

81

"THE CROPHEAD..."

From the marine and tributary city,
The crophead will take the seat
of government
To chase the sordid one who will then
be against him.
For fourteen years he will hold
his tyranny.
C7 Q13

After becoming First Consul of France, Napoleon, the hero of Toulon "the marine and tributary city," shaved off his locks to resemble his favorite ancient Roman dictator, Julius Caesar. In this new image, Nostradamus dates the exact length of time he would hold power, from November 9, 1799 to April 13, 1814 – fourteen years. (Note the date.)

NAPOLEON BONAPARTE (1769-1821)

THE COUP D'ÉTAT

A great swarm of bees will arise
But no one will know from whence they come:
They ambush by night, the sentinel
under the vines,
The city handed over to five bribed babblers...

C4 Q26

Inside the Hall of Mars in St Cloud the five hundred red-robed delegates of the Directory had just unanimously voted to have General Bonaparte, commander of the Paris garrison, arrested for encircling the building with troops. Their cheers were soon drowned out by the sound of drums beating the charge outside. Burly grenadiers cleared the hall. The delegates threw off their robes and jumped out of the windows in a panic.

Nostradamus foresaw that the empty Hall of Mars would be decorated with the bees of Napoleon's coat-of-arms as a symbol of his coming Empire. The coup d'état was planned the night before. The "five babblers" are the Directory's executive counselors. Two of them had conspired with Napoleon, the other three were bribed to look the other way.

TRAFALGAR

82

＊

In 1805, the British Fleet commanded by the Admiral Lord Nelson, defeated the French and Spanish fleets under Admiral Villeneuve off the Spanish coast near the Cape of Trafalgar. Napoleon could not proceed with his planned invasion of England. This was to create a fatal strategic set-back. England remained unbeaten and safe from his victorious armies and was free to invade occupied Spain and incite the Russians to break Napoleon's continental blockade of England. This led to his disastrous war with Russia in 1812. By 1814 his empire had collapsed.

Lord Nelson died in the battle of Trafalgar and on his flagship, the HMS Victory, black sails were unfurled for her homeward voyage. The hapless Villeneuve was captured in the battle. When he was returned in a prisoner exchange, Napoleon had him strangled to death by one of his Mameluke bodyguards. The executioner used a horse's bridle (bit of a horse). Nostradamus saw the murderer's weapon 250 years prior to the crime.

The promontory stands between two seas
(The Rock of Gibraltar is between the
Atlantic and the Mediterranean Sea)
A man will later die by the bit of a horse:
Proud Neptune (England) unfurls a black
sail for his own man.
Through Gibraltar the fleet near Rocheval.

C1 Q77

DEATH OF LORD NELSON
AT TRAFALGAR

Admiral Lord Nelson died on
the deck of HMS Victory at
the Battle of Trafalgar. His
ship returned to England
under black sail.

THE MAN WITH
THE FEROCIOUS NAME

In Quatrain 76 of Century 1, Nostradamus writes: "A man will be called by a ferocious name, that the three sisters will have his name for destiny. He will speak then to a great people (the French) in words and deeds. More than any other man he will have fame and renown." The three sisters are a double pun for the three Graces of classical Greek mythology and the three sisters of Napoleon – Caroline, Pauline and Elisa – to whom he gave crowns and titles. The "ferocious name" they immortalize for destiny is "(N)apalyon," the Greek word for "Destroyer." (A name immortalized in Revelations 9.11 of the New Testament as "the angel of the abyss, whose name, in Hebrew, is Abbadon, and in Greek, Appolyon, the Destroyer".)

Of the three Antichrists, Napoleon was correctly foreseen as the most obsessed with "deeds" of glory and his immortal "destiny." To this day more books have been written about Napoleon than any other despot, except perhaps for the fierce mid-20th century German warlord, Nostradamus' Second Antichrist.

Other clues to the name and the life of the First Antichrist appear in C8 Q1, which says: "PAU, NAY, LORON will be more of fire than of the blood. To swim in praise, the great one to flee to the confluence. He will refuse entry to the Piuses. The depraved ones and the Durance (France) will keep them imprisoned."

From simple soldier he will attain to Empire.
From the short robe he will attain to the long.
Brave in arms, the very worst towards
the church,
He will vex the priests as water does
the sponge.

C8 Q57

Napoleon was a shaggy, underfed artillery officer during the Revolution. The rigid division of class was broken by the fall of the aristocracy, leaving a situation for promotion which was both dangerous and advantageous. Napoleon gambled on his merit and made a meteoric rise to become the Revolution's brightest general. The people of France, tired of years of chaos, accepted this new law and order dictator. Five years after the death of Robespierre, Napoleon overthrew the Directory and proclaimed himself First Consul of France in 1799. By December 1804 he had discarded the "short" consular robe for the long ermine train of an emperor, when he was crowned by a blackmailed Pope Pius VII in Notre Dame.

The anagram PAU NAY LORON swiveled once becomes NAY PAU LORON and twice NAPAULON ROY = Napoleon the King. The spelling for Napoleon in Corsican style is even closer to the anagram, Napauleone. A more sinister decoding has one drop the "N" and the anagram spells out the Greek horror of the Apocalypse, APALUON ROY or "King Destroyer."

This quatrain also describes him as a man of war "fire" more than of royal blood i.e. a commoner. A passionate man, born under the fire sign of Leo, Napoleon distinguished himself in the "fire" of combat and became a holy terror to Pope Pius VI and Pius VII. They were both imprisoned by Napoleon and Pius VI died in captivity in Valence, on "the confluence" of the rivers Isère and Rhône in 1799. "Durance" is an anagram for France.

JOSEPHINE
Napoleon's first significant mistress, later his wife and first empress. She was a Creole born in the French Colony of Haiti.

Of a name never held by a Gallic King:
Never was so fearful a thunderbolt.
Italy, Spain and the English tremble.
He will be greatly attentive to foreign women.
C4 Q54

MARIA WALENSKA
This ravishing Polish princess was perhaps his most faithful mistress. She visited him during his first abdication and also bore him an illegitimate child.

84

MARIE-LOUISE
Daughter of Francis I of Austria, was his second empress. Napoleon divorced Josephine to marry her. She bore him his first male heir.

Quite a different man will attain to great Empire.
Distant from kindness, more so from happiness,
Ruled by one coming a short time from his bed.
The kingdom rushes towards great misfortune.
C6 Q67

Napoleon was a brooding, lonely man. Only the Empress Josephine among many women who loved him was his true confidant. The common people believed Josephine was his good-luck charm. It is said that she was an avid reader of Nostradamus, and may have recognized the anagram PAY, NAY, LORON for her life's love. Napoleon's fortunes faded after he divorced Josephine to marry a more fertile Marie-Louise of Austria. "Not another Austrian!" murmured the common French folk. The last Austrian princess sharing the French throne was Marie Antoinette. An unlucky omen, indeed! It is a fact that Josephine was dead set against Napoleon's invasion of Russia. But her council was lost. By the disastrous year of 1812, another woman – a rather simple-minded little breeder – was coming a short time from the Emperor's bed.

AN EMPIRE IN ASHES

Napoleon's march to Moscow, stretching his army's strength and supplies to the limit, was his greatest mistake. He had gambled everything on its success but disaster awaited him in the great Russian capital. As the exhausted French soldiers camped in a deserted Moscow on the night of 14 September, 1812, a handful of remaining Muscovites set their city of wooden buildings on fire. For three days and nights Moscow blazed. By the end, only a fifth of the once great city was left and Napoleon was forced to turn back and retrace his steps westwards.

A mass of men approach
from Slavonia,
The Destroyer (Napaulon) will ruin the
old city:
He will see his Roman Empire
quite desolated,
Then he would not know how to
extinguish the great flame.
C4 Q82

NAPOLEON'S PYRRHIC VICTORY BEFORE THE APPROACHES OF MOSCOW, AT BORODINO, 1812

85

Ready to fight he will desert,
The chief adversary will be victorious.
The rear guard will make a defense,
Those who falter dying in the
white country.

C4 Q75

Abandoned by their leader the remnants
of Napoleon's army had to make their
own way back after the débâcle of
Moscow. Ambushed by Cossacks,
starving and frozen, the few who came
back were lucky to be alive.

On the long road back from Moscow, Napoleon's Grand Army, now weary, demoralized and almost in rags, deteriorated into an undisciplined rabble. Many soldiers died in the freezing temperatures and gathering snow, while the tattered remnants of the once-great army fought off attacks by marauding Cossack bands. They received no help from their great commander. Napoleon, callously leaving his soldiers to their fate, donned a disguise and rode back to France on a sleigh, determined to rebuild his armies for the anticipated spring campaigns in Germany. The Grand Army of 20 nations and half a million soldiers which had crossed into Russia on a sunny June day in 1812 returned six months later as 20,000 sick, frozen, and broken men.

THE DEMORALIZED FRENCH ARMY RETURNS HOME

FROM ELBA TO WATERLOO

When Napoleon abdicated in 1814 the Congress of Vienna exiled him to the Mediterranean island of Elba. The following year he escaped from Elba to gather forces for a return to France. His route may have been known by Nostradamus over 240 years before since he writes in Century 10, Quatrain 24: "The captive prince conquered in Itales (either Italy or an anagram facsimile of "Aethalia", the ancient word for Elba), (he) will pass Genoa by sea as far as Marseille..." On 1 March 1815, Napoleon with around 1,100 grenadiers and sailors set out for France, sailing close to the coastline through the Gulf of Genoa and disembarking at Cannes, 100 miles south of Marseilles. By 20 March he was back in Paris, being carried into the Tuileries on the shoulders of a rejoicing crowd who hailed him once more as their hero and head of state.

But, as Nostradamus foretells, Napoleon's victory was to be short-lived. "The captive escaped great dangers. The great one has a change of fortune in a short time..." Exactly 100 days after taking power Napoleon suffered his greatest defeat at Waterloo, bringing the armies of Europe into Paris for the second time in little over a year. The prophet says, "By a good omen, the city is besieged." (C2 Q66). For Nostradamus, the 16th-century monarchist, Napoleon's defeat is a good omen as it anticipates the return to the throne of the royal house of Bourbon.

On June 18, 1815, three months after retaking power, Napoleon prepared to do battle with the era's other great general, the Duke of Wellington[1], on the rain-soaked fields of Belgium. Napoleon had defeated the Prussian army under Field Marshal Blücher two days before at Ligny. He had sent a third of his army in pursuit, gambling that Marshal Grouchy's 30,000 men would pursue the Prussians and prevent them from surprising his right flank while he engaged the British.

CATASTROPHE FOR BONAPARTE AT WATERLOO

The battle of Waterloo proved a disaster for Napoleon. Tens of thousands of French soldiers broke ranks and fled before the advancing English and Prussian troops.

87

By dawn on the 18th, the emperor had endured another long night of suffering from a chronic urinary infection. The pressures of sustaining his empire and fighting 50 pitched battles in 20 years had burnt him out. Still he was expecting victory at Waterloo where he planned to engage the British. The red orb of the summer sun rising over the mist-cloaked muddy campgrounds reminded him of an autumn sunrise many years before at Austerlitz, the place of his greatest victory. While watching the 3,480th sunrise after Austerlitz, an older and war-weary Antichrist wanted to believe it was an omen of victory; Napoleon desperately needed the sun that had shone on Austerlitz in December 1805 to rise in June in the approaching winter of his career.

---

[1] Arthur Wellesley, 1st Duke of Wellington (1769-1852), Irish soldier who proved to be Napoleon's nemesis, defeating him in the Peninsula Wars and destroying him at Waterloo in 1815.

THE BOAR AND THE LEOPARD

In the third month, the sun rising,
The Boar and the Leopard meet on
the battlefield:
The fatigued Leopard looks up to heaven,
And sees an Eagle playing with the sun.

C1 Q23

The Sun and the Eagle will appear to the victor,
The vanquished is reassured with an
empty message:
Neither bugle nor cries will stop the soldiers.
In time liberty and peace is achieved
through death.

C1 Q38

The rising sun of Waterloo could not dry out the mud of the rain-drenched fields. As the light increased it was clear that Napoleon's cannons and troops could not maneuver at dawn as they had done at Austerlitz. Precious time would be lost. And no one knew where Grouchy or the Prussians were.

The battle began at exactly 11:30 pm. One hour and several thousand lives later, keen-eyed junior members of Napoleon's general staff spotted a great mass of men on the distant eastern horizon. One sweep of his spyglass told Napoleon that they were not Grouchy's returning forces but Blücher's[1] Prussians coming to the aid of Wellington. Time was running out. If Napoleon could not give Wellington's army the coup de grace by sundown, his own right flank would be overrun by 30,000 Prussians.

Wellington's men held on to the ridge of Mont. St Jean all that bloody afternoon, beating back wave after wave of French Cavalry and infantry assaults. By sundown, Napoleon committed his final reserves, his own Imperial Guard. The grenadiers swept across the corpse-strewn fields with the irresistible confidence of 20 years of victory. A thin red line of British soldiers crouched in the tangled wheat upon Mont. St Jean, poised for the collision. Wellington rolled his eyes and said, "If Blücher doesn't come now, they will break every bone in my body."

In that terrible moment, Wellington could not have known how close he was to victory.

As he watched the eagle standards of the Guard crest the ridge before the setting sun, a prophecy written 261 years before was coming to life:

"The third month..." (June 1815.) "...the sun rising..." (Napoleon's omen of Austerlitz) "...the Boar..." (This is Napoleon) "...and the Leopard..." (What Napoleon called the heraldic lion symbolizing England, here inferring the Duke of Wellington, meeting on the "battlefield" of Waterloo.)

The vision of Nostradamus becomes reality for the exhausted duke as he sees the brass eagle standards of the French playing in the sun, just as the British line discharges the first of several deadly volleys into the advancing lines of the enemy.

Now the lines of the second Waterloo prophecy spring from mere potential to actual reality. "The Sun and Eagle will appear to the victor. The vanquished is reassured with an empty message..."

Before the Imperial Guard advanced, Napoleon passed a false message among his regular troops that the men massing on their left flank were Grouchy's French troops and not the Prussians. The setting sun of Waterloo illuminated an impossible sight to the French regulars of the Imperial Guard emerging from the smoke of British volleys in full retreat off

88
✳

---

[1] Gebhard Leberecht von Blücher, Prince of Wahlstadt (1752-1819), Prussian field marshal whose last minute appearance with his troops at Waterloo saved the day for Wellington.

the ridge. In the waning light they also saw the battle flags and slate blue uniforms of Prussians on their right flank. The truth behind Napoleon's "empty message" registered on the minds of tens of thousands of exhausted Frenchmen. His army broke ranks and ran.

"...Neither bugle nor cries will stop the soldiers. In time liberty and peace is achieved through death."

No bugle call, or command could stop the stampede. Only the retreating Imperial Guardsmen held their ranks, forming battle squares to face the advancing English and Prussians, and buy time for Nostradamus' First Antichrist to escape the ignominy of capture. Within 15 minutes thousands of guardsmen lay dead and dying.

Peace descended on Europe like the gathering darkness, to cloak the bodies of 47,000 dead and wounded men.

CHAOS AND CARNAGE ON THE WATERLOO BATTLEFIELD

CHAPTER SIX

A CENTURY
OF ROMANCE &
REVOLUTION

NAPOLEON'S TOMB ON ST HELENA

NAPOLEON BONAPARTE, exiled to the South Atlantic island of St Helena, had plenty of time to reflect on the past and predict how his actions would cast a giant shadow on the rest of the 19th century. Hidden within his memoirs and apologies to history are several accurate forecasts. He writes that the "19th" would be "a century of revolu-tions" when monarchies would fall, and that the German states would achieve their unifica-tion. He foresaw the French people freed of the Bourbon yoke. Nostradamus' First Antichrist describes the worldwide spread of the French Revolution with a phrase one might expect from the prophet himself: "from this tripod the light will burst upon the world."

90
✴

THE "DÉBONNAIRE" BOURBON

A hundred times will the inhuman tyrant
die
His place taken by a wise and debonair man.
The entire senate is in his hands
He will be vexed by a malicious scoundrel.

C10 Q90

The great Empire will soon be
exchanged for a little place...
A small petty place of tiny area,
In the middle of which
He will come to lay down his scepter.

C1 Q32

"I still don't understand why I lost," Napoleon often remarked during his slow fade into history on St Helena. "I should have died at Waterloo!" In Century 10, Quatrain 90 (above) we may have Nostradamus chronicling Napoleon's inner torture at being out of the loop of history; a workaholic fighting a losing battle against his two great enemies - time and inactivity. Dying "a hundred times" could also stand as a pun that dates the time of his final bid for power in what historians call the "Hundred Days," the three month period between his triumphal return to Paris on 20 March to his final defeat at Waterloo on 18 June, 1815.

Replacing him on the French throne is Louis XVIII, nicknamed "Le Débonnaire." The new French Parliament pledged themselves to their new king but their zeal for the restored monarchy soon cooled with the crowning of his brother, Charles X, a few years later. Charles X is the quatrain's vexed man, tormented by a Republican fanatic who is to kill his son, Charles, Duc de Berri, the legitimate heir to the throne of France.

One of Nostradamus' prophetic strong suits is the murders of various members of the French royal line. The three quatrains displayed right, and on the following page give relatively clear, but unheeded, warnings for the near-perfect dating of the assassination of the Duc de Berri outside the Paris Opera.

The town of Fossano, in Sardinia, contains the palace of Marie Thérèse of Savoy, the Duc de Berri's grandmother, and he spent his vacations there as Prince of Sardinia (Chief of Fossano). On the night of 13 February, 1820, the duke left the Paris Opera early because his wife was ill. As he helped her into the waiting carriage he was stabbed by Louvel, a republican fanatic employed in the royal stables. Although the stables had kennels for hunting and racing dogs, it is clear Louvel did not take care of the dogs. However, as he was employed as a saddler, he did make their leashes.

Nostradamus misses the mark regarding the area of the fatal wound, unless he can be excused for future potentials moving in a slightly less than predictable direction. Louvel did not cut de Berri's throat; he stabbed him in the chest. The phrase "throat cut" could be an example of Nostradamus' poetic frenzies where he is describing Louvel as a "cut-throat." The

91

❋

The Chief of Fossano will have his throat cut
By the guide (with the leash) exercising
bloodhounds and greyhounds.
The deed is executed by those of the Tarpean Rock,
Saturn in Leo, 13th of February.

C3 Q96

Tarpean Rock stands for Louvel's republicanism; it was a term often used by the great revolutionary orator, Marat[1], in his impassioned speeches. He called for the French people to fling the royalists off the Tarpean Rock to their deaths, just as the republicans of ancient Rome had done with their enemies.

The planet Saturn was definitely not in Leo on the night of de Berri's assassination. But Louvel did murder the duke outside the Paris Opera on the night of 13 February, 1820, and the moon was indeed in a "profound shadow" on that night. According to American astrologer, Dan Oldenburg, there was a new moon at 9 pm, (Paris time) on February 13!

The next quatrain (C1 Q84) unlocks further details. Line one concerns Charles X, father of the Duc de Berri. The second line refers to his brother, Louis XVI, killed by the guillotine. Then Charles, as Duke of Artois, will return after the defeat of Bonaparte to later become Charles X. The phrase "profound shadow" could also be a description of Louvel waiting in the shadows outside the Paris Opera, dagger in hand. Louvel leaped upon de

The Moon obscured in profound shadow
His brother becomes the color of stained blood.
The great one hidden for a long time
in the shadows
Will hold the blade in the bloody wound.

C1 Q84

The great nephew by force will prove
the crime
Committed by the coward's heart...
When the comedy takes place in the evening.

C4 Q73

Berri as he was helping his wife into the carriage. As the grooms quickly dragged the assassin away, the duke looked down in horror at his own hand gripping the dagger buried up to the hilt. "I am dead!" he cried, "I am holding the hilt of the dagger!" Nostradamus gives a vivid impression of being the first to hear the duke's last words (Will hold the blade in the bloody wound).

The third quatrain (C4 Q73) is the denouement. Charles X would step down in the revolution of 1830. The "great nephew" who eventually takes the throne is not of the house of Bourbon, nor of its successor, King Louis Philippe, but Louis Napoleon, nephew of Napoleon Bonaparte. This quatrain is numbered after the year of Louis Napoleon's death - 1873. It also correctly implies that he would benefit from the assassination of the Bourbon heir (when the comedy takes place in the evening) as it brings forward the reign of Louis Philippe who, in 1848, was destined to fall from power in a second revolution. Thanks in part to Louvel, Napoleon Bonaparte's prediction that the Bourbon yoke would fall off the French people was fulfilled.

92

DUC DE BERRI ASSASSINATED BY LOUVEL

---

[1] Jean Paul Marat (1743-93) French revolutionary and doctor. He was stabbed to death in his bath in 1793 by Charlotte Corday.

THE BONES OF THE TRIUMVIR

The French grew restless under the Bourbon Charles. He was deposed in the 1830 revolution by Louis Philippe, Duke of Orléans. He too was deposed - in the even bloodier Europe-wide rash of revolutions in 1848. Both Louis Philippe and his successor, Louis Napoleon, feature strongly in Nostradamus' prophecies.

Louis Philippe's first seven years were a period of prosperity and domestic peace. The successful conquest of Algeria during that time brought added glory, both to France and to its royal house. But things began to sour midway in his 14 year reign. By 1838, riots were erupting in Lyons, Grenoble and Paris over the limited right to vote. The new Bonapartists rallied around the dead emperor's nephew, Louis Bonaparte (poetically described by the prophet as "Ogmios," after "Ogmion" the Celtic Hercules, god of eloquence and poetry). Louis Philippe had him imprisoned but to no avail. The French people persisted in their perplexing, paradoxical love affair with Napoleon's dictatorship and, in time, this was to precipitate Louis Philippe's downfall.

Louis Philippe tried to boost his faltering popularity by fostering the growing romance with the myth of Napoleon Bonaparte. In 1840 he ordered the return of Napoleon's corpse to France. The "triumvir" of Century 5, Quatrain 7 is Napoleon, who in 1799 had been a member of a triumvirate of consuls ruling France. Napoleon's former aides, Gourgaud and Bertrand, sailed with the king's son to

The bones of the Triumvir will be found.
Looking for a deep enigmatic treasure.
Those around will not remain at rest
In this hollowing of lead and marble.

C5 Q7

Fortune will favor Philip for seven years.
He will beat down the exertions of
the Arabs.
Then in the middle (of his reign), a
perplexing and paradoxical affair.
Young Ogmios will destroy his stronghold.

C9 Q89

make a positive identification of their long dead master. They found the embalmed body in remarkable condition. Napoleon's face looked just as it had done when he had seized power in 1799. His hair had grown to its youthful shoulder-length. The ravages of cancer had burned away the fat leaving the lean, Grecian face of his earlier days of youth and glory. His body was placed in a coffin of lead and marble and shipped back to France, where it was drawn through the Paris streets on an elaborate bier to its final resting place at the Hôtel des Invalides. The "enigmatic treasure" is the intangible, romantic myth of France's lost glory and the national nostalgia for it. Though Louis Philippe tried hard to reawaken the romantic fever and transfer it to himself, he never succeeded.

93

A death mask taken from the embalmed body of Napoleon Bonaparte.

*Through avarice, through force
and violence
The chief of Orléans will come to vex
his supporters:
Near St Memire assault and resistance.
Dead in his tent they will say he
sleeps within.*

C8 Q42

By the year 1848, avaricious Louis Philippe was universally disliked. He spent the revolution asleep in his canopied bed (tent). The fighting in the streets started near the Rue de St Merri (Memire: in anagram). Philippe did not die in the revolution; however, Nostradamus' description of his being "dead" may be figurative for his psychological death. Witnesses describe him emerging from his bedroom looking more dead than alive. He stood before members of his cabinet in a nightcap and soiled nightshirt, with a two-day-old growth of beard. In this condition he officially signed his abdication.

94

LIBERTY LEADING THE PEOPLE

THE FRANCO - PRUSSIAN WAR

Under one man peace will be proclaimed everywhere, But not long after there will be looting and rebellion. Because of a refusal, town, land and sea will be invaded. A third of a million dead or captured.

C1 Q92

Prussian Grenadiers storm the French barricades at Le Bourget on 30 October 1870 halfway through the Franco-Prussian war.

95

Napoleon Bonaparte was right in his prediction that Germany would successfully resume its efforts to reunite. But he did not foresee what the cost of this development would be to his nephew, Louis Napoleon, and to France's Second Empire.

Nostradamus, however, does foretell the tragic and sudden fall of the nephew who became Napoleon III, the "one man" who called the Second Empire the "empire of peace." The second line aptly describes the rebellion and bloodshed of the Paris Commune of 1871. The refusal is the Prussian Kaiser Wilhelm I's rejection of Napoleon III's humiliating demands concerning the Hohenzollern candidacy for the Spanish throne. The result of this refusal was that

France found itself plunged into a war it was not prepared to fight. The Prussians and their German allies made rapid and deep incursions into French territory ("land and sea will be invaded") and historians estimate that French losses, killed and captured, were around 300,000. (Nostradamus is 33,000 casualties over the mark.) This estimate is, however, conservative since it takes no account of civilian deaths which were not adequately recorded.

The place in 16th-century Paris where tiles were kilned appears twice in Nostradamus' chronicle of future history. Perhaps when the prophet chanced upon the rows of kilns and piles of tiles during his visit to Paris in 1556, he had premonitions that the place of The Tiles, "la Tuile," would become

96

THE TUILERIES IN FLAMES

the Royal Palace of Les Tuileries; the focal point for two future French revolutions. We have already examined (C9 Q35) in Chapter 4, how "the 500" Fédérés stormed the palace and humiliated King Louis XVI by forcing him to wear the "mitered" cap of the Revolution.

The quatrain above once more implies the Tuileries as the ("royal building") destroyed by forces of the Paris Commune shortly after the end of the Franco-Prussian War ("war will weaken"). The palace was set on fire by artillery shells and incendiaries ("fire falls from the sky"). The war raged from July, 1870 to February, 1871 ("seven months"). The cause of death and grief was the irresponsibility of

Fire falls from the sky on to the royal building when the light of war will weaken. For seven months a great war, people dead through an evil spell (i.e. war hysteria). Rouen and Evreux (Normandy) will not fail the king.

C4 Q100

France's military and political leaders who, caught in the "evil spell" of war hysteria, plunged the country headlong into a military disaster. Nostradamus correctly foresees the people of Normandy wishing to restore the monarchy through the National Assembly.

NAPOLEON III AND THE SECOND REICH

To the deserter of the great fortress
(Sedan). After he will have abandoned his
post: His adversary will display great
prowess. The Emperor – soon to die – will
be condemned.

C4 Q65

Quatrain 65 is an overview of the rise and fall of Napoleon III. On his rise to power Louis Napoleon was "condemned" to life detention in the (great fortress) of Ham. He escaped in 1846 to a castle (fortress) in England. Louis Philippe (abandoned his post) as king in the 1848 Revolution, thereby allowing Louis Napoleon to seize power and become Napoleon III. The French Emperor's "adversary" is the Iron Chancellor of Germany, Otto von Bismarck, who lays a political trap for the French with his demands for a resolution of the German unification question. Napoleon III has a poor record as emperor. Bismarck out-maneuvered him politically and militarily. The luckless man was condemned by his countrymen for allowing himself to be captured by the enemy at Sedan.

The French river will change course
And no longer include the city of Agrippina
(Cologne):
All changed except the old language
Saturn in Leo, Mars (the God of War)
plundering Cancer (in July).

C6 Q4

Line one of this quatrain could be a poetic metaphor for the changing current of France's political fortunes which accelerated the unification of German states. For centuries the French have desired (and occasionally succeeded) to make the Rhine a "French river." Both Charlemagne and Napoleon achieved this in empires past. The last line dates France's final loss of territory on the shores of the Rhine through the acquisition of Alsace and Lorraine by the Germans after the war. Agrippina is a classical allusion to the city of Cologne. All political allegience is changed in Alsace and Lorraine except that French "the old language" is still spoken and was to remain the dominant language. The Franco-Prussian war began in the month of Cancer (July 1870).

THE VICTORIOUS KAISER ENTERS PARIS 1871

POST-EMPIRE DEPRESSION

THE DEATH OF NAPOLEON III. THE LEGACY OF EMPRESS EUGÉNIE

She who is driven from the reign will return,
Her enemies found among conspirators:
More than ever her time will triumph
3 and 70, to death assured.

C6 Q74

Empress Eugénie was Napoleon III's chief confidante, she played Josephine to his Bonaparte. She exerted a powerful influence on her emperor's policies and had her fair share of enemies at court, chiefly among her husband's procession of mistresses. When the emperor was deposed by the National Assembly after his capture at Sedan, she followed him into exile to live at Chiselhurst, England. Line four's "three and seventy" may be a dating for the death of Napoleon III in 1873. No other century with "73" saw a great French leader's death coincide with the end of a French Empire. The quatrain number "74" cannot be ruled out as another hint at dating the event. The general slant of this prophecy points to the year Napoleon III died while undergoing surgery. The former empress lived a long and fulfilling life (her time will triumph) and finally passed away in 1920. Though driven out by her people in 1871, she often returned to her adopted homeland and purchased apartments overlooking the open garden at the end of the Louvre where her previous residence, the Tuileries, had once stood.

As Nostradamus ends his future history of the 19th century, the French people, in a state of general exhaustion and disillusion, are trying to come to terms with the truth of their romantic perceptions of Napoleon Bonaparte and with the trauma of losing two empires. In 1894, the noble mask of French chauvinism slipped, revealing its anti-semitic face in the sensational conspiracy and trial of the unjustly accused Jewish army officer, Alfred Dreyfus.

Before America had its "Watergate" France had its "Dreyfus-Gate." The conspiracy, which haunts the French legal services to this day, haunted Nostradamus 300 years before it happened. He gives an accurate account of the trial and was a better judge of Dreyfus' innocence than the avowed anti-semite judge of the case, Waldeck Rousseau, whom the prophet names outright.

We can only wonder what Dreyfus' staunch defender, the eminent writer and thinker Émile Zola[1], would have thought of this quatrain (right) had he been aware of it.

After the first trial had convicted Dreyfus of espionage and treason and sent him to the notorious prison of Devil's Island, new evidence had arrived proving Dreyfus had not sent secret documents to Germany. Zola and

98

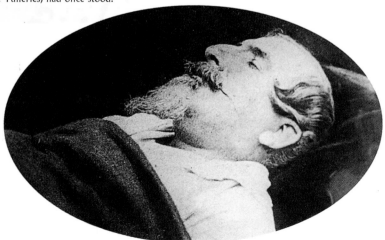

NAPOLEON III DIES AT CHISLEHURST, ENGLAND

[1] Émile Zola (1840-1902). French novelist and political journalist who stood with Dreyfus against the anti-semitism of the French army.

others pressed for a retrial and eventually, in 1899, the government appointed Waldeck Rousseau to re-examine the Dreyfus Case.

Details of the second conspiracy – or "Waldeck-Gate" – surface in the lines of this quatrain.

Line one: "Arrived too late. The act already done..."

The evidence had come too late to save Dreyfus from Devil's Island. Both trials were famous for their anti-semitic overtones. There may be a hidden pun in the first phrase "arrived too late." It implies a missed "schedule", namely a "bodrereau," as the infamous letter disclosing French military secrets to the German military attaché in Paris, was called.

Line two's cliché describes the difficulties of his defense attorneys:

"...the wind was against them..."

Waldeck Rouseau found Dreyfus guilty a second time but, on the strength of Émile Zola's crusade for justice, Dreyfus was pardoned by President Loubet. A new investigation uncovered the true criminals and proved the letters incriminating Dreyfus were forgeries.

"...The letter intercepted on the way.
"...Fourteen conspirators in a body..."

Line three refers to the number of conspirators, although it is not known exactly how many there were. In line four, Nostradamus, the Christianized Jew and prophet, may accuse the noted anti-semitic judge as part of the conspiracy:

"...The enterprise will be undertaken by Rousseau."

RIGHT *Alfred Dreyfus (1859-1935) was accused of passing military secrets to the Germans and imprisoned on Devil's Island. His wife and friends protested his innocence. After a retrial he was still found guilty, but pardoned. His innocence was not established until 1906.*

Arrived too late. The act already done.
The wind was against them. The letters
intercepted on the way
Fourteen conspirators in a party.
The enterprise will be undertaken
by Rousseau .

C1 Q7

With this commentary on the future persecution of Jews, Nostradamus' prophetic chronicle of this romantic and revolutionary century ends. The prophet's First Antichrist, Napoleon Bonaparte, gave us his own chilling prophetic coda to the coming century from his lonely exile on St Helena: "The old system is ended, and the new one is not consolidated, and will not be until after long and furious convulsions."

99

✳

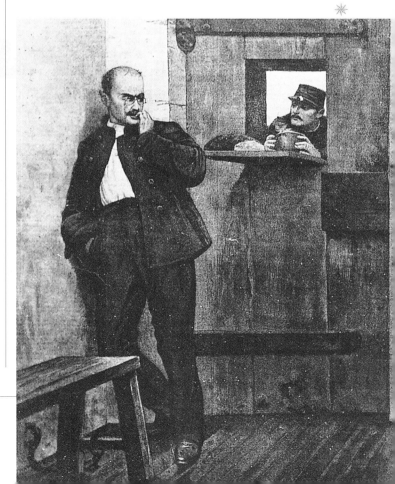

CHAPTER SEVEN

EVIL CENTURY

HITLER AND MUSSOLINI IN UNISON 1938

100

IN THE 20TH CENTURY the details of our lives are recorded as never before. We are organized, numbered, classified, unionized and institutionalized in a way that previous generations could never have imagined.

The foundations of Nostradamus' world - the unassailable sanctity and traditions of the Church, the distinctions of class and wealth, the divine right of kings - have all been transformed, adapted or swept away, and we live in a world dominated by the power of technology. For Nostradamus, the 16th-century man, the visions of our century granted to him in his solitary noctural explorations must have seemed extraordinary and incredible.

"Few will be found who wish to stay in their places." This statement has direct relevance to this century, which has seen the fall of monarchies and the rise of communism and capitalism. From this point onward, the focus of Nostradamus' vision of the future moved away from France to encompass a world that has become, as he says elsewhere, "a small place," where the convulsions of history, for good or evil, affect everyone more completely than ever before.

INVENTIONS

Before long everything will be organized
We await a very evil century:
The lot of the masked and solitary ones (the Clergy) greatly changed,
Few will be found who wish to stay in their places.

C2 Q10

When the animal is tamed by man, after great efforts and difficulty, begins to speak:
The lightning so harmful to the rod will be taken from earth and suspended in the air.

C3 Q44

The blue leader will inflict upon the white leader as much evil as France has done them good. Death from the great antenna hanging from the branch. When (he is) seized the king will ask how many of his men have been captured.

C2 Q2

Would we of the 20th century describe the alien media tools of the 24th century as well as Nostradamus describes the link between modern-day imaging antennas and information gathering implied here? This quatrain describes a near-future event, perhaps a coup d'état in the year 2002 (Q2). Other references in the quatrains to "blue Persian" could infer a coup between a blue or black turbaned Shiite Ayatollah of Iran against a Sunni Moslem leader (White turban). A death is broadcast on TV (antenna...from the branch – i.e. from a tower or aerial). Many European television stations call themselves "Antenna."

Weapons will be heard fighting in the skies.

C4 Q43

...People will travel safely through the sky over land and seas...

C1 Q63

It will rain blood, milk, famine, war and disease.
In the sky will be seen a fire, dragging a trail of sparks."

C2 Q46

By 1943 (Q43), hundreds of German fighters battled Allied bomber fleets numbering up to 1,000 planes in the first great air battles over Germany. International air travel was in full swing by 1963 (Q63); the year 1946 (Q46) saw America ship a number of V-2 rockets and their scientists from Germany to the deserts of the Southwest to begin testing and developing what have become today's intercontinental ballistic missiles. Perhaps in some near-future nightmare we may yet avoid what could be a 16th-century description of lethal chemical weapons (the rain of blood and milk), and their aftermath (famine, war, disease) carried across the skies by the descendants of V-2 rockets, today's intermediate-range and intercontinental ballistic missiles.

Nostradamus tries his bewildered best to describe the 20th century's amazing inventions. The vision of cars, planes and the mysterious powers of nature harnessed for our daily use strain his vocabulary and 16th-century conditioning for an explanation. To him, the disembodied voice of mankind on the air waves is a tamed animal. The sights we pay little attention to, such as power lines, must have fascinated him.

THE HYDROGEN BOMB

Through lightning in the box of the central life fire, gold and silver are melted. The two captives will devour each other...When the fleet travels under water.

C3 Q13

Ships melted and sunk by the Trident.

C5 Q62

This may be no less an act of wanton gibberish than attempts by modern visionaries to describe the future mechanics of Warp drive and transporter beams. The first quatrain is clearly trying to describe the nuclear engines of submarines. The first sentence may be a description of the electrical output coming from the implosion of atoms in a nuclear reactor (captives, i.e. harnessed energies, will devour each other).

The new START II agreement promises a two-thirds cut back of nuclear weapons by 2003. A majority of the remaining 7,000 nuclear devices will be on submarines (many of them are stationed on U.S. Trident nuclear submarines). In World War II air-power decided the outcome of the war. If there is a third world war, the outcome may be decided by submarine power.

THE NUCLEAR SUBMARINE

The incendiary trapped in his own fire...

C5 Q100

There will be let loose living fire and hidden death – horror inside dreadful globes. By night the city will be reduced to dust by the fleet. (Submarines?) The city on fire, helpful to the enemy.

C5 Q8

The mechanics of a nuclear trigger could be described here. In the case of a fission bomb, a hollow sphere of plutonium is surrounded by a second sphere of conventional TNT explosive. The entire outer sphere is ignited by an electrical charge which blasts inward from all sides at once, thus compressing (or in the prophet's words, "trapping") the plutonium in a critical mass. With hydrogen or thermal nuclear bombs a core of deuterium and tritium is ignited by the explosion of an atomic bomb. The radiation from the atomic bomb is focused on a styrofoam explosive surrounding the hydrogen bomb. The hydrogen incendiary, like the fission process, is trapped and compressed by the surrounding atomic explosion which raises the temperature of the deuterium-tritium core to around 20 million degrees Fahrenheit. By being "trapped in its own fire" the hydrogen bomb undergoes fusion and becomes a miniature sun (living fire) as it explodes.

Energy is neutral. The evil or the good is in the user. Here again we have another warning that despite any future ratification and success of the START (Strategic Arms Reduction Treaty), naval forces of the new millennium will still have more than enough weaponry to destroy the planet.

MODERN WARFARE

"LINE WILL ATTACK" ON FRENCH BATTLEFIELDS

Portuguese soldiers taken prisoner during an attack by the German army in April 1918.

*Toward Aquitaine (France) the British
make assaults,
They make great incursions:
Rains and frosts make the terrain
unsafe and uneven,
Against the port of those of the Crescent
(The Turks)
they will make mighty invasions.*

C2 Q1

Nostradamus warns future generations of the great evils of modern warfare. World War I inspired a prophecy of huge battles, fought between vast armies (the size of a whole country's population in his day), and stretching across thousands of miles. Instead of knights in dazzling armor and baggy-sleeved pikemen Nostradamus sees the hell of the **Western Front**. In one line he may describe the terrified soldiers of the future, surrounded by swollen corpses, dying like rats in a barbed wire wasteland of mud. In the next line, he transports us 1,000 miles east, to the outskirts of Istanbul, where the sun beats down on soldiers scrambling up the Dardanelles hills to die under a burst of Turkish machine gun fire.

THE GREAT RED ONE

So many evils committed by means of the great Red One. Holy Icons placed over burning candles. Terrified by fear, none will be seen to move.

C8 Q80

Thousands of Russian Orthodox churches were systematically dynamited and countless religious icons were burned by order of the early Bolshevik government of Lenin and later by the "Great Red" of all communist dictators, Joseph Stalin.

104

BOLSHEVIK GUARDS PROTECT LENIN AND TROTSKY'S PETROGRAD OFFICE

RASPUTIN

Through feigned fury of a divine emotion,
The wife of the great one will be violated.
The judges wishing to condemn such
a doctrine
The victim sacrificed to the ignorant
people.

C6 Q72

Rasputin, like Nostradamus, had the gift of future sight. In his last letter to the Czarina he predicted his murder would take place before New Year's Day, 1917. If he was killed by peasants (ignorant people) he promised the Czarina and her family would flourish, but if he was killed by princes, then she and all her family would be killed inside of two years by the peasants (ignorant people). Nostradamus backed up Rasputin's either-or prediction over 350 years before when the Czarina and Czar Nicolas II (wife...great one) were imprisoned and shot by the Bolsheviks (judges) and "sacrificed to the ignorant people."

Grigoriy Rasputin, the controversial monk and faith healer, is claimed to have healed the young Czarevich of Russia, Alexis, from serious hemophilia attacks. This healing power gained him great influence over the boy's mother, the Czarina Alexandra. Rasputin also had a reputation for seducing many Russian princesses, perhaps even the Czarina herself, with his hypnotic powers and eventually the aristocrats, angry at his domination of the Czar's family, conspired to murder him. Around Christmas 1916 they lured Rasputin to a party in St Petersburg, promising an evening of debauchery. Late in the party, as a phonograph played "Yankee Doodle" in the background, Rasputin's hosts plied him with cyanide-laced drinks. When the poison had no effect, they shot, stabbed and bludgeoned him. Still Rasputin survived. Finally, they threw him bound and chained into the Neva river through a hole in the ice. When his body was recovered it was clear that he had died from drowning.

Grigoriy Rasputin (1871-1916) was a
low-born peasant who became a monk.
He enthralled Czarina Alexandra over
whom he had a magnetic hold.

GRIGORIY RASPUTIN (CENTRE) – ROYAL FAVORITE

THE ROMANOV MURDER MYSTERY

106

THE CZAR AND HIS FAMILY IN 1902
The fall of the Soviet Empire has brought
new opportunities to re-examine the
assassination site and the remains of the
Czar and his family.

Nostradamus may shine some prophetic light on this murder mystery with his remarkably close description of the Romanov murders: "Instead of a bride the daughters are slaughtered. Murder of such wickedness, no survivors to be; the vestal virgins are drowned in the well. And the bride poisoned by a drink of Aconite," C4 Q71. Nostradamus gives us little hope that any of the Czar's virgin daughters were to survive. Yet his last comment may support recent evidence, uncovered in 1991, to support the rumor that Anastasia survived the hail of bullets shot by Cheka[1] guards in the Ekaterinburg basement. Exhumation of remains, believed to be those of the Romanov family, from a muddy pit in a birch forest outside of town showed that those of Anastasia were not among them.

According to William Maples, a biological anthropologist who heads the C.A. Pound Human Identification Laboratory in Gainesville Fla., none of the skeletons is young enough to have been Anastasia or the Czarevich. Nostradamus gives little support to those who believe the woman who claimed to be the grand duchess was in truth the real Anastasia. He seems adamant that she was poisoned (by Aconite).

There may be more figurative meanings to "Aconite." It may stand for its Greek root *akonitos*, "dustless, unconquerable" which may take the meaning beyond the deadly properties of monkshood herb, and apply it to the Romanov murder mystery itself: *a* - without = *konitos*, "dusty," from *koniein*, "to raise dust" or "struggle." In other words, all further investigations, exhumations or the search for a fire pit in the surrounding region, where forensic scientists believe that the bodies of Anastasia and Alexei were cremated, will only raise more controversy and not provide solutions. The mystery of Anastasia will remain forever "akonitos" – unconquerable.

It is believed that Czar Nicholas II and his entire family were shot by Red Guards in Ekaterinberg near the Ural mountains, a few days before the town was liberated by pro-Czarist forces. Circumstantial evidence for the last 70 years indicates that their remains were doused with acid and thrown down a flooded mine shaft. In the following decades stories spread that the Czar's daughter, the grand duchess Anastasia, had survived the assassination. A woman claiming to be the grand duchess bore scars and bunions similar to those possessed by the child but her claim was never adequately proven.

---

[1] Cheka. Secret police of revolutionary Russia.

According to long-suppressed Bolshevik accounts, sometime after midnight on 17 July, 1918, eleven members of the Czar's family and entourage were directed down into the basement of Ipatyev house in Ekaterinberg. There they waited in mounting tension, not knowing what would happen next. Suddenly, a dozen executioners armed with pistols choked the doorway. The Czar stood up, the children clutched hold of each other. The basement air roared with gunfire for 20 minutes. Alexei and three of his sisters were still alive, groaning and writhing on the floor. The guards repeatedly stabbed them with bayonets, but the points hardly penetrated. Later, after stripping the corpses, they found that the women had sewn pearl necklaces, diamonds, and gold coins into their underwear. Their corsets had acted like flak vests, prolonging their death agony. The

The blood of innocents, of the widow and virgin...by the Great Red One...

C8 Q80

...murder of such wickedness, no survivors to be...virgins drowned in a well...

C4 Q71

assassins took the jewellery and money, cut up the bodies, burned the remains, threw what was left into a pit of acid and lobbed a hand-grenade into the pit. Perhaps Anastasia and Alexei were not in the pit. Nostradamus does not shine much more light on the mystery, except that one might infer that Anastasia, if not Alexei, was poisoned.

107

ROMANOV FAMILY SHOT IN BASEMENT ROOM

ABDICATION OF EDWARD VIII

The young heir to the British realm
Which his dying father had recommended
to him,
When the latter is dead, London will dispute
with him,
And from the son, the realm is demanded back.

C10 Q40

THE DUKE AND DUCHESS OF WINDSOR IN 1967

Nostradamus noted a modern concept far beyond the 16th-century mind: an English king abdicating the throne for a twice-divorced commoner, not wishing to remain in his social "place" without the woman he loved.

Edward, Prince of Wales was considered one of the most eligible bachelors of the 1930s. But, in Parliament and in the higher echelons of London society, many disapproved of his comings and goings from nightclubs, first in the company of an attractive, dark-haired American socialite and her English husband, then later without the husband. The prince's father King George V was dying of cancer and soon Edward would be king. He would also be moral defender of the Anglican faith, which required that he marry a girl of suitable blood and moral integrity. When, as King Edward VIII, he continued to see American divorcée, Wallis Simpson, Parliament sent him an ultimatum: drop Wallis or relinquish the crown. Millions heard the king announcing his abdication through the radio - Nostradamus' "tamed animal." Edward declared that he could not continue his responsibilities of office without the help and support of the woman he loved. After his abdication he was given the title Duke of Windsor and left England for a life of exile. As soon as she had finalized her second divorce he married Wallis Simpson.

Nostradamus' opinion of Edward's successor, George VI, is not flattering. Perhaps he disliked the new king's stutter which he "heard" in his visions. It was believed, particularly by George VI's wife, Queen Elizabeth, that the king was unprepared for the stressful job and, in consequence, suffered a premature death. We may therefore infer from Nostradamus that a different and better future for the British royal line could have come from Edward VIII. As he saw it, the pressure to force abdication upon him would later be viewed as "unworthy."

For not wishing to consent to the divorce
Which afterwards will be recognized
as unworthy,
The king of the isles will be driven out
by force
One is put in his place who will have no
mark of kingship.

C10 Q22

HIꭍTER, DUCE, FRANCO

*From the deepest part of
Western Europe
A young child will be born to
poor people:
Who by his speech will seduce a great
multitude,
His reputation will increase in the
Kingdom of the East.*

C3 Q35

*Near the Rhine from the Noricum
Mountains (Austria)
Will be born a great one of the people
come too late,
One who will defend (his conquests)
between Poland, the Baltic and Caspian
Seas and Hungary,
One will not know what became of him.*

C3 Q58

Hitler believed he was Germany's savior. He made people aware "too late" of how abusive the Treaty of Versailles was to Germany after its defeat in World War I. Hitler declared himself the protector of Poland in 1939. He used his "protection" as an excuse to invade Poland. This triggered World War II. Hungary was a German ally during the war. He would later meet disaster through forcing his generals to defend every foot of his conquests in European Russia (between the Baltic and Caspian Seas). Mystery still surrounds the death of Hitler. To this date there is no conclusive evidence to prove that the bodies found burned before his bunker in Berlin were those of Adolf Hitler and his long time mistress, Eva Braun.

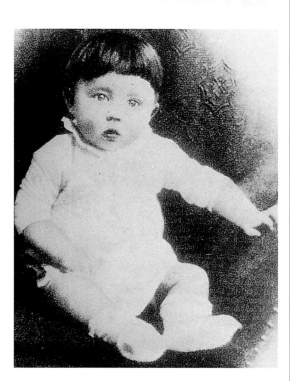

THE YOUNG
ADOLF HITLER

Born in Braunau, Austria, this child of a poor customs official was destined to seduce the entire German nation through eloquent lies and half-truths. Imperial Japan would join his Axis Alliance during World War II.

After warning future generations of the communist revolution, the "Big Red One," Nostradamus foresees the failure of another Utopia, one that will cause the deaths of nearly 50 million people in a second world war. The three great dictators of Fascism appear in his quatrains behind the cryptic names: "Duce," "Hiꭍter," and "Franco."

"Hiꭍter" is probably Nostradamus' most famous enigmatic name, encapsulating the birthplace and name of Adolf Hitler in one word. Hiꭍter is the Latin name for the river Danube, near whose shores Hitler grew up in Linz, Austria. In the original manuscript of *The Centuries* Nostradamus has the "s" written in the old Gothic form of "ꭍ," implying a spelling clue to make the anagram resemble the German dictator's name more closely, "Hister – Hi(*f*)ter – Hitler."

The identification of Mussolini as "Duce," for Il Duce, witnesses to the extraordinary visionary power of Nostradamus. The images he received from this period must have been so strong that he could hear the chorus of Italian voices rhythmically shouting "Duce! Duce!" whenever this posturing buffoon appeared in public. Mussolini led the way in his theatrical manipulation of hysterical crowds but Hitler soon outclassed him with even more sinister and histrionic public spectacles in his bombastic torch-lit rallies. Four centuries before the prophet had described the two men in these words: "Roman power will be quite abased following in the footsteps of its great neighbor; hidden civil hatred and disputes will postpone the follies of these buffoons." C3 Q63. "...They are said to have come from the Rhine and from Hi*f*ter..." C4 Q68.

From Castille, Franco will bring out
the assembly,
The ambassadors will not agree and cause
a schism.
The people of Rivera will be in the crowd,
and they will refuse entry into the Gulf.

C9 Q16

The Cimbrians allied to their neighbors will
come to ravage almost all of Spain...

C3 Q8

Franco[1] and his chief adversary in the Spanish Civil War, Primo de Riviera, are mentioned outright. The republicans (people of Rivera) had Franco exiled to Spanish Morocco. The Cimbrians were an ancient tribe of Germany. Hitler and Mussolini used the Spanish tragedy as a trial ground to test weapons and sharpen strategies for world conquest. Nazi and Italian armaments helped kill 600,000 Spaniards between 1936 and 1939. Franco survived the war by remaining neutral. He would not allow Axis forces free access to attack the British at Gibraltar (refuse entry into the Gulf). This was a strategic loss that Mussolini and Hitler's forces in North Africa could not survive.

Adolf Hitler met Francisco Franco in 1940 for talks. Franco adamantly refused to be drawn into World War II, although he was pro-German in attitude.

[1] Francisco Franco (1892-1976), Spanish military dictator who kept Spain neutral through World War II. After the war he granted the USA rights for military bases in Spain in return for economic help.

THE DICTATOR OF THE THIRD REICH

Liberty will not be regained; it will be occupied by a black, proud, villainous and unjust man.. When the matter of the Pontiff is opened. The republic of Venice (Fascist Italy) will be vexed by Hitler.

C5 Q29

Line two depicts the Italian and German fascists in their black shirts and Gestapo uniforms. It represents Mussolini and indirectly, perhaps his ally, Hitler. The quatrain positively identifies the future intrigues and tacit support of Mussolini and Hitler by the Papacy of Pope Pius XII. The final line is not only a synecdoche for Mussolini's fascist empire, but also covers the many conferences between Hitler and Mussolini in Italy, giving this Latin grammatical device even more poetic impact. The Axis Alliance would be a pact that binds the Italians body and soul to Hitler's self-destruction.

BENITO MUSSOLINI 1883-1945

The great one will be born of Verona and Vicenza, who will bear a very unworthy surname. He who at Venice will desire to take vengeance. He himself is taken by a man of the watch and the sign.

C8 Q33

Mussolini was born in Northern Italy (Verona and Vicenza). His name means "muslin maker," a lowly profession in Nostradamus' time. Mussolini and Hitler's first meeting in Venice in 1933 was a flop. Hitler was dressed in shabby civilian clothes while Il Ducè stood resplendent in military uniform. A diplomat watching Hitler deplane on Lido Airport said "I was fascinated to watch the expressions on their faces. Beneath the obligatory cordiality I found I could see an expression of amusement in Mussolini's eyes and of resentment in Hitler's." Hitler could not understand Il Duce's florid German and Mussolini could not follow Hitler's sharp Austrian accent. Few witnesses at the time could imagine that a few years after that Venetian comedy, Hitler would forge an Axis pact with Mussolini. Hitler, the man of the sign (the Swastika), would get his revenge by turning Mussolini and his regime into a puppet satellite of nazi Germany.

THE GATHERING CLOUDS OF WAR

A great number of people will be condemned,
When the monarchs are reconciled.
But one of them will be so embarrassed
and harmed
That they will hardly remain allies

C2 Q38

The German/Soviet Non-Aggression Pact, signed in 1939, was a tacit agreement between the nazi and communist dictators to postpone war between their two nations. It suited Stalin to believe in Hitler's promises because it gave him time to start modernizing his backward armed forces. In *Mein Kampf*[1], however, Hitler had made it clear that, after France and England were sufficiently devastated, he would turn his forces east and attack the Bolsheviks. Like many other world leaders, Stalin was content to believe that Hitler was bluffing when, in fact, he told the truth. Stalin ignored intelligence reports of mass movements of German forces near the Soviet Union's western frontiers. Even after acquiring the plans of Hitler's imminent invasion of the Soviet Union from a crashed German reconnaissance plane, Stalin remained deluded that Hitler would not strike so soon. But Hitler relentlessly proceeded with his plans, in a way that even his general staff found difficult to believe. After defeating France and isolating England, and just two years after signing the Non-Aggression Treaty with the Soviet Union, he hurled 3,500 tanks and three million men across the Russian border. In his memoirs Nikita Khruschev relates how a chagrined Stalin, contemplating his greatest blunder and faced with catastrophic military losses, confided to Khruschev that they had turned Lenin's revolution "into shit" (so embarrassed and harmed).

As the prophecy states, many people would be condemned as a result of the German/Soviet Non-Aggression Pact. It paved the way for the rapid conquest of Poland by Germans from the West and Soviet troops invading from the East. Millions of Jews would be trapped. On 22 June, 1941 Stalin's self-deception ended at the news of a surprise German offensive along a 1,000 mile front. Within the first year of combat he would lose 20,000 tanks, 15,000 planes, and six million

112

LEFT TO RIGHT *Gaus,*
Von Ribbentrop, Stalin and
Molotov sign the doomed
non-aggression agreement in 1939.

[1]Mein Kampf. *My Struggle*, Hitler's autobiography and political theory, written in Landsberg prison in 1923-4 and published in 1925.

Soviet soldiers would be killed, wounded or missing. Millions of Soviet POWs were condemned to death by starvation in German concentration camps. In three years of battle on the Eastern Front 2.5 million Germans and 20 million Soviets would be killed and vast numbers of Jews and Gentiles from that Eastern European war zone contained within the Hitler-Stalin Pact would be destined to die in Hitler's concentration camps.

Nostradamus' predictions were to become a key factor in French military policy before the war. During the late 1920s the Minister of Defense planned to build a great defensive wall on France's eastern frontiers with Germany. He based his plans on an interpretation of C4

Near the great river, a vast trench, earth excavated,
It will be divided by water into 15 parts:
The city taken, fire, blood, cries and battle given
The greater part involving the collision (of forces).

C4 Q80

The great river is the Rhine. The Maginot Line was broken in 15 places by rivers. Two years before the outbreak of the Second World War, Dr E. de Fontrune, a noted scholar of Nostradamus, believed this quatrain predicted the fortress line's failure. His disturbing interpretation turned out to be correct. The city in the quatrain is Paris, taken by a sudden collision of battles fought by German Panzers side-stepping the fortifications with a plunge through Belgium.

Q80 made in the 19th century by Abbé Torné who, in his analysis of the quatrain, wrote that the next German invasion would swing through Switzerland. The defensive wall, known as the Maginot Line, was built at a cost of two million dollars per mile (1930's costs). This marvelous feat of engineering comprised a network of self-sufficient forts built seven storeys deep into the earth, all interconnected by underground railways. The French government and their military advisors, convinced that the Maginot Line was impregnable, declared that France was safe from invasion. But by its very existence the Maginot Line led to a false sense of security, known throughout the 1930s as the "Maginot mentality."

113

The Maginot Line, considered unbreachable by the French, did not save them from German invasion, as Nostradamus had foreseen.

CHAPTER EIGHT
"HIƒTER"
THE SECOND
ANTICHRIST

THE GATES OPEN AT AUSCHWITZ

114

❋

Marshal Foch, one of the finest French generals of World War I once commented on the Treaty of Versailles that it was "not a peace, but an armistice of twenty years." It can be argued that the harsh terms it inflicted on Germany sowed seeds for revenge, opening doors of opportunity for hate-mongers like Adolf Hitler.

World War II followed exactly 20 years later in 1939, an interval that left the victorious allies of World War I unprepared for the war of Nostradamus' Second Antichrist - the fearsome "Hifter" - who would unleash the "tumult" of modern warfare and open the hellish gates of the concentration camps.

Nostradamus wrote this first commentary on the mid-20th century catastrophe that was World War II (C9 Q90) in the remote 1550s. The quatrain contains many clues to support this interpretation. "Greater Germany" was the name Hitler used for his nazi empire "Grossdeutschland." He promised the German people that he would help them become masters of the world. After 12 years of his tyranny they had nothing and were left trying to survive in the smoke and rubble of his "false" dreams and delusions.

The Captain of Greater Germany will come to deliver false help...his war will cause a great shedding of blood...

C9 Q90

Great discord in the Adriatic (Italy, Yugoslavia and Greece), warfare will arise...unions will be spit apart...including England and France in (the year) '45 and other (broken unions) in '41, '42 and '37...

In that time and in those countries an infernal power will rise against the Church of Jesus Christ, this shall be the second Antichrist...

Epistle

Shortly afterwards, not a very long interval A great roaring storm will be raised by land and sea, The naval battles will be greater than ever: Fires, creatures which shoot making more tumult.

C2 Q40 *1940?*

Many major events, including the dissolution of many "unions," took place on or near the Epistle's dates: In 1936 the Treaty of Versailles was broken by the nazi occupation of the Rhineland, in 1938 by the occupation of Austria; in 1937, full-scale war broke out between China and Japan; the nazi usurpation of Czechoslovakia broke the Munich Pact of 1938; the British saw their alliance with the French split asunder with the defeat of France in 1940-41. The next union to crumble, through Hitler's invasion of Russia in "41," was the notorious Soviet-Nazi Non-Aggression Pact. A long union of trade between Japan and America was broken in 1941 with the Japanese attack on Pearl Harbor. The second Antichrist's union of Japan, Italy and Germany was finally destroyed with the total defeat of the Axis alliance in 1945.

115

Warsaw waifs after the German occupation.

THE PHONY WAR

One autumn night in 1939, Frau Goebbels was tucked up in bed with a good book on her favorite subject, the occult. When she reached a chapter on a certain French prophet named Nostradamus she became very excited. She was stumbling repeatedly on the familiar "Hister" and was soon convinced that the name referred to her husband's boss. Unable to contain herself any longer she shook her husband awake and read aloud to him the most important passages.

Goebbels[1], Hitler's Minister of Propaganda, although he despised all things occult, was impressed. His interest was not, as was later related in his diaries, because he was a

The people gathered to see a new spectacle,
Princes and Kings among many onlookers
Pillars and walls fall, but as if by a miracle
The King and thirty of those present
are saved.

C6 Q51

Ernst Krafft, a Swiss citizen and a fervent believer in the Nazi Party, moved to Germany to offer his already well-known and respected astrological and intuitive services. While working for Himmler's secret service as an astrological consultant, Krafft submitted a paper at the beginning of November, 1939 warning of an assassination threat hovering over Hitler's stars between November 7th through the 10th. The paper was filed and locked away since horoscopes on the Führer were forbidden. On the evening of November 8th, Hitler made his annual speech at the Munich Beer Hall which was the scene of the 1923 "Putsch." Pressing business forced him to cut short his speech. Eight minutes after Hitler and a number of other key nazi leaders left the hall a time bomb hidden in a pillar behind the rostrum exploded killing 7 and wounding 63. On hearing about the Führer's close brush with death, Krafft reminded Himmler's office of his forecast. This time the Gestapo arrested him and brought him to Berlin. He was released to Joseph Goebbels, to work on the Nostradamus project as chief interpreter. It is said that the above quatrain helped Krafft pinpoint the time and place of the assassination attempt.

HITLER AND HIS NAZI HENCHMEN

born-again occultist, but because he saw great propaganda potential in misusing the obscure predictions to feed the growing defeatism of the French. The next morning he ordered his subordinates to hire the astrologer Ernst Krafft to dig out more clues concerning Hitler in the prophecies of Nostradamus. Thus began the famous propaganda war between the nazis and the allies, based on some far-fetched and, occasionally, ingenious interpretations of the quatrains of Nostradamus.

[1] Joseph Goebbels (1897-1945). Hitler's Minister of Public Enlightenment and Propaganda. When the end of Hitler's Reich was inevitable, Goebbels shot his family and himself.

During the lull in fighting after the fall of Poland, between December 1939 through April 1940, German planes flew over the Maginot Line and deep into French airspace, dropping leaflets containing Krafft's interpretations of French defeat. Copies of the pamphlet were soon popping up in England and even as far away as Iran. The allies took Nostradamus seriously after the fall of France. The British Prime Minister, Winston Churchill, had his own interpreter, Ludwig de Wohl, primed and ready to fire back at Krafft's propaganda with pamphlets of his own and, when America joined the conflict, newsreels were shown proclaiming Nostradamus the prophetic champion of democracy.

Ernst Krafft's fortunes turned for the worse in 1941. In that year Rudolph Hess, Nazi Party official and follower of the occult, flew to England on a self-deluded errand of astrologically or psychically-approved peace. Hitler instigated a purge of occultists and

During the "phony war," while both sides waited for battle to commence, France was bombarded by air with leaflets explaining that the country was doomed to defeat, according to the forecasts of their own countryman Nostradamus.

The royal bird over the city of the Sun (Paris)
By night will prophesy warnings for seven months
The wall of the East will fall (Maginot Line)...

C5 Q81

astrologers and Krafft was imprisoned. While in prison he was coerced by the Gestapo into continuing his writing on Nostradamus. Krafft was sincere in his examination of the prophecies and his gift for astrology and interpreting Nostradamus had opened doors for him in the Reich. Now his inability to find a genuine prediction supporting nazi victory stretched him tight as a string. Finally, he succumbed to a nervous breakdown and in January 1945 died from typhus while on his way to the Buchenwald concentration camp.

It is possible to interpret Quatrain 36 of Century 2 as a prophecy about Krafft. It says: "The letters of the great prophet will be seized and fall into the hands of the tyrant. His enterprise will be to deceive his king; but soon his thefts will trouble him."

117

THE FALL OF FRANCE

When the great one carries off the prize
of Nuremberg
Of Augsburg, and those of Basel;
Frankfurt retaken by the leader of Cologne.
He will go through Flanders right into France.

C3 Q53

Here is a sweeping overview of Hitler's political and military successes. Line one refers to his imperious performance before the Nuremberg rallies in 1933-34. Augsburg, Frankfurt and Cologne are each a synecdoche for Hitler's seizure of the Rhineland in 1936. We can even speculate whether "Basel" is a synecdoche for a future trend never followed - a union of Swiss Germany with Hitler. During the seizure of the Rhineland, Hitler correctly concluded that the French did not have the stomach to fight another war. He therefore invaded Poland with little fear that the 45 French divisions stationed on his western borders near the Siegfried Line would dare to attack him in the rear.

Long before the Nuremberg rallies sanctified the cult of Hitler, the French seer appears able to augur its catastrophic results, right down to the Panzer maneuvers. The first stage of Hitler's invasion of France began on 10 May, 1940, with an western invasion of Holland and Belgium (Flanders) all the way to the French Channel coast at the Pas de Calais.

The Germans (and Nostradamus, apparently) saw the fatal flaw in the French defensive plan which had them leave the approaches to the Ardennes forest region near Sedan thinly defended by second-class troops. The French general staff could not believe any large armored force could cross the hilly, forested terrain. They had not read their Nostradamus. Here we have an unobscured reference to the forest of the Ardennes as the pivotal attack point of Hitler's invasion plan. The great empire and colonies of the French would fall through a surprise attack emerging from the Ardennes forest at Sedan. The French Ninth Army would be overrun by waves of Panzers and Stuka dive bombers. The two men earning the prophet's condemnation as "bastards"

Paris fell to the nazis in 1940.
Hitler himself came to stamp
his mark on the city of the sun.

118

The great Empire will soon be desolated
And transferred near the forest of
the Ardennes.
The two bastards will be beheaded by
the oldest
Aenodarb will rule, the hawk nosed one.

C5 Q45

could be the commanders of the French Ninth and Second Armies, Generals Corap and Huntzinger respectively, who did not respond fast enough to prevent the Germans from crossing the Meuse River and splitting the French defensive line in two. After this ignominious failure Corap was dismissed for incompetence and the able Huntzinger was given the humiliating task of signing the armistice on behalf of the vanquished French at a meeting with Hitler. The most senior (oldest) French officer, the commander-in-chief, General Weygrand, tried in vain to staunch the flood of Germans breaching the French front. As a result, Hitler occupied and ruled France. "Aenodarb," as we will see later, could be an enigmatic name used for Adolf Hitler. Nostradamus may be metaphorically naming him after the medieval German emperor, Frederick I, known as Frederick Barbarossa (red beard). The "hawk nosed one" is Charles de Gaulle, the only French tank commander to briefly check the advance of Rommel's Panzer Corps at Montcornet.

...He will launch thunderbolts – so many and
in such an array
Near, and far, then deep into the West.

C4 Q99

...The wall of the East will fall, thunder
and lightning.
In seven days the enemy directly at the gates.

C5 Q81

The great eastern "ditch" of the Maginot Line was made strategically irrelevant by Hitler's lightning thrusts through Flanders and surprise thunderstroke through the Ardennes. Two relatively moderate sorties by German forces breached the fortifications and overcame their demoralized defenders. After the British Expeditionary force abandoned its heavy equipment on the beaches of Dunkirk, Hitler's blitzkrieg (i.e., "lightning war" – called "thunderbolts" by the prophet) turned southwest, plunging through France. Applying an overwhelming force of arms, artillery and air strikes on small sectors of the French lines, he broke through and advanced deep into the rear sectors.

The old man mocked and deprived
of his position,
By a foreigner subordinating him.
The powers of his sons are devoured
before him,
He who will betray his brother at Chartres,
Orléans, and Rouen.

C4 Q61

The purgatory of France under German occupation and Marshal Pétain's puppet Vichy government did not escape the attention of Nostradamus. By the summer of 1944, Hitler had stripped the sons of France and their leader, the "old man" as Pétain was nicknamed, of all their powers. Pétain was deported to Sigmariggen on 19 August, the same day the allies (brother[s]) liberated Chartres, Orléans and Rouen. Note that Quatrain "61" could be upside down for "19."

THE BATTLE OF BRITAIN

They will think they have seen the
sun at night
When they see the half-pig man.
Noise, chants, battles seen fought in the sky
The brute beasts will be heard talking.

C1 Q64

Here is another example of Nostradamus' uncanny accuracy when forecasting English history. He records future battles of great air fleets, piloted by "half-pig men" (pilots in their masks) "Noise, chants...brute beasts...heard talking." (radio transmissions in coded messages, i.e. chants).

From where he thought to cause
famine to come,
From there will come relief supplies.
The eye of the sea watches like a greedy dog,
While one gives the other oil, and wheat.

C4 Q15

If certain actions did not create the necessary future reactions, this riddle-filled quatrain might be just another bit of gibberish. The key to its secrets lies within the right interpretation of "greedy dog." It represents groups of German U boats, which hunted down cargo ships in what were called "wolf" packs. The "eye of the sea" is the submarine periscope. The indexing may also apply this future vision to German submarines of the first world war in 19(15). In either conflict the strategic goal was the same, to cut off American military supplies, fuel and food to Britain, starving her into submission. In both wars the German submarines failed.

Babies starve to death in
Warsaw ghetto.

German submarines patrolled the seas hunting the convoys of merchant ships
bringing supplies to Britain from America.

Londoners, who bore the brunt of the "blitzkrieg" watch the vapor trails as fighter pilots pursue the enemy.

Those of the islands besieged for a long time
Will unleash great violence against
their enemies.
Those outside (of Britain) overcome,
die of hunger
By such starvation as has never been known.

C3 Q71

Britain fought on virtually alone after the fall of France between the summer of 1940 through the summer of 1941, resorting to night bombing raids on German cities. The controversial strategy indiscriminately to bomb urban populations would escalate (unleash great violence) into the great fire-bombings of Hamburg and finally Dresden where tens of thousands died in firestorms. Of the estimated 3,350,000 German civilians killed in the war a large proportion of the fatalities came from Allied bombing raids.

Starvation was one of Hitler's greatest weapons against what he labeled the "subhuman races" – those outside the protection of England. Over 13 million Russians, Poles and Jews from all occupied countries were detained and willfully killed or starved to death.

JEWISH FAMILIES ROUNDED UP FOR TRANSPORTATION

THE FINAL SOLUTION*

*The shocking and infamous armed one will
fear the great furnace
First the chosen one (the Jews), the captives
not returning:
The world's lowest crime,
the Angry Female "Irale" (Israel?) not
at ease,
Barb(arossa), Hitler, Malta. And the
Empty (souless) One does not return.*

P15

To the 16th-century, western European mind-set, cremation was the most disgraceful act that could be inflicted upon the dead. Nostradamus, the Christianized Jew, forewarns us of the Holocaust and its perpetrator's ultimate defeat, in this often overlooked prophecy. It is taken from the collections of quatrains called Presages which were scattered through his annual almanacs published from 1554 through 1567.

The "infamous one" is Hitler, who based his power on manipulating people's fear. He would sanction the German SS commander, Heinrich Himmler, to apply German technology to the creation of an efficient "great furnace" to burn millions of Jewish corpses. No order was written for the final solution, as Hitler feared leaving behind any incriminating evidence. The nazis succeeded in influencing many Jewish community leaders to calm their people with false hopes that their "captivity" in concentration camps was only temporary. But those who passively left the ghettos of Eastern Europe in the endless trains of cattle box cars never returned. Mother Israel is still not "at ease" in a world that still betrays signs of anti-semitism.

The final line, naming the strategic disasters that caused Hitler to lose the war, leaves no doubt that this quatrain foretells the fall of the Second Antichrist.

"Barb" is another allusion to the medieval German ruler "Barbarossa," Hitler's favorite German king. From this reference we may infer that Nostradamus is drawing a parallel between Hitler's obsession with conquering and colonizing the East. Operation "*Barb*" arossa was the code name for Hitler's disastrous Russian campaign.

"Malta" was the linchpin for Hitler's military catastrophes in the south. He never grasped the strategic importance of the small Mediterranean island. Throughout the North African campaigns, ships carrying men and supplies to Rommel's Afrika Korps were sunk by Allied ships and planes based on Malta. Thanks to Malta, Rommel could not sustain his offensives or capitalize on his remarkable victories in the desert, and he could not defeat the British and seize the Middle Eastern oilfields for Germany. At the same time German forces were overextended in Russia and could not reach the Baku oilfields. Hitler would lose the war because he could not cut off the flow of oil to the Allied war effort or sustain his own oil supplies. He is (the empty one) the inhuman messiah of fear no longer able to fuel his world conquest. Hitler's final solution was defeated and the Christianized-Jewish prophet promises Israel that such evil will not return.

---

* "Human flesh through death is burned to ashes . . ." Century 5 Quatrain 16.

BARBAROSSA

Frederick I, nicknamed "Barbarossa," or red beard, was Holy Roman Emperor from 1152 until his death in 1190. He led the Third Crusade against Saladin.

123

On 22 June, 1941, almost 129 years to the day that Napoleon invaded Russia, Hitler unleashed "Operation Barbarossa" against the Soviet Union. The invasion was named for the medieval German king who had tried to extend German domination eastward and to co-lead the Third Crusade into the Middle East. Operation Barbarossa's long-term strategic objectives were to defeat the Soviet Union and open a northern access to the Middle East and its recently discovered oil reserves. Prophetically, the name "Barbarossa" (meaning "red" or "bronze beard," after the king's long red beard) is rich with potential interpretations. Plays on the "Barb" or the "Aeno" (bronze) "darb" anagram for "Barbarossa" appear in five quatrains. Most modern interpreters believe they are metaphors for one or all three of Nostradamus' Antichrists. If we turn to the classics we find it was the name of the Emperor Nero's father, Domitius Aenobarbus. The nickname "bronzebeard" comes from a legend in which one of Nero's ancestors has a black beard that suddenly turns red. Black swastikas on red flags play strongly in Nazi insignia and Nazi standards are modeled after those of Nero's Imperial Rome. The name "Nero" even in his own time, was synonymous with mad, monstrous despotism. Hitler and Nero are both mad rulers who would burn down their own capital cities for their deluded dreams.

Many underground traditions of prophecy, including those influencing Nostradamus' prophetic bias, believed St John the Divine, author of The Book of Revelation, meant Nero as the Antichrist. Since St John there have been off-beat interpretations that Nero did not die from his wounds and would rise again. Nostradamus may be using this myth as a metaphor for a future Antichrist – a new "Bronzebeard" – who would lead a dark Christian crusade against the Bolsheviks and the Jewish killers of Christ.

ARMAGEDDON ON THE STEPPES

He will gather into Greater Germany
Brabant and Flanders, Ghent, Bruges
and Bologne,
The truce feigned, the great Duke of
Armenia (Stalin)
Will assault Vienna and Cologne.

C5 Q94

Hitler's great Russian gamble would fail. He could not shatter the Soviet Empire in eight weeks as planned. Stalin would have time to harness Russia's vast manpower and industrial potential to bring total defeat to Hitler's empire. In a few words this quatrain gives us a prophetic coda to Hitler's successes and catastrophes. First, he lists all the pre-war successes: the occupation of the Rhineland, Austria and the Sudetenland which would "pass" into his "Gross Deutschland" (Greater Germany) empire. Next, Nostradamus lists the early nazi conquests: The Netherlands, Belgium, Northern France. The Italian city of Bologna would be occupied by nazi forces later in the war when Mussolini's government finally collapsed.

Stalin and Hitler had a tacit understanding that their Non-Aggression Pact of 1939 was a postponement for the final battle to be waged between fascism and communism. Hitler had only jumped the gun on Stalin and exposed the pact for what it was, a "feigned" truce. The title "Great Duke of Armenia" is a synecdoche for Joseph Stalin who was born in Soviet Georgia and spent much of his formative years in neighboring "Armenia."

By 1945, the full consequences of Hitler's Operation Barbarossa were clear. Three years after facing near defeat before Moscow, the Russians had pushed the nazis back into Europe and had themselves advanced as far as Berlin and Vienna.

Nostradamus' mention of Cologne is either an interesting mistake, or a future potential aborted. It implies the Allies may have faltered in the Normandy invasion, or perhaps lost the Battle of the Bulge, leaving the Russians to completely overrun Germany.

While the eagle is with the cock at Savona,
The Eastern Sea and Hungary will
be united.
The army at Naples, Palermo, the
marches of Ancona,
Rome and Venice – a horrible outcry by
the Barb.

C8 Q9

Except for the fact that American (Eagle) and French (Cock) forces were not present to liberate Savona, Italy, the quatrain adequately describes Allied advances during in the final weeks of the war in 1945. The Soviets by that time had completely liberated Hungary and the Black Sea region from the nazis. At the same time Allied forces were marching up the Northern Italian peninsula past Ancona, as a result of their successful victories of 1943 in Sicily (Palermo) and Southern Italy (Naples). Rome could stand for the Vatican which gave so much tacit support to Mussolini's fascist empire (Venice). The horrible outcry from Barb(arossa) comes from Hitler in the last days of his life, which were noted for the Führer's rabid outbursts against the German peoples' betrayal of his Third Reich.

THE GREATER PART OF THE BATTLEFIELD AGAINST "HIƒTER"

It has often been said by those who either have an attitude about Nostradamus — or simply don't deeply study these quatrains — that the prophet fairly well describes how World War Two begins but doesn't pinpoint who wins. On these pages are four quatrains that detail the maneuvers of the victorious Allies in the final years of the war.

The inhabitants of Marseilles completely changed,
Flight and pursuit right up to the approaches of Lyons.
Narbonne, Toulouse outraged by Bordeaux;
Killed and captive are almost a million.

C1 Q72

In 1940 the French government fled Paris for Bordeaux leaving the capital to Hitler's panzers. The "outraged" towns later belonged to the hated Vichy puppet government. It appears that Nostradamus foresaw the peaceful town and hills of his native Provence becoming the battlefield of a distant, future war. In 1944, the great steel monsters firing and making tumult landed on the shores of Provence in Operation Dragoon. The forces of the Free French initially pushed the Germans out of Marseilles and all the way back to Lyons. Official French casualty estimates for World War II put their losses at 863,145.

Rain, wind, forces, Barbare (Barbarossa),
Hitler, the Tyrrhenian Sea,
Vessels to pass Orkneys and beyond Gibraltar,
grain and soldiers provided:
Retreats too well executed by Florence,
Sienna crossed,
The two will be dead, friendships joined.

Presage 31

Because of his losses in winter battles of 1941 Hitler could not resume his Russian Campaign along the entire front. The "Tyrren" stands for Naples and the region of the Mediterranean sea. Line two maps the major convoy routes from America through the North Atlantic and Gibraltar which eventually supplied the Allies with enough food, fuel and soldiers to win. By the end of 1944 both Sienna and Florence were liberated by the Allies (crossed). The final line relates the fateful Axis alliance of Nostradamus' Duce and Hitler, joining them in a friendship and death.

Beasts wild with hunger will cross the rivers,
The greater part of the battlefield will be against Hitler.
He will cause the great one to be drawn into an iron cage,
When the child of Germany observes no law.

C2 Q24

A total of over 100 million men from over 50 nations were united against the Axis forces of Hitler and his allies, Italy and Japan. Using Europe's vast rivers as natural obstacles played a major part in Hitler's "Fortress Europe" defense plan, especially on the Eastern Front. Titanic battles thick with the thunder and tumult of planes tanks and tens of thousands of artillery pieces were fought by the Soviets to cross the Volga (Stalingrad, 1942), the Neva (Leningrad, 1943), the Dnieper (Kiev, 1943), the Danube (Budapest, 1944, and Vienna, 1945) the Oder (Berlin, 1945); and from the Western Front came the two great battles to cross the Rhine (Arnhem, 1944, and the Battle of the Rhine, 1945). The third line most likely stands for the fate of Mussolini who will be actually encaged as we will see later. The final line is a coda to the madness befallen Germany under the Third Reich. Hitler even said that he wanted the children of Germany to become good "German Barbarians."

THE DEATH OF MUSSOLINI

Duce loses his eyes in an iron cage in Milan

C9 Q95

MUSSOLINI KILLED AND HANGING IN THE PIAZZOLE

By 28 April, 1945, the Axis forces were routed on all fronts. Hitler remained in Berlin trying to muster his last reserves for a final stand against the Soviet steamroller. The same day, Mussolini and his mistress, Clara Petacci, fell into the hands of communist partisans. After a few words of mock trial they were gunned down in the street and their bodies hauled to Milan to be strung upside down from the charred steel frame of a bombed-out gas station. The gathering crowd vented years of repressed rage at "Il Duce's" body: throwing stones, shooting and even urinating on the corpses. One man pummeled Mussolini's face beyond recognition (loses his eyes) with a board.

In C6 Q31 Nostradamus may have recorded the coup which precipitated Mussolini's execution. The quatrain says: "The King will find that which he desires so much...the reply to Duce will make him angry." King Victor Emmanuel III was no friend of the Italian premier and the Allied invasion of Italy in 1943 finally gave him the political clout to dismiss Mussolini in person. The final outcome is related in the quatrain's last line, "He (the king's action) will put several to death in Milan."

The great Empire will soon be desolated
And transferred near the forest of the Ardennes.
The two bastards will be beheaded by the oldest
Aenodarb, will rule, the hawk nosed one.

C5 Q45

Nostradamus continues to pinpoint the Ardennes Forest region of Luxembourg as the invasion avenue where the fortunes of two great empires fail in the space of a few years. As we examined earlier this quatrain targets France and its colonial empire defeated by a German surprise thrust through the Ardennes in 1940. The quatrain can also apply equally to the Nazi Empire falling because the next German thrust would backfire in the Battle of the Bulge. The quatrain is appropriately numbered "45" for the year the battle ended and dates the Nazi Empire's total annihilation down to the month: C5 Q45 = (May) of (19)45.

THE DEATH OF
THE SECOND ANTICHRIST

The beginning and end of World War II are foretold in two quatrains numbered 40. They may be a message to France that 1940, the year of their greatest defeat, will be avenged. The last quatrain describes Hitler's final moments deep inside his fortified Berlin bunker while, above him, the great city was bombarded. It says,

"The fortress of the besieged sealed and sunk to its depths by explosives. The traitor will be entombed alive, never did such a pitiful division happen to the Saxons (Germany)..." C4 Q40.

Adolf Hitler shot himself two days after Mussolini's death in Milan. The terrible war would end with Eastern portions of Nazi Germany (the Saxons) divided from the rest of Germany by the Iron Curtain.

The photograph below is taken from a recently discovered archive film. It is said to show the corpse of Adolf Hitler clutching a photograph of his mother. It is believed to have been taken by Hitler's nazi henchmen, just prior to their cremating his body outside the Berlin bunker.

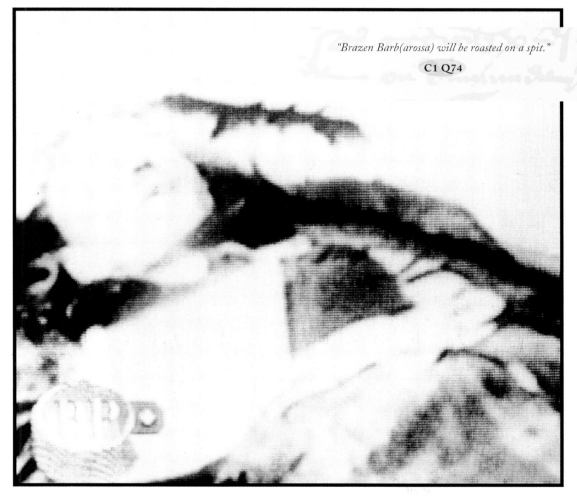

"Brazen Barb(arossa) will be roasted on a spit."
C1 Q74

127

HITLER'S SUICIDE ENDS NAZI TYRANNY

THE SUN FALLS ON HIROSHIMA

*Those of the Sun will not cross the
sea in safety
...part of Asia will change.*

C5 Q11

Japan lost the war because it could not adequately supply and reinforce its island fortresses when its maritime and naval fleet were sunk by American submarine and air power dominating the Pacific theater of war.

*Near the harbors within two cities,
There will happen two scourges the like of
which was never before seen,
Famine, pestilence within, people put
out by the sword.
They cry for help from the great
immortal God!*

C2 Q6

In other quatrains Nostradamus may reveal the date(s) when a new and terrible nightmare weapon would obliterate two port cities: August 6, 1945, the day Hiroshima was irradiated and perhaps even August 9th, the day Nagasaki suffered the second nuclear attack. Turn the "6" upside down and one gets the date for the bombing of Nagasaki three days later on August 9th. The words of this quatrain capture some of the prophet's horror while witnessing the two Japanese ports sacrificed on the altar of the dawning Nuclear Age.

*Hiroshima was devastated
by the atomic bomb dropped
on 6 August 1945.*

CHAPTER NINE

TENSION IN A SHRINKING WORLD

THE PLANET EARTH AS SEEN FROM THE MOON

129

*

THE PROPHECY of Century 1, Quatrain 63, gives a perfect description of the post-war world. By 1963, modern medicine had almost eradicated the great killer diseases of previous centuries. The jet age, by making global travel fast and safe, had made the world smaller. Developments in communications technology facilitated contact between different peoples and cultures.

For nearly half-a-century, fear of atomic war has deterred the world's leaders from launching into another global conflict. The struggle between the superpowers has been played out in the developing countries of the Third World. Since 1945, their arguments and tensions have found expression in local wars and confrontations between the Arab nations and Israel, or India and Pakistan. With the end of the Cold War, tensions in the Third World are increasing, as are wars in the ethnic hotbeds of the former communist bloc.

The technological and medical advances foretold by Nostradamus have their darker consequences. The record growth of industrial production has improved our quality of life but its pollution threatens the earth's fragile ecosystem. The computer which has revolutionized our lives is capable of transmitting a message of peace – or global nuclear destruction – at the stroke of a key.

ISRAEL AND PALESTINE

*Pestilences extinguished, the world
becomes small
For a long time the lands will be
inhabited in peace.
People will travel safely by air, (over)
land, seas and wave.
Then wars will start again.*

C1 Q63

*Newcomers build a place without defense,
Occupying a place (which) until then
(was) inhabitable.
Meadows, houses, fields, towns to take
at pleasure,
Famine, plague, war, extensive arable land.*

C2 Q19

Palestinians rioting in 1991 after rumors spread through the Arab quarter of Jerusalem that Jewish ultra-nationalists, called the Temple Mount Faithful, were planning to put the cornerstone of the new Temple of Solomon next to the Dome on the Rock, one of Islam's holiest shrines.

The newcomers (C2 Q19) are the Jewish survivors of the Holocaust establishing their own state in the "promised land" of Palestine. Prior to the Holocaust the slow-but-steady colonization of Palestine by the Zionist movement saw Jewish pioneers establish communes (kibbutzim) which were always vulnerable to attack from hostile Arab neighbors, thus the term "without defense." This early experience of vulnerability, compounded with the horrors of the Holocaust, has understandably deepened the Israeli feeling of being "without defense" in a hostile gentile world.

It can be argued that the cryptic phrase "until then (was) inhabitable" dates the creation of the Israeli state in 1948 as the beginning of a period when life in the Holy Land is in danger of annihilation. The Jewish state was achieved at the price of expulsion for the Palestinians and, since its establishment, there have been Arab-Israeli wars in 1948, 1956, 1967, 1973, 1982 and the second Gulf War of 1990-91. The quatrain's meadows, houses, fields and towns taken with pleasure could be a criticism of Israeli's policy of occupation in the West Bank, Gaza Strip, South Lebanon and the Golan Heights.

The final line of this prophecy could be a warning to a people once persecuted, of the consequences of becoming persecutors themselves. It could signal the breaking point of a nation which, itself armed with a nuclear capability, will go to any lengths to prevent its neighbors from acquiring such power. The final line of the quatrain hints of horror and hope. Either "famine, plague, war..." will come as a result from this regional doomsday arms race or a continued strengthening of global government and ethics, ensuring security and peace for Arab and Jew, will monitor the creation of a regional nuclear free zone, creating a happy future of "extensive arable land" for all those living in the Middle East.

THE HUNGARIAN REVOLUTION
1956 – 1990

On 1 November, 1956, as the people of Hungary struggle with another dreary winter of communist domination, their Premier Nagy[1] sets off a brief flash fire in the Cold War by declaring Hungary free of the Warsaw Pact Alliance with the Soviets. Three days later celebrations in the streets of Budapest are replaced by mobs hurling Molotov cocktails at invading Soviet tanks. Castor and Pollux, the twins of Greek mythology, stand as a double meaning for pro and anti-communist Hungarian brothers killing each other in the rubble of the "twin" city of Buda and Pest.

As fighting raged in the streets of Budapest, the Suez Canal crisis was gathering pace, leaving the United States, Britain and France divided on what to do. Desperate calls for Western assistance from the Hungarian freedom fighters went unheeded. President Eisenhower would not wage nuclear war with Russia over Hungary. Once the rebellion was crushed, Nagy and thousands of supporters of the uprising were shot and Hungary was to endure long decades of repressive Soviet-backed governments.

Nostradamus may have left a clue of hope for the Hungarians. Consider the indexing of this quatrain. Number "90" could be intended for the time Hungary achieved democracy. Just two months prior to 1990 the Hungarian Communist Party was dissolved and the Hungarian parliament passed legislation legalizing freedom of assembly and association. The year 1990 saw Hungary break away from communism to become a fledgling democracy. It was also the year that marked the beginning of the withdrawal of Soviet military forces from Hungary, a process completed by 19 June, 1991.

> *Through (a) life and death (struggle), the rule of Hungary changed.*
> *The law will be more harsh than slavery.*
> *Their great city calls out with howls and laments,*
> *Castor and Pollux are enemies in the arena.*
>
> **C2 Q90**

PROTEST AND UPRISING IN HUNGARY 1956

---

[1] Imre Nagy (1895-1958). Hungarian politician who was a keen revolutionary and Soviet citizen in his youth. He became Prime Minister of Hungary in 1953 and again in 1956 when he supported the revolutionaries. When the Soviets put down the uprising, Nagy was removed from power and later executed.

CHARLES DE GAULLE
1958 – 1970

*...for three times one surnamed de Gaulle
will lead France...*

C9 Q33

In 1940, Charles de Gaulle (center) distinguished himself by leading France three times. First as head of the Free French forces; then as the leader of the provisional post-World War II government until 1946, and again in 1958 during the Algerian crisis, where he gained voter approval to become the first president of the newly established French Fifth Republic. During his long presidency (1958-70) he was responsible for the dismantling of the French colonial empire, which was a major step toward the formation of the future's global village. However, De Gaulle also resisted the creation of a global village by pulling France out of the NATO alliance. His famous "non" policy in foreign affairs made De Gaulle a nagging thorn in the side of those making efforts to form a European Community.

CHARLES DE GAULLE, PRESIDENT OF FRANCE 1958-70

From the Albert Hall, General de Gaulle rallies the Free French, French soldiers and airmen based in London, in 1942.

CHINA'S CULTURAL REVOLUTIONS
1949 – 1989

毛澤東的勝利旗幟下前進

在毛澤東的勝利旗幟下前進

MAO TSE TUNG

Far distant from his realm, sent on a
dangerous journey
He will lead a great army and keep it
for himself,
The King will hold his nation hostage
He will plunder the whole country on
his return.

C8 Q92

In the early 1930s Chiang Kai-Shek's Nationalist forces tried to encircle and annihilate the Chinese Red Army. Mao Tse Tung heroically lead the communists on a six-thousand-mile journey through the Chinese hinterlands to safety during what is popularly called the "Long March." Later, he kept the hardened Red Army for himself at last defeating the nationalist Chinese in 1949. In the 1960s, the aging demigod of communist China threw the world's highest populated country into the destructive catharsis and social turmoil of the Cultural Revolution. Ever since that time China suffers from the bloody spasms of a political identity crisis. How she balances free economy with rigid adherence to Marxist communism will define her critical role in the coming global village as she is destined to fill the superpower void left by the collapse of the Soviet Empire. Before the next millennium China will take up her role as the developing Southern world's protector against the Northern bloc of developed–and formerly colonial – master nations. How she is treated will either see her wage Armageddon with the Northerners or help bridge the economic gap dividing the wealthy and developing nations.

Mao Tse Tung. The near deified founder of communism, a regime which was ultimately responsible for the unanimously vilified massacre of Tiananmen square – "The King will hold his nation hostage."

THE THREE MURDERED BROTHERS
1963 – 1968

With his remarkable sensitivity to major upheavals in our future history, Nostradamus would have been unlikely to miss the assassinations of President John F. Kennedy (JFK) and his brother, Senator Robert Kennedy (RFK) which so shocked the world. With the President's assassination in 1963 the American post war age of innocence ended and the nation faced the new realism of war in Vietnam and turbulent protest at home. But in 1968 hopes were renewed by the political rise of the Robert Kennedy who won a decisive victory in the California primary. The Kennedy charisma was back and, riding on a wave of political support and public euphoria, Robert seemed destined for the White House. A few minutes after delivering his victory speech Robert Kennedy was assassinated.

A plethora of plausible-though-controversial assassination theories have circulated since the 1960s, ranging from an underworld conspiracy to kill the Kennedy brothers to a state-sanctioned assassination of President Kennedy by Fidel Castro[1], Cuba's Marxist dictator. In the 1990s such conspiracy theorizing was given a new lease of life by Oliver Stone's blockbuster movie "JFK" which proposes that a rogue element in the United States Government assassinated the President in a coup d'état. Stone's dramatization has us believe the assassination was committed to forestall Kennedy's efforts to pull American forces out of Vietnam and end the Cold War 30 years early. There is no denying that the deaths of John Kennedy and his brother directed the world down a new prophetic pathway of chance. Their assassinations may have aided those with a vested interest in the continued expansion of a military industrial complex with its highly profitable business of armaments and weapons development. If Kennedy had lived, there may never have been a Vietnam and 60,000 American and two million Asian deaths would have been prevented.

134

FAMILY CHRISTMAS AT THE KENNEDY HOME

"It should be clear by now that a nation can be no stronger abroad than she is at home. An America which practices what it preaches about equal rights and social justice will be respected by those whose choice affects our future." Kennedy's undelivered speech at Dallas, Texas.

[1] Fidel Castro (b. 1927). Cuban revolutionary who waged relentless guerilla war on President Juan Batista and finally became leader of his country in February 1959.

JOE

The antichrist very soon annihilates the three (brothers)...

C8 Q77

The lands populated by humans will become uninhabitable... Nations given to men incapable of prudence. For the three brothers, death and dissension.

C2 Q95

135
✳

BOBBY   TEDDY   JACK

A common oversight is to assume that the last living brother of the slain President, Senator Edward Kennedy, is the third brother foreseen by Nostradamus to be killed by evil, anti-Christian forces. The Kennedy patriarch, Joseph Kennedy had

earmarked the oldest brother, Joseph Jr., as the number one choice for the presidency. Young Joe was killed while fighting "anti-Christian" nazi forces in World War II. Interesting theories abound implicating the pro-war and "anti-Christian" forces of

the Cold War military industrial complex and the Mafia as responsible for assassinating John and Robert Kennedy. It can be argued that Teddy Kennedy, the youngest brother, was never part of the prophecy.

Both Kennedy and Khrushchev[1] were changed by the trauma of the Cuban missile crisis. The experience of being the only men to have come within a hair's breadth of pushing the "button" of thermo-nuclear war seems to have scared the two world leaders into sanity, resolving them both to initiate political moves toward nuclear disarmament. Three months before President Kennedy was shot (and 16 months before Khrushchev was overthrown by the vested interests of his own military industrial complex), the two men signed the Nuclear Test Ban Treaty, prohibiting nuclear tests in space or in the oceans.

Who knows what could have happened if bullets had not ripped the air at Dealey Plaza in Dallas on that November day in 1963; or what future course history might have taken if a madman in the Los Angeles Ambassador Hotel had not shot Robert Kennedy in 1968. Nostradamus gives prophetic hints that John Kennedy was destined to be a great president. It may be that quatrains which we now find undecipherable might, given a different direction of history, describe Kennedy as a two-term president. Kennedy might have had enough time to end the Cold War a generation earlier. Robert Kennedy could then have become president in 1968 and kept the superpowers on a short path to peace. Prophecy aside, the rehabilitation of Russia would have been more secure had there been a move toward more "glasnost" (openness) and "perestroika" (restructuring) in the late 60s, instead of two decades later when the Soviet economy was in a state of terminal decline.

Conspiracy theories continue to haunt the work of the formal committees investigating the Kennedy assassinations. The Warren Commission concluded that President John Kennedy was shot by Lee Harvey Oswald from the sixth floor of the Texas Book Repository Building shortly after noon on 22 November. According to the Commission, Oswald had worked alone and there had been no conspiracy. But a detailed inspection of a home movie made by a spectator at the Dallas shooting shows that the Commission's theory of one assassin and one gun is a physical impossibility.

The key to discovering the truth about a conspiracy was Lee Harvey Oswald but, on the day Kennedy's body lay in state in the U.S. Capital rotunda, Oswald was shot dead by Jack Ruby in Dallas. The Dallas chief of homicide announced that the Kennedy assassination case was closed.

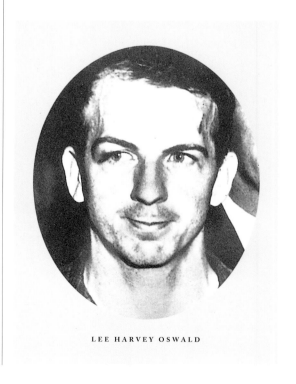

LEE HARVEY OSWALD

Lee Harvey Oswald, after he was arrested for the assassination of President Kennedy in November 1963. Oswald was himself shot by Jack Ruby.

---

[1] Nikita Sergeyovitch Khrushchev (1894-1971). Soviet politician who joined the Communist Party in 1918 and rapidly rose to become first Secretary in 1953 and premier in 1956. He was deposed in 1964.

The sudden death of the first
personage
Will have caused a change and put
another to rule:
Soon but too late he comes to high
position, of young age,
It will be necessary to fear him by land and sea.

C4 Q14

At age 43, Kennedy was the youngest person ever elected president. His masterful handling of the Cuban missile crisis in 1962 made him feared on land and sea by the Soviet Union. Nostradamus may infer here that Kennedy would have become one of our century's greatest leaders if he had survived assassination and finished his term.

Before the battle the great man will fall,
The great one to death, death too sudden and lamented.
Born imperfect, he will go the greater part of the way:
Near the river of blood (i.e. The Red River: synecdoche for northern Texas)
the ground is stained.

C2 Q57

Perhaps these quatrains imply an alternative destiny for young Kennedy's Camelot? One where America never knew a Vietnam war, or the social breakdown of the 60s. Young President Kennedy was known for his "imperfect" moral conduct as well as being born with an "imperfect" adrenal system and lower back. Perhaps if he had "not" been assassinated we would have also known him as the president who went the extra mile in ending the Cold War, and championed the Black American advance toward equal civil rights to its completion. If JFK had lived, Senator Johnson, would have fallen into political obscurity as a two-term vice president, rather than become the slain president's successor and the captain of a failed administration overwhelmed by the debacle of Vietnam. After John Kennedy's tenure in "Camelot" ended in 1968, the political dynasty would continue with Robert Kennedy. With the Cold War over, Robert's dream of bringing peace to the Middle East might have been realized by 1976. Maybe then, Senator Edward (Teddy) Kennedy would have had the time to mature and be a president through the tute-

lage of his "living" brothers, rather than struggle along as a psychological victim of assassination's tragedy?

President John F. Kennedy may have defined that murdered future when he once said, "What kind of peace do we seek? Not a Pax Americana enforced on the world by American weapons of war. Not a peace of the grave or the security of the slave. I am talking about genuine peace, the kind of peace that makes life on earth worth living, the kind of peace that enables men and nations to grow and to hope and to build a better life for their children – not merely peace for Americans, but peace for all men and women; not merely peace in our time, but peace for all time." (*The Burden and the Glory* - Allen Nevins, ed.)

If the Kennedy brothers had lived much more time and effort would have existed to bring about a Global Village by the 90s. Because their future was terminated we now live with the ever clearer and always present danger that there will be Armageddon before the new millennium "because" the Cold War ended a generation too late!

Over a dozen witnesses to the Dallas assassination said they heard the fatal shot issue from a small grass covered hill. In the controversial documentary "The Men Who Killed Kennedy" (Bill Kurtis Production: 1988) a computer-enhanced photograph dimly distinguishes a man dressed as a police officer, aiming a rifle from the grassy knoll. The puff of smoke is clearly displayed. In the years following most of the witnesses who heard the shot from the mysterious policeman died violent deaths. Nostradamus implicates another man as the real murderer of Kennedy, rather than Oswald. He says, "The guilty one is hidden in the misty woods."

138

KENNEDY MOTORCADE DRIVES THROUGH DALLAS

The great man will be struck down in the day by a thunderbolt,
The evil deed predicted by the bearer of a petition
According to the prediction another falls at night time.
Conflict in Reims, London, and pestilence in Tuscany.

C1 Q26

President John Kennedy was shot shortly after twelve noon in Dallas, Texas on November 22, 1963. Senator Robert Kennedy was assassinated a few minutes after 1 a.m., moments after his victory speech for winning the California primary election in his run for the U.S. presidency in 1968. Jean Dixon, one of the foremost prophets of modern times, earned international notoriety for predicting JFK's assassination as early as 1956. The "bearer of the petition" could be Dixon. Nostradamus may have chronicled her unsuccessful attempt to forewarn the president and later Senator Kennedy, who was her friend. The last line dates RFK's murder through events occurring around the time of his murder: student riots in France and London during 1968-9, (Reims – is a synecdoche for France) and the Florence flood in 1966 when authorities were afraid of pestilence in Tuscany following the disaster.

*Jack Ruby shot Lee Harvey Oswald at point
blank range while he was in police custody.
Ruby later died of cancer.*

*Before the people, blood will be spilt,
It will not come far from the high heavens:
But for a long time it will not be heard,
The spirit of a single man will bear
witness to it.*

C4 Q49

Few now believe that Oswald was the true assassin but according to Nostradamus whoever actually killed Kennedy was seen only by one witness – "The spirit of a single man will bear witness to it." On the day that President Kennedy's body lay in state, Jack Ruby, a Mafia man, killed Oswald in Dallas. Shortly after, the Dallas chief of homicide declared the Kennedy case closed.

According to Stephen J. Rivele, an noted investigative reporter on the Mafia, it was Lucien Sartee, the Corsican Mafia hit man who was contracted to kill Kennedy. His favorite ballistic signature for a kill was the dumb dumb bullet; the kind of hollow ammunition that shatters on impact making horrible wounds like the one which ripped the president's head wide open. Examining Nostradamus' "spirit" riddle in another way, perhaps he is saying that conspiracy buffs of the future can do no more than wonder what tales the ghost of Sartee could tell about who really marked Kennedy for assassination. And then there is Jack Ruby, who before dying of cancer admitted with a tantilizing tip of an iceberg of conspiracy when he repeated the following to the Warren Commission: "The world will never know the true facts of what occurred, because, unfortunately, the people who had so much to gain will never let the true facts come out, above-board, to the world."

139

A hasty cover-up of the Warren investigation only served to strengthen conspiracy rumours. A favorite was that the assassination had been plotted by a conspiracy involving the Mafia, Cuban nationals, and military industrial interests. Perhaps we shall never know the full story but, in Century 4 Quatrain 49, Nostradamus strongly implies that there is one man who knows the truth of the Kennedy tragedy. He may still be alive today.

Hundreds of years before President Kennedy's asassination Nostradamus may have known the concealed details about the third bullet. He wrote: "The ancient work will be accomplished, and from the roof evil ruin will

fall on the great man. Being dead they will accuse an innocent of the deed; the guilty one is hidden in the misty woods." C6 Q37.

Both Kennedy brothers had declared war on Mafia chief Sam Giancanna and his right hand man Jimmy Hoffa, leader of one of America's most powerful unions. As U.S. Attorney General in his brother's administration Robert Kennedy announced that his top priority target in his fight against crime was to be Sam Giancanna's underworld empire. Jimmy Hoffa, sent to prison for crimes of extortion, was heard to say after his trial, "Somebody needs to bump that SOB off..." implying Robert Kennedy. The Mafia had strong Cuban connections and it is possible that the organization may have helped Fidel Castro's agents to murder the president as a retaliation for CIA plans to kill Castro. The FBI chief J. Edgar Hoover, who had little affection for his chief, Attorney General Robert Kennedy, may have helped cover up the murder.

In 1978 a second examination of the assassination case was held before the U.S. House Select Committee on Assassinations. Witnesses testified to hearing a third bullet pass them from behind the grassy knoll; they further testified that they had withheld this information from the Warren Commission hearings because of FBI threats of reprisals if they spoke up. The House Select Committee came to the conclusion that, although the evidence pointed to the possibility of a conspiracy, it was not hard enough for prosecutions to be brought.

There is clear evidence that Lee Harvey Oswald was connected to Jack Ruby and the Cubans, but serious doubt remains as to whether he was Kennedy's assassin. According to a voice stress test made on a recording of Oswald's voice during a press interview, Oswald was telling the truth when he stated that he did not kill the president.

It is known that Jack Ruby was a Mafia agent working under the control of Sam Giancanna. The "ancient work accomplished" implies that Ruby killed Oswald on the orders of the Cosa Nostra, in return for favors granted him by his Mafia godfather. The phrase could also have a wider application, referring to the influence of secret societies such as the Freemasons, the Prior of Sion, the Illuminatus

and the Ashoka Nine, on governments throughout history.

When Nostradamus writes, "they will accuse an innocent of the deed," he may mean Lee Harvey Oswald. Of Kennedy's real assassin he says, "The guilty one is hidden in the misty woods." In his vision of this event Nostradamus perhaps saw a blurred "misty" picture of a man beneath the trees of the grassy knoll taking aim behind the wooden fence. If so, it would be very like the "misty" computer-enhanced image portrayed in investigative reporter Bill Kurtis' ground-breaking television documentary "The Men Who Killed Kennedy".

Similar conspiracy theories hover around the death of Robert Kennedy in 1968. The assassin Sirhan Sirhan's gun held only eight rounds but 10 bullets were fired in the crowded passageway of the Ambassador Hotel. The fatal shot was fired from a distance of four inches away but Sirhan Sirhan was standing at between two and 15 feet from Robert Kennedy when he fired. According to his mother's testimony Sirhan Sirhan had, eight months prior to the assassination, fallen into bad company and become involved with strangers of whom she did not approve. The strangers were not identified. In both assassinations, those alleged to have organized the conspiracy, Jimmy Hoffa and Sam Giancanna, are now dead: the union boss is presumed murdered after his release from jail, the Mafia chief was gunned down in New York City.

Within three years of President Kennedy's assassination 17 witnesses to the event had died: two committed suicide, three died in car accidents, three suffered fatal heart attacks, six were shot, one had his throat cut and one died from a karate chop to the throat. Only one death out of the 17 can be attributed to natural causes. An article in the London *Sunday Times* analyzed the odds in this seemingly bizarre sequence of deaths. The newspaper report concluded that the chance of the deaths of this number of witnesses to the same crime being pure coincidence was one-thousand-trillion to one.

The Kennedy conspiracy is a controversy that just will not go away. Even President George Bush, a former director of the C.I.A., had to make official comments about Oliver Stone's "JFK" movie. (Bush had been appointed to the post of chief "spook" in 1976 by President Ford who had been a member of the Warren Commission.)

In 1992, the controversial movie "JFK" played a significant role in the passing of the U.S. Assassination Materials Disclosure Act. It was the popular response to the movie that prompted the federal government to release 800,000 heavily blacked-out pages of documents in August 1993. At the time of writing, the Assassination Archives & Research Center, a non-profit organization run by conspiracy buffs, says the CIA has withheld over 160,000 documents for "security reasons." A special committee will, no doubt, be appointed to decide which documents can be released.

THE FUNERAL OF
JOHN F KENNEDY

Five years after the murder of President Kennedy, a second tragedy left the Kennedy family once more in mourning. JFK's younger brother Robert was felled by an assassin's bullet at the Los Angeles Ambassador Hotel and the "Camelot" dream was finally shattered. Conspiracy theories continue to surround the Kennedy assassinations.

APOLLO ON THE MOON
1969

He will come to take himself to the
corner of Luna (the moon)
Where he will be taken and placed
on alien land...

C9 Q65

"...to the corner of Luna." How must it have looked to a 16th-century man to watch our first steps on another world from a time when the fastest form of transport was a post horse.

In a 16th-century Europe dominated by the Church it would have been heresy to suggest that the earth was not the center of the known universe. Yet, in this time of limited scientific understanding and widespread superstition, Nostradamus dared to propose that, one day in the future, men would be able to walk upon another planet.

Even at the beginning of the 20th century the idea that, within 70 years, men would be able to travel in a man-made vehicle through space to "Luna" was unimaginable.

An astronaut from Apollo 12 walks
on the surface of the moon.

142

CHERNOBYL – THE OMEN OF CHANGE
1986

The law of More will be seen
to decline,
Followed by one more pleasing.
The Boristhenes (Dnieper) first will
give way,
Through gifts and tongues more
attractive.

C3 Q95

...The communal law will be made
in opposition.
The old order will hold strong, then
are removed from the scene:
Then communism put far behind.

C4 Q32

Nostradamus was a contemporary of Sir Thomas More[1]. There can be little doubt that he read a Latin copy of More's Utopia, which was one of the first socialist manifestos ever written. These quatrains are a prophecy-in-progress. They first predict the Czarist old order then communism itself replaced by a new and apparently more agreeable way of life.

Boristhenes is the 16th-century name for the Dnieper River, the Ukraine region. Interpreters of this century could not decipher the importance of the Ukraine in the downfall of communism. That was before the Chernobyl nuclear disaster of 1986 changed the lives of hundreds of thousands of Ukrainians and Belorussians who will live with the specter of radiation sickness for the rest of their lives.

The devastated nuclear reactor at Chernobyl sent clouds of silent death drifting over the northern hemisphere.

CHERNOBYL

[1]Thomas More (1478-1535). English statesman and political thinker. A member of Henry VIII's circle of advisors, he became Lord Chancellor in 1529, but resigned when Henry broke with Rome. He refused to recognise the king as head of the English church and was beheaded on 7 July 1535.

THE END OF COMMUNISM FORESEEN
1990

Quatrain 14 of Century 1, usually interpreted in terms of the French Revolution, has equally strong application to the revolutionary upheavals in Russia. "Enslave" in the first line can mean "enslaved" or, more literally, "Slavic." In the steaming waters of his prophetic bowl Nostradamus saw the locations changing but the themes of history repeating themselves. Narrow Parisian streets and alleys gave way to the frozen boulevards of Moscow and the song of revolutionary fervor changed from the Marseillaise to the Internationale.

Once again, a monarchy is under threat and a new breed of "headless idiots" imprison and kill a royal family. The new revolutionary leaders - Lenin, Trotsky and the other Bolsheviks - are later to be purged themselves in a new Reign of Terror masterminded by a new Napoleon/Robespierre, Joseph Stalin.

Conventional wisdom would tag the "scythe bearer" in Quatrain 54 of Century 1 (right), as Saturn, which exerted its negative

From the enslaved (Slavic) people, songs chants and demands. The Princes and Lords are held captive in prisons; In the future by such headless idiots. These (demands) will be taken as divine utterances.

C1 Q14

influence in the French and Russian revolutions. In astrology, however, Saturn also has constructive ways to represent uncompromising change by being the planet of "reality checks." In the light of Saturn's positive utility, the two revolutions mentioned here concern not only the rise and fall of Marxist communism, but also point to the revolutions taking place at the beginning and ending of this century. The first Russian Revolution of 1917, was Saturn's "reality check" concerning the corruption of the Czar's autocratic rule. In

144
✳

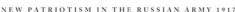
NEW PATRIOTISM IN THE RUSSIAN ARMY 1917

Banners, mottos and strong graphic images attested the popularity of the revolution in Russia at its birth.

"Two revolutions will be caused by the evil scythe bearer, making a change in reign and centuries. The mobile sign of Libra thus moves into its house (i.e., its earthly expression), equal in favor to both sides."

C1 Q54

August 1991, 74 years later, a second Saturnian revolution exposed the social and political bankruptcy of the Bolshevik Utopia signalling the disintegration of the Soviet bloc.

The quatrain indexing (Q54) could be interpreted as a fulcrum point in time, the mid-point in the pendulum's swing from one extreme revolution to the coming of another. The death of Stalin in 1953 (a near-miss for Q54), made it a pivotal year in the Cold War and communist hegemony, as it saw the election of Nikita Khruschev to First Secretary of the Central Committee. In this powerful position Krushchev could begin the "de-Stalinization" of Soviet society.

The mobile sign mentioned is Libra's scales of Justice and Balance which, in other quatrains, Nostradamus uses as a symbol for democracy. Perhaps this prediction hints at the kind of "change" Nostradamus is referring to here - a form of democratic government which affirms that all people are created equal (equal in favor to both sides).

A wider interpretation of the two revolutions of the hammer and (scythe-sickle) sees them as descriptions of the fates of the Russian and the Chinese communist revolutions. Communism in those countries will completely collapse as a result of Chinese and Russian efforts to democratize before the coming millennium, "making a change in reign and centuries."

REVOLUTION FOR DEMOCRACY, RUSSIA 1991

Once again Russians take to the streets, this time to celebrate the death of the Communist dream-turned-nightmare.

THE CHALLENGER DISASTER
1986

Nine will be set apart
from the human flock
Separated from judgment
and counsel:
Their fate to be determined
on departure.
Kappa (K), Thita (TH), Lamda (L) dead,
banished and scattered.

C1 Q81

...The unripe fruit will be the source of
great scandal
Great blame, to the other great praise.

C9 Q65

"Their fate to be determined on departure..." Although Nostradamus saw nine deaths the balance of this quatrain aligns exactly with the tragic circumstances of the Challenger disaster.

On 28 January, 1986, just over a minute after lift-off, the US space shuttle Challenger exploded. The tragedy, witnessed by shocked millions around the world, was caused by the leakage of volatile gases from the left solid rocket-booster. Seven astronauts were killed. In an era when space flight would have been the stuff of fairy tales Nostradamus, apart from a mistake in numbers, makes an uncannily accurate description of this disaster.

In the months of investigation following the explosion, the National Aeronautics and Space Administration (NASA) came under close scrutiny. The inquiry revealed that there had been flaws, both in the shuttle itself and in command decision-making.

The American space effort was castigated for sending their astronauts on the "unripe fruit" of faulty rocket boosters all to trim the budget to suit the accountants.

At the time of the Challenger disaster, however, the Soviet space program was running smoothly with the complete support of its government and people (to the other great praise).

The final line of C1 Q81 with its riddle of Greek letters has puzzled interpreters for centuries. I would venture that they are an anagram for some of those involved in the Challenger scandal: K, TH, L = (TH)io(K)o(L) = Thiokol. This could stand for the rocket manufacturers Morton Thiokol Inc., who designed and built the faulty solid rocket boosters. Neither the company management nor NASA officials took much interest in the doubts expressed about the booster design by junior engineers at Morton Thiokol Inc. In the scandal many company heads and engineers, along with senior NASA officials, were fired (banished and scattered).

THE EXPLOSION OF SPACE SHUTTLE CHALLENGER

THE SHOOTING OF ROY REB
1981

During the late 1950s Harold Macmillan, the British prime minister, conceded to American wishes and allowed the establishment of the first ballistic missile bases in Great Britain. In the 1980s, Prime Minister Margaret Thatcher's government allowed the Americans to station another "cold thing" – the new Pershing II intermediate nuclear missiles – on the British Isles.

"Roi Reb" may be an enigmatic phrase for Ronald Reagan. The president made clear his Christian faith and his view of the Soviet Union as "The Evil Empire" and, throughout the Reagan era, his get-tough foreign policies against "anti-Christian" communism and terrorist leaders like Libya's Colonel Mohammar Qaddafi increased world tension. The final line could also be an unheeded warning to the Reagan administration, and to subsequent administrations, not to continue the American Middle Eastern policy which succors and strengthens one dictator to destroy another as, for example, in the case of arming Saddam Hussein of Iraq against Ayatollah Khomeini of Iran, during the Iran-Iraq conflict of 1980-88. Reagan and his cabinet were brought into further "troubles" through the bombing of the Marine barracks in Lebanon, and the notorious "arms for hostages" policy, which led to the Iran-Contra scandal. This scandal was to damage the credibility of President Reagan, and his successor, George Bush ("bring them all into troubles").

On 30 March, 1981, 20 days prior to Easter Sunday, President Reagan was shot by William Hinckley Jr. while exiting the VIP door of the Washington DC Hilton Hotel. Along with the bewilderment and trauma felt in America on that terrible day, there was also confusion about how badly the president had been injured. As six shots rang out the president was immediately pushed into a waiting limousine by Jerry Parr, the senior secret ser-

*The Chief of London through
American power
Will burden the island of Scotland with
a cold thing.
Roy Reb (Reb the King) will have so
dreadful an antichrist,
Who will bring them all into the conflict.*

C10 Q66

The delivery of Pershing II missiles on British soil. Note the ironic and retroactive coincidence in the quatrain numbers dating the Norman victory at the battle of Hastings in 1066, the last time England was successfully invaded by enemies.

PRESIDENT RONALD REAGAN

147

vice agent on the scene. As the car made for the White House a few critical minutes passed before either Parr or the president knew he was seriously wounded. Reagan assumed his shortness of breath and the pain he felt under his arm were caused by the security agent's shove. Then he coughed bright red blood, indicating a serious lung wound, and Parr immediately ordered the car to drive to

REAGAN ASSASSINATION ATTEMPT
"NEAR EASTER"

148

The seducer will be placed in a ditch
And will be tied up for some time.
The theologian joins the chief with his cross.
The sharp right will attract
the contented ones (American citizens).

C8 Q95

This could be a prophetic coda to the end of the Reagan years which saw his presidency suffer (tied up for some time - and - placed in a ditch) through political scandals like Iran-Contra. Reagan will also be remembered as a strong advocate for Right-wing Christian fundamentalism. He was proud of the title, "American Dreamer" and his "feel-good-with-the-flag" sentiments satisfied the American public's collective need during the 80s to wax patriotic and restore pride whenever possible to a country so traumatized by the Vietnam war and the Watergate conspiracy.

The great king captured by the hands
of a young man (Hinckley)
Not far from Easter, confusion,
incision of the knife (surgery on Reagan?)
Everlasting captives, times when the
lightning is on the top,
when three brothers will be wounded
and murdered. (Joe, John, & Robert
Kennedy?)

C9 Q36

George Washington University Hospital. At the hospital the president's natural vitality continued to work against him, concealing the seriousness of the wound. Although he walked unaided into the emergency room, he had lost three pints of blood from internal bleeding. The bullet had ricocheted off the limousine, entered Reagan's left side under the arm and bounced off the rib, puncturing and collapsing a lung and lodging an inch above his heart. Two hours of surgery were required to pull the president out of danger.

The final two lines could define the general time window for the Reagan assassination attempt: the turbulent latter half of the 20th century ("when three [Kennedy] brothers will be wounded"). The "everlasting captives" might represent the 63 American hostages held in Iran for 444 days, released minutes after President Reagan was sworn into office. The phrase can also double for the next, seemingly "everlasting," hostage crisis in Lebanon which plagued Reagan's two terms of office. "Lightning on the top" works well as a description of the aerials televising both the Kennedy assassinations and the attempt on Ronald Reagan's life.

STOCK MARKET CRASH
1929

The imitations of gold and silver will
become inflated
which after the rape are thrown into the fire,
After discovering all is exhausted and
dissipated by the dept.
All scripts and bonds are wiped out.

C8 Q28

The prophecy of the quatrain above (C8 Q28) has only been fulfilled in part but stands every chance of complete realisation in the near future. It has relevance both to the Stock Market crash of 1929 and to a future day of reckoning when America's huge deficit goes out of control.

In Nostradamus' day there was no paper money, only coins. His description of money "imitating" gold and silver is, therefore, a triumph of foresight. The quatrain number, 28, could be a near-miss for the actual year of the Stock Market crash.

The last two lines may foretell the outcome of today's spiraling inflation and America's global deficit; a kind of economic Judgement Day. The efforts of political prophet Ross Perot and President Clinton to conjure economic reform may have come too late to stem the karmic results of extending credit for credit. Despite the 1993 stalling of inflationary trends, prophetic warnings predict a drastic return to inflation in a few years. If America does not support the call for "change," paper money may not be worth the wood to burn it by 1996 onward. The world's trade deficit might turn into the "rape" of line two. The phrase "after the rape" could augur the coming consequences of the American S&L (Savings and Loan) bank scandal of the late 80s. The U.S. Government had to rescue the faltering Savings and Loan industry by enacting legislation which would provide 166 billion dollars over 10 years to close or merge hundreds of insolvent S&Ls. The total cost was put at 400 billion dollars over 30 years, most to be paid by U.S. taxpayers. This strain on the American banking system may result, by the mid-late 90s, in an economic crash.

149

STOCK MARKETS UNDER PRESSURE

*The great credit of gold and abundance
of silver
Will cause honor to be blinded by lust:
The offense of the adulteress will
become known,
Which will occur to her great dishonor.*

C8 Q14

The prophet's derogatory descriptions of adultery and financial greed may be directed toward what in other quatrains is America, the "adulterous lady" symbolized by the Statue of Liberty.

REWARDS AND RISKS ON "WALL STREET"

*Where all is good, all well abundant,
In Sun (gold standard) and Moon (silver
standard), its ruin approaches.
It comes from the sky as you sift through
your exhausted fortune
In the same state as the seventh rock.*

C5 Q32

There are several repeated and cryptic references in the quatrains to a catastrophe coming "from the sky" or "fire from the skies." Conventional 20th-century interpretations have attributed this disaster to nuclear war. James Laver believed this quatrain stood for the abundant economy and life of the French Second Empire suddenly destroyed by the Franco-Prussian war. But this cannot apply because the final line is a clear metaphor for the biblical Apocalypse. The fall of economy and wealth may indeed go to blazes in some future nuclear war, but one cannot rule out an interpretation of global warming as the catastrophe that descends with a different "fire" to overtax the world's economies through the expected super-hurricanes and rising oceans waiting for us in the next century. The quatrain indexing could even stand for two different worldwide depressions, the first being that of the early 1930s and the more apocalyptic being set for the year 2030s – the time many scientists and climatologists believe we will reap the uncontrollable fury of the Greenhouse Effect if we have not curtailed our throw-away consumerism-unto-doomsday habits in the final years of this century.

STRATEGIC ARMS REDUCTION TREATIES

The picture of Presidents George Bush Sr. and Boris Yeltsin joyously waving the signed papers of the two nuclear disarmament START (Strategic Arms Reduction) treaties at the end of 1992, carries disturbing echoes of the British PM Neville Chamberlain's waving of his signed agreement with Hitler in 1938, claiming it signaled "Peace for our time."

According to Nostradamus and the warnings of other proven forecasters, we could not be living in more dangerous times. The fulfillment of Armageddon is assisted by the ignorance or collective denial of some basic facts about both START I and II.

Beyond the long delays, by Russia and the US to finally ratify the treaty, and beyond the fact that Russia can little afford the cost of dismantling an arsenal that has already a number of un-accounted for nuclear weapons, the expected reduction of both US and former Soviet arsenals by 75 percent will leave 7,000 warheads for use in a future nuclear conflict. The START treaties do not even begin to prevent Third World nuclear proliferation. Since Britain, France, China, North Korea, India, Iran, Iraq, Pakistan, Libya and Israel will continue to develop and retain their arsenals, we can add another several thousand nuclear weapons to that new millennial arsenal.

Even if, by the end of the first decade of the new century, a new age of "peace" sees Russian and US arsenals cut to a quarter of their doomsday bang, START will leave an economically stressed America and a collapsing Russia, many more intercontinental ballistic missiles and submarine launched warheads to throw at each other than existed during the Cuban Missile Crisis of 1962.

The bloody wars in former Yugoslavia continue despite attempts by the UN to stop them.

The speeches of Lake Leman (Geneva) become angered.
The days drag out into weeks,
Then months, then years, then all will fail,
The authorities will damn their useless powers.

C1 Q47

Interpreters have claimed this quatrain for the League of Nations which disbanded in 1946 and became the United Nations. (Note the quatrain indexing). Today, the same city is the scene of further debates between American and former Soviet diplomats over nuclear disarmament as well as the place where much endless and impotent discussion drones on about how to stop the global plague of ethnic cleansing and ethnic wars, primarily the conflicts currently raging in the Balkans, Chechnya, Kurdistan and Indonesia.

There will be let loose living fire and hidden death, horror inside dreadful globes...

C5 Q8

152

A Pershing missile lifts off, bearer of the "dreadful globes"

COUNTDOWN TO CATASTROPHE OR TRANSFORMATION

Halley's Comet, which appears every 76 years. It last appeared in 1986.

Saturn joined with a pond (Scorpio)
Transiting toward Sagittarius at
its highest ascendant
Plague, famine, death through military hands
The century as well as the Age
approaches its renewal.

C1 Q16

In the year when Saturn and Mars are
equally fiery,
The air is very dry, a long comet;
From hidden fires a great place burns
with heat,
Little rain, hot wind, wars and raids.

C4 Q67

...Thirst, and famine when the comet
will pass.

C2 Q62

These three quatrains date the beginning of Nostradamus' final years of tribulation before the new age of peace. The countdown to catastrophe or transformation has already begun. It is triggered by three factors taking place simultaneously in what is a clearly predicted date:

1. The transit of the planet Saturn from the constellation of Scorpio to Sagittarius, a fire sign.

2. The transit of Mars through Sagittarius (equally fiery) around the same time.

3. Both planets can perform this transit when a great comet appears at the end of a century, or when an astrological epoch is approaching its renewal.

Both planets often transit the constellation of Sagittarius – Saturn every 29 years and Mars every two years. The comet is the key linking these quatrains together. Saturn moved into Sagittarius on 17 November, 1985. Halley's comet became visible in the skies a few days later. Mars "joined" Saturn in Sagittarius from 2 February to 29 March of 1986, when the comet was at its brightest.

Nostradamus may be telling us to watch for apocalyptic warning signs during this countdown period. We will begin to see world plague, famines and droughts of unparalleled intensity, many wars and raids (perhaps representing terrorist attacks), the hidden fires of volcanoes, and the invisible fire of the "greenhouse effect" (hot wind). All these begin to exert their terrible influence between late 1985 through the spring of 1986.

The theme of plague, famine, drought, war and
renewal of the century is repeated throughout the
quatrains. Over a dozen prophecies have one or two
lines carrying this apocalyptic sequence alongside
contemporary-sounding messages.

*Religions, famine, nations, plagues,
confusion...
(When Paris is attacked from the sky and
sea in a future war.)*

C1 Q55

*Famine, plague, war, extensive arable land...
(A great slaughter over disputed territories,
perhaps those of the Middle East, or any
number of ethnic civil wars.)*

C2 Q19

*Great plague and war, famine and
drought will be seen...
(When plague of "blood and milk" rages in
Italy, possibly a toxic plague or a plague
affecting the blood, such as AIDS.)*

C3 Q19

*Hunger, plague, war, the end of
extended evils...
(When a nuclear disaster, an act of nuclear
terrorism or the use of chemical and biological
weapons in some future Balkan War
sends a poisonous cloud over south eastern
Europe, forcing a complete evacuation of the
entire region for nine months.)*

C7 Q6

*When the great cycle of the centuries is renewed,
It will rain blood, milk, famine, war and
plague...(This death and renewal of a great era
begins when a great comet is
seen – most likely Halley's Comet. Therefore
the Tribulation is
between 1985 through 2000.)*

C2 Q46

*Thirst and famine, when the comet will pass...
(Around the time of a great comet's passing,
when the world
experiences unprecedented famines and drought,
Nostradamus' third
Antichrist, "MABUS" will begin his
mayhem and possibly
trigger a Third World War "after" the
Cold War is over.)*

C2 Q62

*The great Ethiopian famine and a rash of some of the
world's worst cases of drought in Africa, Asia, Southern
Europe and the North American grain belts all peaked at
the sighting of Halley's Comet in 1985-86. During that
time the Third World was suffering from over 50 wars,
the worst being the Iran-Iraq conflict. In 1985 through
1986 there were many successful terrorist raids: civilians
were gunned down by terrorists in two international
airports. America replied with two retaliatory "raids" on
the terrorist-sanctioning state of Libya.*

THE SHADOW OF FAMINE HAUNTS ETHIOPIA

155

The creative process is always inherently destructive to the old order. Michelangelo's David, for example, rises from the chaos that destroyed the rock from which it is sculpted.

According to many traditions of prophecy, we are now living through the final chaotic and violent stages of the world as we have known it for the past 10 millennia. Our world, moving towards the birth of a new humanity, is like that rock being chiseled away by a great sculptor's strokes. We may despair at seeing the shards of old and hallowed traditions, ecosystems and social systems fly off into oblivion. We are bound to feel anguish at what is being forever lost and fear for what is yet to come.

For Nostradamus, the mysterious and divine sculptor is the cosmos. The stars and planets are "its" language. Through them, the prophet sets before us dates that mark the final tribulation-strokes leading to the millennium and the revelation of a new humanity.

CHAPTER TEN

THE CATHOLIC APOCALYPSE

THE CATHOLIC CHURCH, DESPITE ITS POMP, MAY WEAKEN

156

IN A LETTER to Henry II of France Nostradamus confronted the king with a vision which, no doubt, seriously perturbed the 16th-century monarch. The prophet confided that, sometime around the year 2000, the religious world as the king understood it would either be changed beyond recognition or be completely destroyed. In the following selection of quatrains, Nostradamus implies that there would be three major steps along the Catholic Church's path to self-destruction. First, through its relationship with fascism the Papacy would forfeit its spiritual integrity. Secondly, it would be further weakened by the murder of a Pope who is on the verge of revealing corruption in the Vatican Bank. Thirdly, the Catholic clergy would be decimated by a new kind of plague.

THE FIRST SCANDAL
FLIRTING WITH FASCISM

POPE PIUS XII RULED 1939-1958

It is now widely acknowledged by historians that Pope Pius XII was sympathetic to the fascist cause and that, by the time he became pope, his reputation for being able to deal successfully with fascist governments was well known. In 1933, as Vatican secretary of state, he had played a major role in the conclusion of a Vatican treaty with nazi Germany and, despite worldwide pressure, refused to excommunicate either Hitler or Mussolini during the war. In his communications with his French and German clergy concerning the papal position on "just wars" his arguments were so cleverly constructed that the leading priests of these two opposing nations could each assure their governments that their military endeavors had the Church's blessing. In justification of his reluctance to condemn Germany's invasion of Poland, Pope Pius XII said: "There are 40 million Catholics in the Reich. What would they be exposed to after such an act by the Holy See?"

The warlike party, by the great Pontiff.
Who will subjugate the frontiers of the
Danube (Hister)
Those of the crooked cross (OR: the cross
pursued by hook or by crook)
Captives, gold, jewels, more than one
hundred thousand rubies.

C6 Q49

The Danube in Nostradamus' time was also known by its Latin name, the "Ister," sometimes spelled with a silent "H." As we have seen in other verses the chief of the war-like party is said to be born on the banks of the Danube and named "Hister." Adolph Hitler was born in Braunau on the river Inn, near the Danube. He spent his early childhood along its banks. Hitler would later subjugate those countries one could consider as being within the frontiers of the Danube. Czechoslovakia and Austria were swallowed up by nazi Germany while Hungary, and Romania became nazi satellites.

The swastika-symbol of the Nazi Party was commonly described as a "crooked cross". The double meaning of "crooked" as evil is not missed by Nostradamus who foresaw the vast crimes of the nazis and the uncountable wealth they robbed from their victims. He points a damning finger at Pope Pius XII.

Pius XII also lent his support to Bernardino Nogara's business-(and fascist-) related efforts and three of Nogara's nephews were on the boards of Vatican-controlled companies in Italy.

In Germany today one legacy of the Vatican agreement with Hitler still remains. This is the Kirchensteuer, or church tax, which, automatically deducted from the wages of all Germans who do not renounce their religion, is given to Germany's Catholic and Protestant churches. In 1978, the Catholics' share of this tax amounted to 1.9 billion dollars, of which a significant portion was passed on to the Vatican in Rome.

...Some changed, the greater part reformed....when Rome has a new Leopard..

C6 Q20

In Quatrain 20 of Century 6 Nostradamus implies that the pope to follow Pius XII will come as a leopard. The family coat of arms of Pope John XXIII was dominated by an Heraldic Lion (which is a leopard). The prophet is also accurate in his prediction of the four-year duration of John XXIII's papacy, and of the new pope's popularity and attempts to help the church move with the times. The "more worldly" pope mentioned is Pope Paul VI, a man whose urbane character and political sophistication was in great contrast to the innocence of Pope John.

After a pontificate of seventeen years,
five years will see changes (W.W.II)
that put an end to the war.
At the same time one will be elected
Who will not be too conforming to
the Romans.

C5 Q92

For four years, the Seat will be held
for some little good.
One will accede to it who is more worldly.
Ravenna and Pisa, Verona will
support him,
desirous of elevating the Papal cross.

C6 Q26

158

POPE JOHN XXIII

The succession of Pope Paul VI is inferred in the first quatrain. His tenure of the papal throne is described as one in which the Church is wracked with pressures to change. Pope Paul's conservative slant and his anti-abortion policy did much to exacerbate the growing divisions in the Catholic Church during the turbulent 60s.

However, it is also true to say that Pope Paul VI traveled more widely than any previous pope and made strenuous efforts to calm growing world tensions.

A pope in radical contrast to his popular predecessor, Paul VI was both more worldly and more politically astute. During his papacy an old friend of his – a Sicilian banker with close ties to the Mafia – was taken on as financial advisor to the Vatican Bank. The activities of banker Michele Sindona, and of others involved in his schemes using Vatican money, led to a major scandal in 1982. When a bank controlled by Sindona's group was found to be on the brink of collapse, a huge network of corruption, murder and fraud was exposed. This network had been made possible and financed through Sindona's manipulation of the Vatican's enormous wealth.

One of Nostradamus' verses can be read as an ironic jibe at

After the very aged Pope's death
Will be elected a Roman of good age:
He will be accused of weakening
the Holy See and will last a long time,
doing controversial work.

C5 Q56

Paul the Celibate shall die three
leagues from Rome...

C8 Q46

Paul VI's piety. "Paul the Celibate," he says, "shall die three leagues from Rome." It was widely rumored that the pope had a homosexual lover and, in this verse, Nostradamus predicts the exact distance between the city limits of Rome and Castel Gandolfo, the papal summer residence just outside the city, where Paul died in 1978.

159

POPE PAUL VI

THE SECOND SCANDAL
PAPAL ASSASSINATION

When Albino Luciani became pope on the death of Paul VI the world was surprised and delighted. His beaming smile and warm, approachable manner were worlds away from the kind of steely political maneuvering that usually accompanied a rise to the papal throne. But he counted cardinals throughout the world as his friends and had made a great success of a tenure in Venice. The candidates in the papal election included a number of Vatican "insiders" so it was to his great surprise - and that of many experienced Vatican watchers - that he emerged victorious.

Immediately on his election Pope John Paul I demonstrated that the new papal style was not to be autocratic and remote, but down-to-earth and approachable. In his first speech he dispensed with the customary royal "we" to refer to himself and, in his papal inauguration, he rejected traditional pomp and ceremony. In place of the papal crown he wore a simple cap and, instead of being carried on the elaborate peacock-feathered throne designed for the ceremony, he chose to go on foot.

John Paul I was pope for just 30 days but in that short time he paved the way for the re-examination of many traditional religious convictions. He once remarked that "God is not only your father, but your mother" – not a statement guaranteed to find favor with the existing Vatican hierarchy. He also angered the Curia and worried church conservatives by his support of women's rights and his readiness to take a new look at the Catholic church's traditional and very conservative opposition to artificial means of birth control.

John Paul I had also planned to examine the Vatican's financial affairs, and to re-locate several Vatican insiders who were major players in the operations known as "Vatican Inc." His investigation would, no doubt, have uncovered the Vatican connections with the Mafia and with the right-wing Freemason's group known as "P2." But before he could set his plans for this investigation in motion Pope John Paul I died suddenly of a heart attack.

POPE JOHN PAUL I

Pope John Paul I lying in state after his unexpected and mysterious death in 1978.

When the great Roman's tomb is found.
The day after a Pope shall be elected.
The Senate (i.e. the Conclave) will not
approve of him.
His blood is poisoned in the
Sacred Chalice.

C3 Q65

Here is a quatrain that may try to name the relative date and victim of a crime. In 1978 archaeologists believed they had found the tomb of the first pope, the Apostle Peter, said to be buried somewhere beneath the Vatican. Pope John Paul I indeed was elected shortly afterward by the Senate of Cardinals, a select body of several hundred cardinals which is called together from all over the world when a pope dies, to elect a new pontiff. By tradition the Conclave of Cardinals is sealed into their apartments and cannot leave until they have secretly and successfully voted in a new pope. It is customary that their paper ballots are deposited in a golden chalice. They elected Albino Luciani, the Patriarch of Venice as Pope John Paul I.

According to the quatrain (above) many of those in the conclave would rue the votes they cast. Among the voters were some of the 12 cabinet ministers of the Papal Curia, led by Cardinal Villot.

John Paul always had a bottle of Effortil at his bedside to alleviate his low blood pressure. The morning he was found dead in his bed witnesses testify that Cardinal Villot had the Effortil immediately cleared from the bedroom. Line four's figurative description may infer that the heart attack was triggered by poison.

The one elected Pope
will be mocked by his electors,
this enterprising and prudent person
will suddenly be reduced to silence.
They cause him to die because of his
too great
goodness and mildness.
Stricken by fear, they will lead him
to his death in the night.

C10 Q12

A born reformist, John Paul I immediately enraged the conservatives in the Curia and threatened those who had secretly abused the privileges of power in the previous years. On the night before his death, he had given a list to Cardinal Villot. It contained many dismissals and a complete reshuffle of the staff in the power structure of the Vatican.

The night before the pope planned to start his reformation of the Vatican bank and other key posts, he retired for bed at 9:30 p.m. His servants found him the following morning (4:45 a.m.) dead in his bed, with the papers listing who was to be dismissed, scattered over the covers and the floor. As soon as Cardinal Villot (the papal secretary of state) was summoned to the bedroom he pocketed his papers, along with his last will and testament (which had been in the desk in his study). Then he issued false statements to the police and the press about the circumstances surrounding the death of the pope. The controversial list has never been disclosed to anyone.

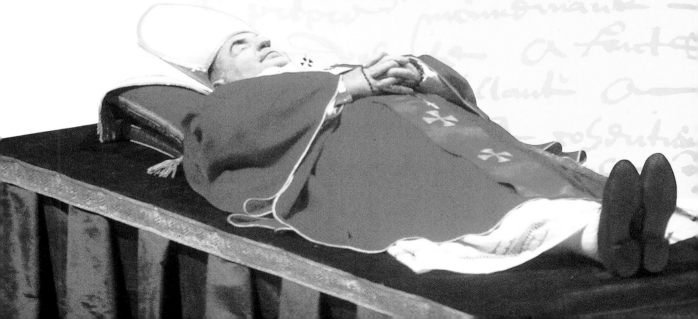

"UNDER MURDER, MURDER WILL BE PERPETRATED"

*He who will have government
of the great cape will be led
to execute in certain cases.
The twelve red ones
will spoil the cover.
Under murder,
murder will be perpetrated.*
C4 Q11

"J'accuse!" four centuries before the crime. Nostradamus gives an overview of a revolutionary reformer who's activism and life was cut very short by the 12 "red ones" the cardinals of the Curia who "spoil" his semi-secret investigation into the infiltration of the Mother Church by neo-fascist elements of secret societies. The "cases" of corruption in the Vatican would not be executed. First the pope, then many of the perpetrators and the investigators would die. What follows is the chronology of events. The following data is taken from David Yallop's *In God's Name*, an excellent work of investigative reporting on the murder of John Paul I.

EARLY SEPTEMBER, *1978*

Pope John Paul I asks his secretary of state, Cardinal Jean Villot, to initiate an investigation into Vatican Bank operations. He also agrees to meet with a U.S. Congressional delegation on the subject of population and artificial birth control.

SEPTEMBER 28, *1978*

John Paul I presents Cardinal Villot with a list of people who are to be transferred, asked for their resignations, or reassigned. All the people on the list are suspected to be members of the Freemason's group "P2." The reshuffle of power will have major implications for the existing Vatican power structure and its financial dealings.

SEPTEMBER 29, *1978*

John Paul I found dead in his bed. Villot issues false statements to the press about the circumstances surrounding the death, removes key evidence from John Paul's room, and orders the body to be embalmed immediately without an autopsy.

OCTOBER, *1978*

Pope John Paul II elected to replace John Paul I. None of John Paul's instructions to Villot before his death are carried out.

JANUARY 21, *1979*

Murder of Judge Emilio Alessandrini, the Milan magistrate investigating the activities of Banco Ambrosiano, whose director, Roberto Calvi, has close ties with Michele Sindona and the Vatican.

MARCH 20, *1979*

Murder of Mino Pecorelli, an investigative journalist in the process of publishing articles exposing the membership and dealings of "P2" – a powerful group of Freemasons whose membership was involved in Vatican financial dealings, and whose founder, Lucio Gelli, was deeply connected with Roberto Calvi.

MARCH 25, *1979*

Arrests on false charges of Mario Sarcinelli and Paolo Baffi of the Bank of Italy. The two men were pressing for action on the investigation of the financial dealings of Roberto Calvi and Banco Ambrosiano.

JULY 11, *1979*

Murder of Giorgio Ambrosioli, following his testimony to law enforcement agencies concerning Michele Sindona's financial dealings with Roberto Calvi and other Vatican interests, the activities of the "P2" and its members among powerful government and business circles, and the connections between Calvi, Sindona and Bishop Paul Marcinkus of the Vatican Bank.

JULY 13, *1979*

Murder of Lt. Col. Antonio Varisco, head of the Rome security service, who was investigating the activities and membership of "P2" and had spoken with Giorgio Ambrosioli two days before Ambrosioli's death.

JULY 21, *1979*

Murder of Boris Guiliano, the Palermo police deputy superintendent and head of Palermo CID. Guiliano had spoken with Giorgio Ambrosioli two days before Ambrosioli's death concerning Michele Sindona's laundering of Mafia money through the Vatican Bank into Switzerland.

OCTOBER, *1979*

Bomb explosion at the apartment of Enrico Cuccia, managing director of Mediobanca and witness to Michele Sindona's threat to the life of Giorgio Ambrosioli.

FEBRUARY 2, *1980*

The Vatican withdraws at the last moment its agreement that Cardinals Guiseppe Caprio and Sergio Guerri and Bishop Paul Marcinkus will provide videotaped depositions on behalf of Michele Sindona in his trial in the U.S. on charges of fraud, conspiracy and misappropriation of funds in connection with the collapse of Franklin National Bank.

MAY 13, *1980*

Michele Sindona attempts suicide in jail.

JUNE 13, *1980*

Michele Sindona sentenced to 25 years.

JULY 8, *1980*

Roberto Calvi attempts suicide while in jail on charges of fraud, etc. Later released on bail and reconfirmed as chairman of Banco Ambrosiano.

SEPTEMBER 1, *1981*

The Vatican Bank – apparently at the request of Roberto Calvi – issues "letters of comfort" acknowledging its controlling interest in, and assuming responsibility for, more than 1 billion dollar debt of a number of banks controlled by Calvi.

JANUARY 12, *1981*

A group of shareholders in Banco Ambrosiano send a letter to John Paul II, outlining the connections between the Vatican Bank, Roberto Calvi and the "P2" and the Mafia. The letter is never acknowledged.

*In the sacred temples scandals will
be committed
They will be thought of as honors and
praiseworthy
Of one of whom they engrave on
silver, gold and medals.
The end will be very strange torments.*

C6 Q9

It seems that there will be continued success of the scandal's perpetrators, to avoid justice and even turn their crimes into noble acts. When John Paul II took office, he was briefed about the same revelations contained in the reports found spread across the bed of his dead predecessor. Instead of dismissing Bishop Paul Marcinkus, the man in charge of the Vatican Bank, a prime suspect for masterminding the scandal and participating in the conspiracy to kill the pope, the new pontiff had him promoted to archbishop and kept him in firm control of the Church's finances throughout the rest of the 80s. Marcinkus retired with honor after the long standing threat by police authorities to detain him for questioning if he ever stepped outside of the Vatican was lifted. The final lines may reprise the commentary on the long list of mysterious murders reverberating from the poisoning of the first John Paul.

APRIL 27, *1982*

Attempted murder of Roberto Rosone, general manager and deputy chairman of Banco Ambrosiano, who was trying to "clean up" the bank's operations.

JUNE 17, *1982*

Roberto Calvi found hanged to death from a bridge in London. A few days later, a 1.3 billion dollar "hole" is discovered in Banco Ambrosiano, Milan.

OCTOBER 2, *1982*

Guiseppe Dellacha, executive at Banco Ambrosiano, dead of a fall from a window of Banco Ambrosiano in Milan.

MARCH 23, *1986*

Michele Sindona found dead of poisoning in the Italian jail to which he had been extradited on charges of ordering the murder of Giorgio Ambrosioli.

ARCHBISHOP MARCINKUS

Archbishop Marcinkus, heavily implicated in the financial scandals at the Vatican.

THE THIRD SCANDAL
PLAGUES UPON THE HOLY BLOOD

As we have already seen, Nostradamus was a firm believer in divine retribution. He sincerely believed, for example, that London suffered plagues and fire as a divine reprisal for the execution of King Charles I. His harsh view of the future of the Church may, therefore, be not so much anti-Catholic as pro-Christ. The plague of which he speaks may be a multifaceted attack on the spiritual blood and substance of Christ's teachings by profane alliances of fascists and drug money launderers – the final line may be the prophet's attempt to describe the plague of intravenous drug use.

The "harsh one of letters" is the investigator(s) into Vatican conspiracies whose revelations will expose the corrupt custodians currently destroying the spiritual substance of the Church. In my opinion, David Yallop will be remembered as a prime candidate for that "harsh," though uncompromisingly brave, ("one of letters") who risked his life to expose the extent of drug money laundering in the Vatican Bank.

If Nostradamus is describing divine retribution here, he may be suggesting that the first two corruptions - of fascism and drugs - will lead the Catholic clergy toward a literal plague affecting the blood in their veins. The "lifeblood" or vitality of the body could be, in modern terms, the human immune system. Towards the end of this century several plagues of the blood will decimate the clergy and clearly, the one that springs readily to mind is AIDS. This could be spread through their ranks through intravenous drug use or homosexual acts; current estimates, by homosexual activist priests such as AIDS-sufferer Father Robert L. Arpin, indicate that over 40 percent of the priesthood are practising homosexual behavior in secret.

O vast Rome, your ruin draws near
Not that of your walls
but of your lifeblood and substance.
The harsh one of letters will make so
horrid a notch,
pointed steel all wounding up the sleeve.
C10 Q65

Clergy in crisis. Allegedly over one third of Catholic priests are practising homosexual behaviour and are therefore vulnerable to sexually transmitted disease.

166

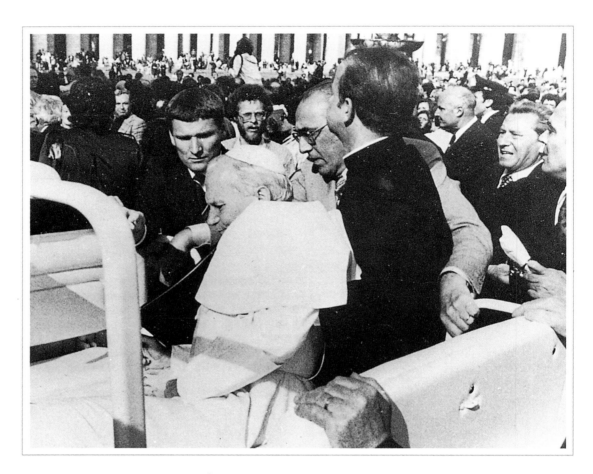

On 13 May 1981, Pope John Paul II was
seriously wounded in an assassination attempt carried out
by a Turkish gunman, Mahmet Ali Agca.

A short while before the Holy
Monarch (John Paul I) is murdered
Castor and Pollux (Twin named Pope,
John Paul II)
In the papacy, a bearded star
(Halley's Comet)
Public treasure by land and sea is emptied...

C2 Q15

In one complex verse Nostradamus describes and dates a sequence of events which perhaps relate to the Vatican bank scandal; we see the murder of John Paul I, the rise of his successor and the transit of Halley's Comet in 1986 when world attention about the bank scandal reached a climax. "Castor and Pollux" is a good example of Nostradamus using the classics to paint layers of meaning in very few words. The Twins of Gemini may be a poetic description of two popes side by side with twin names (John Paul) who will run the papal ship of state. According to classical lore one twin was divine while the other all too human and corrupt. We might infer that Nostradamus views the second John Paul with disdain.

When the election for John Paul I's successor was under way it was widely anticipated that the next pope might not be an Italian. There were several non-Italian candidates in this papal election, including one from Poland and one from Latin America. The election ended in victory for the candidate from an area of southwest Poland which had once formed the boundary of Charlemagne's empire - "from ancient France." The unsuccessful Latin American candidate is also referred to in C5 Q49. In the time of Nostradamus Latin America was thought to be part of Spain; hence the new pope is to hail "not from Spain but from ancient France."

In his Epistle to Henry II, Nostradamus had warned that, some time in or near the period of John Paul's II papacy, the priests of the Catholic church would be threatened by plague. Shortly after the election of Pope John Paul II the world began to be aware of the great modern plague of AIDS. During the ensuing years churches of all denominations have had to reassure their flocks that the disease cannot be passed by the sharing of a communion cup.

Since we do not yet know the origins of the AIDS virus, Nostradamus' "enemy" (C5 Q49) has still to be identified. Theories abound, including one in an off-beat periodical that AIDS was some manufactured horror of the Cold War. However, in the light of events occuring since the first publication of this book, it could be argued that "the enemy" is the nations of the former Soviet Empire which have now forsaken communism. In 1989 John Paul II received a visit in Rome from Michail Gorbachev at which the last leader of the Soviet Union gave the pope a tacit assurance that Ukrainian Catholics would be granted recognition by the outgoing communist régime. In the summer of 1993 John Paul II visited the former Soviet Baltic states.

> *Not from Spain but from ancient France,*
> *Will be elected for the trembling ship.*
> *He will make a promise to the enemy*
> *Who will cause great plague during his reign.*
> **C5 Q49**

Nostradamus variously calls Pope John Paul II "Pol," in a pun on his name and his Polish origins, and "Mansol, the work of the sun," possibly a designation which tallies with the medieval prophet St Malachy's description of John Paul II as "The Sun's Labor." Nostradamus frequently warns that John Paul II will be pursued by enemies, and that his supporters will be captured and killed.

167

GLOBE-TROTTING POPE MEETS THE FAITHFUL

St Peter's Church in Rome, built over the tomb of St Peter, the first pope of the Catholic Church.

168

Nostradamus' parallel prophecy on a theme from St Malachy

Very near the Tiber death threatens,
Shortly after the great flood.
The head of the church
will be taken prisoner and cast out,
the castle (St Angelo)
and the Palace (Vatican) in flames.

C2 Q93

"...a torrent to open the tomb of marble and lead to the great Roman with the Mendusine Device..." (C9 Q84) In the spring of the year 2000 the tomb of St Peter will be uncovered in the ruins of the Vatican after the flood. The "Great Roman" is interpreted as St Peter since "Mendusine" is an anagram for "Deus in Me," Peter's motto.

Nostradamus' quatrains on the final six popes before the apocalyse closely resemble the prophetic visions recorded by St Malachy[1] of Ireland. In 1138 this Irish priest made a pilgrimage to Rome; during the course of his visit to the papal city he experienced an ecstatic trance in which he uttered 112 Latin phrases. Each phrase stands as a prediction for the entire succession of 111 popes, from his contemporary Celestinus II to doomsday. After John Paul II (whom he calls "The Labor of the Sun") there are only two popes remaining on Malachy's list. Malachy's original manuscript was not discovered in the Vatican Archives until 1590 – 24 years after the death of Nostradamus – yet the words of both prophets give parallel clues to the harrowing life and times of the final pope.

Foreseeing the final Catholic apocalypse, St Malachy said:

"In the final persecution of the Holy Roman Church, Peter the Roman will occupy the See, who will guide his flock through numerous tribulations. These tribulations past, the town of seven hills will be destroyed and the terrible Judge shall judge the people."

---

[1] St Malachy (c. 1094-1148). Irish monk who introduced the Cistercian Order to his country in 1142. The Prophesies of St Malachy, published in Lignum Vitae by the Benedictine monk Arnold Wion in 1595 may not be by him.

CHAPTER ELEVEN

PLAGUE OF BLOOD

THE PLAGUE DEVASTATES LONDON IN 1625

IN HIS FIGHT against the bubonic plague Nostradamus employed medical techniques which were centuries ahead of his time and there has been much speculation as to whether he was able to use his prophetic skills to save lives. Particular interest has been shown in Quatrain 25 of Century 1 where the prophet writes: "The lost thing, hidden for many centuries, is discovered. Pasteur will be honored as a demigod. This happens when the moon completes her great cycle. He will be dishonored by other rumors as foul as farting."

When the 19th-century French medical pioneer Louis Pasteur first suggested that diseases were caused by bacteria and other germs he was subject to spiteful attacks from the medical establishment of his day. Once his theories had been proved, however, he was hailed by his contemporaries as a "demigod."

Nostradamus correctly dates the establishment of the Institut Pasteur by reference to the last great lunar cycle which ran from 1535 to 1889, the year Pasteur's institute was set up.

It may have been Nostradamus' interest in medicine which prompted his visions of a future plague of the blood. He refers to this disease as one that will rain "milk, blood and frogs." In Nostradamus' 16th-century world, "milk" was often used in folk medicine as a slang term for lymphatic fluids and semen, "blood" as the vitality-giver or the immune system, and all viral diseases were blamed on "frogs." In the light of this alternative reading of the prophecy the riddle becomes a description of the modern plague AIDS (Acquired Immune Deficiency Syndrome) which is passed from victim to victim chiefly through blood, semen or intravenous drug use.

"A VERY GREAT PLAGUE...
WITH A GREAT SCAB"

*Louis Pasteur (1822-1895). The
medical pioneer of immunology and
micro-biology. Nostradamus
commented on his discoveries over
335 years earlier and dated the
inception of the Institut Pasteur. Luc
Montagnier (box), led the Institut
Pasteur's viral oncology unit which
isolated the virus in early 1983.*

BELOW *Pasteur at work
in his laboratory.*

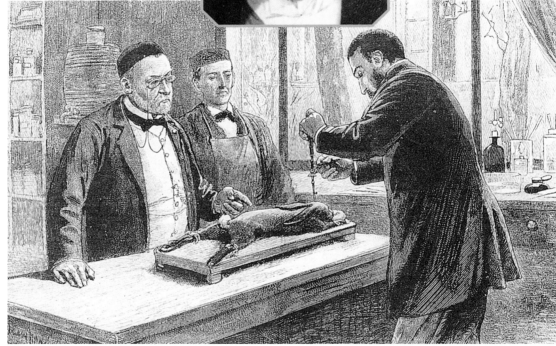

170
✳

In Century 3, Quatrain 75, Nostradamus may have predicted the spread of AIDS through France, Italy and Spain – "...Swords damp with blood from distant lands. A very great plague will come with a great scab. Relief near but the remedies far away."

Scientists working in both America and at the Institut Pasteur in France were able to identify the retrovirus associated with AIDS very quickly. Photographs taken under the microscope reveal a virus chillingly close to the prophet's term "gousse" which means "scab." Also one symptom of AIDS is a rare skin cancer which covers the body in purple scabs. In the language of magic the sword is the symbol of the male phallus. Here the word may portray the male phallus as the chief vector in the spread of AIDS.

THE SPREAD OF AIDS

Scientists investigating the origins of the AIDS virus have traced it back to a virus afflicting green monkeys in Central Africa as far back as 1945. These monkeys probably passed the virus by biting each other and humans. Over the next four decades the disease spread throughout Africa.

The virus is then thought to have moved into North America and Europe via Haitian laborers employed in Zaire in the early 1960s through to the mid-1970s. (Note the quatrain dating: Q[19]75). The disease surfaced first in the homosexual community, then in other sections of society, and over 9,500 fatalities were recorded between 1979 and 1986 in America alone. The worldwide estimate of infected victims stands at over 10 million.

As the prophet says, relief for AIDS sufferers has been "near" - thanks mainly to the fast isolation of the virus which enabled medical scientists to produce drugs such as AZT and DDI. These drugs, however, only slow down the effect of the virus on the immune system and in 1993 AIDS activists branded AZT as little more than a placebo.

Sadly, we do not yet have a cure for AIDS; the most optimistic estimates project little progress in the search for a remedy before the year 2000. There is also a strong possibility that new and virulent forms of the disease will mutate just as a cure becomes possible. In 1990, Sir Donald Acheson, the British Government's chief medical officer, predicted a "Hundred Years' War against AIDS" before it is eradicated. According to Nostradamus' predictions, the plague may spread over half the world and kill two-thirds of humanity before a vaccine is finally ready – "relief near, but the remedies far away."

In 1987, many criticized *Nostradamus and the Millennium* for its alarming interpretations of Nostradamus concerning the apocalyptic threat of AIDS. Unfortunately, as we approach the 1990s, those dire forecasts sound all too plausible as 20th-century statistics catch up with the augury of the 16th-century doctor. Late 1980s estimates of 20 million infected with the AIDS virus by the end of the century are proving to be far short of the actual infection rate. The early 90s has seen a dramatic and more widespread incidence of the disease. It has spread out of Africa to affect many other countries and is now appearing in the heterosexual mainstream. Shocking estimates released in 1992 from Harvard University's School of Public Health suggest that the infection from AIDS will spiral out of control by the first decade of the next century and that 110 million adults and 10 million children will be infected by the year 2000.

There is no guarantee that even these numbers are correct, as the disease seems to be spreading faster than the data collectors can compute them. The Harvard report estimates the current rate of infection to be 5,000 people per day and, until recently, the fastest infection rate was in Africa. Now the disease is spreading fastest in South Asia; in Bombay's red light district, male laborers are contracting AIDS from a prostitute community with the highest per capita infection rate in the world. From Bombay the transient laborers return to their wives and families, exposing the vast population of rural India to AIDS. The Bombay red light district is also the plague's staging ground for a huge increase of AIDS in the Middle East, as many wealthier Arab clients, college students and cheap laborers working in India are carrying the virus back to their wives and families at home. If these trends continue, the situation in South Asia could, by the early 21st century, parallel that of Uganda, with 20 percent of the population exposed to AIDS. South East Asia, North Africa and the Middle East could all go the way of Uganda by the 2020s.

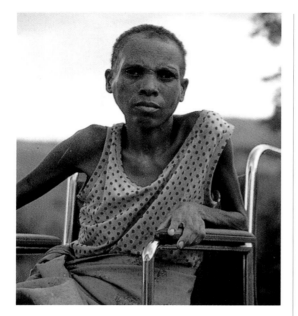

AIDS sufferers in Africa, where the disease is called "Slim" because it emaciates its victims. Perhaps the many parallel references to "Plague" and "Famine" stem from Nostradamus mistaking one for the other?

In the deadly, rapid spread of AIDS and mankind's inability, so far, to fight it, we see the mathematics of a doomsday plague rise to meet Nostradamus' threat of two-thirds of humanity falling prey to this terrible scourge during the next century.

Current medical research shows AIDS to be transmitted primarily through anal intercourse and blood-on-blood and sperm-on-blood contact. According to this research, the highest First World risk group is the homosexual community. The second largest high risk group includes drug users sharing needles, hemophiliacs, and others needing blood products. AIDS is thought to have been carried to the Western hemisphere by Haitians returning from regular employment in Central Africa where the disease is transmitted through the heterosexual community by prostitution, ritual blood rites, scarification and doctors at impoverished rural medical centers re-using needles.

New revelations also show that prostitution is becoming a major bridge of AIDS transmission to the heterosexual communities of the developed world. The gravity of this development can be seen in the story of a male prostitute living in the conservative mid-Western American city of St Paul, Minnesota in 1986. Upon discovering that he had AIDS, the man held a press conference on television so that his clients could recognize him and get tested for the disease in private. The AIDS sufferer admitted that he had had intercourse with 1,000 married men with families in the previous 12 months. It is possible that tens of thousands of similar cases exist throughout America and Europe.

New evidence also frighteningly points to another possible source of infection. Although dentists steam-clean their dental tools in an autoclave it has been proved that simple disinfection of dental equipment will leave 20 percent of the bacteria hidden in the microscopic pitting of tools. At the time of this writing, tests and findings to discover how many AIDS viruses survive the disinfecting process are slow in coming. The U.S. government states that all American dentists are ordered to carry out regular steam sterilization with an autoclave, but several secret investigations, with hidden cameras, have shown that this regulation is often ignored. Dentists who have been shown by these investigations to be lax in the sterilization of their dental tools say that the autoclave is hard on the equipment, necessitating more expensive replacements. In the developed world this problem could be solved by a 10 to 20 dollar increase on the average dental bill.

"TWO THIRDS OF THE WORLD WILL FAIL & DECAY"

In his Epistle to Henry II Nostradamus presents a nightmare vision of the end of the 20th century to the King and to future generations. There will be fierce global conflicts over faith and ethnicity and over all this chaos will loom the dark shadow of the greatest plague mankind has ever experienced:

"...Then the impurities and abominations will be brought to the surface and made manifest...towards the end of a change in reign (perhaps implying the English 'reign' when Elizabeth II gives way to Charles, or the Papal 'reign' when Pope John Paul II gives way to a future pope.)

"The leaders of the Church will be backward in their love of God...Of the three sects the Catholic is thrown into decadence by the partisan differences of its worshippers. The Protestants will be entirely undone in all of Europe and part of Africa by the Islamics, by means of poor in spirit who, led by madmen (terrorists?) shall through worldly luxury (oil) commit adultery... in the meantime (there appears) so vast a plague that two thirds of the world will fail and decay. So many (die) that no one will know the true owners of fields and houses. The weeds in the city streets will rise higher than the knees, and there shall be a total desolation of the Clergy." (Epistle, ibid.)

173

✳

CLUES OF A CURE COMING FROM THE "SKY"

A great famine through a
pestilent wave.
(It) will extend its rain over the length
of the arctic pole,
Samarobrin, one hundred leagues from
the hemisphere,
They shall live without law, exempt
from politics.

C6 Q5

As best as one can divine the wild poetry of Dr Nostradamus, this quatrain may give up some clues for future doctors to consider in the cure of AIDS. Unlocking this prophetic riddle may show a cure coming from the skies themselves. Preliminary radical experiments using ozone infusion into the blood stream show promising potential for killing the AIDS virus. A more mainstream but no less farsighted alternative is research in new vaccines manufactured in zero-gravity in a lab orbiting Earth.

The name "Samarobrin," which appears in Quatrain 5, Century 6, has mystified interpretors of Nostradamus for years. According to the quatrain, whatever Samarobrin is, it is hovering some "100 leagues" or 270 miles above us. However, experienced interpretors of Nostradamus often find that a word or phrase which has remained stubbornly obscure is suddenly illuminated by the appearance in our vocabularies of new words or names. In effect, we are waiting for our world to catch up with Nostradamus' visions. This may be the case with the decoding of Samarobrin. For example, two early anti-AIDS test drugs, Suramin and Ribavrin, could stand for "Samarobrin." An alternative reading is suggested by Erika Cheetham, who records an intriguing interpretation from one of her readers who thinks the word describes a Russian satellite: "samo" meaning "self" and "robrin" meaning "operator" in Russian, hence self-operator. "Samarobrin" could then stand for the Russian space station MIR.

It has been customary to apply Quatrain 55 of Century 9 to the Spanish influenza epidemic of 1918 which followed World War I. In our own times, however, it can be more readily applied to AIDS - a disease which is capable of mutating into a form that could eventually rain on us from the air.

Quatrain 55 of Century 9 could also date the time of the last conjunction of Mercury and Jupiter - in September 1993 (just one year after the release of the Harvard Medical Report). Although at that time Mars is sitting 28 degrees in the constellation of Libra and misses the conjunction by a few degrees, it is still close. Astrologer Dan Oldenburg says that this conjunction takes place every two to three years on average. The next conjunction is 12 December 1995. The next window for a terrible, explosive spread of plague and war is 23 February 1998 when Mercury and Jupiter con-

join the Sun at five degrees Pisces with Mars at 23 degrees Pisces. This conjunction has extra malefic strength as it is squared by Pluto at eight degrees Sagittarius. The Moon joins this conjunction on 27 February. The next windows for major global plague events will be seen in July of 2002 and September of 2004. A "Blood Plague," however, need not be caused by AIDS alone. These conjunctions could date the coming of a second immuno deficiency plague, perhaps caused by pollution creating holes in the atmosphere's protective ozone layer. The "invisible swords" of such a plague are ultraviolet radiation waves which will cause "scabs" of skin cancer, cataracts, and break down the immune systems of human, vegetable and animal life on earth. Perhaps this is another reason why Nostradamus often follows warnings of "plague" with "famine," and visa versa, in his prophecies.

Returning to C6 Q5 and the suggestion that Suramin and Ribavarin could stand for the enigma, "Samarobrin," perhaps Nostradamus is trying to tell future physicians not to abandon work on those drugs. The word could imply that a combined effect of these two drugs is in some way related to zero-gravity laboratories in a satellite – in other words, a permanent "self-operating" space station may produce a cure for AIDS.

A horrible war which is being
prepared in the west,
The following year the pestilence will come,
So very horrible that young nor old,
nor animal (may survive)
Blood fire Mercury Mars Jupiter in France.
C9 Q55

CHAPTER TWELVE
"MABUS" THE FINAL ANTICHRIST

175

Saddam = Sudam = subaM = Mabus?
Usama bin Laden = Usama b = Usaam b = MaabUs = Mabus?
George W. Bush = W Bush = M Bus = MaBus = Mabus?

UNRAVELING THE "MABUS" ENIGMA

Mabus will soon die, then will come
A horrible undoing of people
and animals,
At once vengeance is revealed coming
from a hundred hands.
Thirst, and famine when the comet will pass.

C2 Q62

"Mabus" is one of Nostradamus' most famous prophetic enigmas. It may provide a clue to the name and the identity of the prophet's third and final Antichrist. If one accepts that Nostradamus only lightly scrambled the real names of the first two Antichrists – Napoleon (Napaulon) and Hitler (Hi*f*ter) – then the letters masking the real name of "Mabus" the Third Antichrist must be relatively easy to decode. It may already be too late to positively decode who "Mabus" is and how to prevent his terrible destiny. The final line dates the beginning of his legacy of terror around the time of the appearance of Halley's Comet in 1985–1986 or the comet Hale-Bopp in 1997. Other references put his appearance on the world stage on or a few years after July of 1999 through July of 2000.

Some interpreters believe that Nostradamus' use of the phrase *sept mois* (seven months) in Century 10 Quatrain 72 may be a pun hiding the month of the attack that would trigger the Third Antichrist's 27-year war of terrorism. Not only does *Sept mois* mean seven months, it may also stand for "September month." Terrorists linked directly to Saudi terrorist leader Usama bin Laden's al-Qaeda organization hijacked four civilian jet airliners on the morning of 11 "September", 2001, and, using them as suicide bombs, flew them into the Pentagon building in Washington DC and the World Trade Center in New York.

The Advent of three "Antichrists" is a powerful theme running through Nostradamus' prophecies. The Third Antichrist has yet to be positively identified. Yet he may have shown his bloody hand when guiding the devastating attack on New York on 11 September, 2001.

The people of America and Europe view this surprise attack as the second Pearl Harbor in a new world war of terrorism. One hundred nations have joined ranks with the United States in a coalition to fight terrorism that initially U.S. President George W. Bush indelicately defined as a great "Crusade." Such terms only serve to deepen the divide between Western and Islamic nations in the coming war, foreseen by Nostradamus. He may have viewed this new war over 446 years ago as a catastrophe of many decades in duration. The man we know as "Mabus" may be some obscure future terrorist responsible for triggering World War III and the extinction of civilization as we have known it, if he is not identified and isolated in time.

In earlier editions of this book I stated my view that Nostradamus believed this third, and last, evil demagogue was a Middle Eastern or North African terrorist who may obtain enough nerve gas or uranium to make the world his hostage. The prophet supplies clues for the Antichrist's place of birth, religion, military theater of operations and dates the beginning and ending of his war. It is important to understand that Nostradamus, by implicating someone coming from the Islamic world as his Third Antichrist does not immediately imply that he was seeing the future from an anti-Islamic bias. If that were so then one could judge this French prophet as anti-French for predicting the first Antichrist would be Napoleon. Indeed, at the onset of the new war there are many Nostradamians in Europe and Islam who believe the anagram "Mabus" spells out the name of the American President, George W. Bush. Perhaps this is biased thinking. True, one could take Nostradamus' basic laws of anagram and reverse the "M" to make an "W," then drop the "a" and replace it with an "h" to get W Bus(h). All imaginative, if a bit too obvious. Word crunching aside, I still hold the same view today as I did back in 1986 when I wrote most of the following dissertation on decoding Mabus. I believe most of the clues point to a man born in the Islamic Near East as the next and final Antichrist.

A good place to start our prophetic detective work is by playing one of Nostradamus' favorite word games of factual hide-and-seek: the decoding of classical metaphors and ancient names to find their modern parallels. Consider quatrain C2 Q30 (See Clue #1). The Punic and Phoenician peoples worshiped an all-powerful God they called "Baal", or Lord. Each region gave him a personalized name. Nostradamus may be hinting that the Antichrist comes from a modern-day region which, in former times, was a colony of the wide-ranging ancient Phoenician empire. This is an area that today includes Tunisia, Libya, Palestine, Lebanon, Israel, Iraq and Syria.

Nostradamus' most famous doomsday prediction (C10 Q72) warns future generations of a "King of Terror" descending from the skies in July 1999. This holy terror linked to Mabus and Hannibal's "God" could point to an important location for the final Antichrist. Hannibal's "Baal" was called "Hammon," the patron deity of Carthage. When Baal Hammon was angered, he is described as a reigning "Terror coming from the skies." The Romans had a custom of adopting the patron gods of a conquered nation and Latinizing their names. After the Romans had sacked the city of Carthage at the close of the Third Punic War in 146 BC they built their own city over its ashes and named both city and God "Thurbo Majus." The enigmatic name M-A-B-U-S may stand as a classic anagram for "Majus," another link to the Antichrist and the "The infernal Gods of Hannibal."

From the early 1970s until the early 1980s the chief headquarters of the Palestine Liberation Organization (PLO) was but a few miles beyond the ruins of Thurbo Ma(b)us'

CLUE #1

One who the infernal Gods of Hannibal
(Baal Hammon)
Will cause to be born, terror to all mankind;
Never more horror nor the newspapers
tell of worse in the past,
Then will come to the Italians through
Babel (Iraq).

C2 Q30

city. A number of radical factions in, and evolving beyond, the PLO remain dedicated to destroying Israel and establishing a Palestinian state. These same freedom fighters (or Baal's terrorists) have a reputation for considering any means to obtain their ends, from diplomacy to nuclear, biological or chemical blackmail, or terror from the sky. (Update: I might add that terror from the skies can also come from hijacking planes and turning their frightened hostages and flight crews into the fiery fodder for gasoline bombs roaring out of the skies with the force of nearly 1 kiloton of TNT.)

The concept of newspapers was unheard of in the time of Nostradamus. This fact makes it clear to anyone reading today's newspaper stories from the early 1970s onwards about Saddam Hussein, Abu Nidal, Muammar Qaddafi, Usama bin Laden, or the bombing of the New York World Trade Center in 1993 – and its annihilation in 2001 – that C2 Q30's reference has contemporary relevance. In these quatrains Nostradamus may be hiding a warning of a future plague of world terrorism – mainly based in North Africa and the Middle East. Taking the worst case scenario, a handful of terrorist-sanctioning nations drags the world into nuclear war not "by" 1999 as I stated in earlier editions but "after" 1999.

CANDIDATES FOR THE ANTICHRIST

CLUE#2

In the year 1999 and seven months (July)
The great King of Terror
will come from the sky (Baal Hammon)
He will bring back Ghengis Khan
Before and after War (or Mars) rules happily.

C10 Q72

The message of the quatrain above, if left unheeded, chronicles the apocalyptic consequences to come from a third Gulf War triggered by Iraq (Babylon) mentioned at the end of C2 Q30. As we will examine, there are many prophecies pointing to a breakdown of the Western and Arab coalition that defeated the Iraqi dictator, Saddam Hussein, in his bid to seize Kuwait in the Second Gulf War (1990-1991). Many prophets point to a third Gulf War coming before the millennium. It will pit the Western forces of Operation Desert Storm against their former Arab allies who, by 1999, will have formed a powerful Sino-Islamic alliance with China.

(Update: that war began in late 1998 when Saddam Hussein threw out UN weapons monitors and incurred the wrath of U.S.-led coalition air forces in Operation Desert Fox. Initial air raids on Iraq were the largest and most destructive since the Gulf War in 1991. Since that time Iraq has suffered almost daily attacks on its military anti-aircraft installations. The shadow air war against Saddam's regime has only strengthened his stature among the more desperate and radical factions in the Arab terrorist world. The Sino-Arab alliance I spoke of has yet to happen, but as I write this in October 2001, just one month

after the terrorist attack on America, I would still hold to such an alliance coming in the near future. The so-called Arab moderate governments of Egypt, Saudi Arabia and the United Arab Emirates are pulling away from Western pressure to use their bases for operations against what they call "fellow Islamic nations." George W. Bush is at present making a historic shift in U.S. strategic policy to expedite his war against terrorists. He is pulling away from allies in the Middle East while cultivating alliances with Russia and the other petroleum rich Central Asian republics of the former Soviet Union. This, along with the expected Western counterattacks in the Near East, may lead to further distancing between America and the West from Islamic nations as the war drags on. Thus we may see China, the burgeoning superpower, bring the Arab/Islamic world into its sphere of influence between now and 2008.)

Saddam Hussein's regime still remains one of the chief bases for the most extreme elements of Arab terrorism. In the 1986 edition of this book, written at a time when Saddam's Iraq was a tacit ally of America against Iran in the First Gulf War (1980-1988), I warned that Iraq would build – and use – the first Islamic bomb. We can only hope that the U.S.-Arab Coalition air strikes smartly bombed this potential future. By the summer of 1993, the United Nations weapons monitors stressed that Iraq's nuclear capability had been completely destroyed.

The final line of C2 Q30 could imply that terrorists, based in and supported by Iraq, will target Italy for a future act of nuclear terrorism. In 1991, UN Special Commission (UNSCOM) weapons inspectors declared that Saddam had built a bomb, before the war destroyed his nuclear industry. Two years later, UNSCOM denied its existence. As we will see, the results of air strikes during the nineties

TERRORIST ATTACKS THREATEN WORLD PEACE

will show whether Coalition forces did indeed destroy the bomb that UN-weapons monitors are now claiming Saddam Hussein never built. (Update, October 2001: a full three years since UN monitors were thrown out of Iraq, Saddam Hussein has resumed his clandestine efforts to either make a few crude nuclear devices or procure them on the black market. New UN estimates made in 1999 say that Iraqi chemical and biological weapons arsenals are back to their pre-1990 levels of lethalness, and Iraq could have nuclear weapons in less than five years.)

The name "Mabus" is rich in possibilities to decode phonetically spelled Arabic names. For instance, many shadowy Near Eastern terrorist figures hide their true identities under code names beginning with "Abu" (Arabic for "father"). The wide use of Abu fits the prophet's rules of solving anagrams. You can drop one or two letters in a word, for instance, the "m" and "s" from "mABUs" and you get "Abu." The Majus-Mabus link implies those individuals or organizations using the PLO North African base next door to the ruins of (Thurbo Ma[b]us), or those organizations and their operatives who are code named "Abu" – such as Abu Amar, Abu Nidal, or Abu Abbas, etc. – as candidates for the Third Antichrist.

The enemies of peace, the dissolute ones, after having overcome Italy, the bloody black one of the night... (C6 Q38) Roman power will be quite put down (by Abas), following the footsteps of it great neighbor. Secret hatreds and civil disputes will delay the crassness of these buffoons.

C3 Q63

Abu Abbas was the PLO hard-liner and leader of the Palestine Liberation Front (PLF). Phonetically, this man's name comes closest to Nostradamus' Mabus enigma – Abu Abbas = (M)abu(S) (M)abbas. In an interview held after Abu Abbas' successful attack on the Italian pleasure cruiser *Achille Lauro*, in 1985, our next candidate, Sabri al-Banna (code named Abu Nidal) redefined himself as well as his organization as a father – "abu" – of evil. Since he severed ties with the PLO in 1974 he has masterminded terrorist attacks on 20 nations, killing 900 people. These include bloody assaults on civilians at the airports in Rome and Vienna in December 1985, the Neve Shalom synagogue in Istanbul, the Pan Am Flight 73 hijacking in Karachi in September 1986 and the City of Poros day-excursion attack in July 1988. Currently, Abu Nidal seems to have retired into the wings, but many of his disciples in the Abu Nidal organization continue to network with other organizations. His operatives have secret bases in all the areas of the Middle East where that terrible ancient god had dominion. Asia Minor (Turkey) saw many terrorist events during the Second Gulf War. Iraq and Iran provide the Abu Nidal organization with bases. The growing link between terrorist groups and the Kurdish war for independence against Turkey, Iraq and Iran is also implied.

The 1990s saw Libya isolated with economic sanctions for not delivering up two Libyan secret service men to stand trial for planting the bomb on Pan Am Flight 103. The prophecy implies that Qaddafi and his sect of extremists should fear what revelations come from these two "wounded" men during their trial in Scotland in 2001. The clue "aleph and/or Alif" stand for the Hebrew and Arabic letters for "a," and might be an attempt to name the double "a" named Libyans implicated in the attack. They are (A)l (A)min Khalifa Fhimah and (A)bdel-baset (A)li Muhammed al-Megrahi.

179

*The Religion named after the ocean
will overcome,
against the sect of the son Adaluncatif:
The obstinate, deplored sect will be
afraid of the two wounded Aleph and
Aleph (Alif).*

C10 Q96

*Adaluncatif = Cadafi Luna = Qaddafi Moon
Colonel Qaddafi of Libya*

Quatrain 96 of Century 10 has baffled interpreters for the last half century. In the previous edition I took it to be a riddle about Libyan leader, Muammar Qaddafi, and the consequences surrounding the bombing of Pan Am flight 103, which crashed into the town of Lockerbie, Scotland, in 1988. The term "Oceanic religion" could be somewhat awkwardly describing Qaddafi's bed on the night of the U.S. bombing raid on his home in 1986. Author and former British Parliament member, George Tremlett, has been one of the few Westerners invited into Qaddafi's house in the center of a military barracks outside of Tripoli. The bombed bedroom is enclosed in glass, like a shrine, without one shard of shrapnel or piece of broken masonry disturbed since the night of the bombing. Tremlett's book *Gaddafi: The Desert Mystic* contains a photograph of the bed; at the head we see an illuminated and vividly colored panoramic photo of ocean waves crashing on the rocks. Adaluncatif is one of the prophet's classic anagrams. Reshuffle the letters and they form "Cad(t)afiluna." Allowing for phonetic spelling changes, it is possible to get Qaddafi Luna," "Qaddafi of the Moon," or "Qaddafi of the Crescent of Islam. Qaddafi has long been a harborer of terrorist leaders and organizations, such as Abu Nidal.

The 1990s saw Libya isolated with economic sanctions for not delivering up two Libyan secret service men to stand trial for planting the bomb on Pan Am Flight 103. The prophecy implies that Qaddafi and his sect of extremists should fear what will come from these two "wounded" men. The clue – "Aleph and/or Alif" stand for the Hebrew and Arabic letters for "a," and might be the prophet's attempt to name the double "a" named Libyans implicated in the attack. They are (A)l (A)min Khalifa Fhimah and (A)bdelbaset (A)li Muhammed al-Megrahi.

The Mabus = Abu clue may reveal just who can bring either peace or Armageddon to Israelis and Palestinians, the Palestinian, Chairman Yasser Arafat. Before he became a peace broker for his people, his PLO secret code name was "Abu Amar." Drop the last two letters "ar" and replace with "s" to get "Maabus." The "aa" phonetically stands for one "a" = Mabus.

Given the volatile situation in the Middle East, an observation I made back in late 1997 deserves review. It speculated on how the successor to Pope John Paul II may be drawn into collapsing Middle Eastern peace efforts to play a significant part as a peacemaker in the near future. On page 334 of my book *The Last Pope* (a study of the Latin papal prophecies attributed to the medieval Irish St. Malachy), I said the following:

"Arafat and the Palestinian leadership are preparing for a defensive war they cannot win codenamed Field of Thorns. The pope's role as peacemaker may be set in motion after Israeli troops get bogged down in bloody warfare and negative global public opinion when they fight an intifada of lead bullets rather than stones in street wars with West Bank Palestinian police."

If, in the coming days, Yasser Arafat were to "soon die" in Israel's expected retaliation – or he dies in subsequent fighting as the current intifada becomes a full-fledged war – the vengeance sought for Arafat's martyrdom could trigger a 27-year war of terrorism.

Then there is Saddam Hussein of Iraq. You can find his name matching that of Mabus by using a simple occult word game. First spell m-a-b-u-s backwards; then turn any letters around that can represent a new letter once reversed, such as "b" turned to a "d." Thus, "Mabus" spelled backwards is "Sudam." Use the law of replacing one letter and you get "Sadam." Phonetic redundancies allow you to spell it with an extra "d" and it becomes "Saddam."

Abu Amar (Yasser Arafat)

Despite the current bellicose climate between Israelis and Palestinians and the world attention given to Saudi terrorist, Usama bin Laden, I still hold that Saddam Hussein of Iraq is the chief candidate for Mabus, to date. He considers himself the protector of extremist Palestinian aspirations – namely the deep rooted desire to push Israelis into the sea and take back all Palestinian lands seized in Israel's 1948 war of independence. He has pledged a force of up to 5 million armed Iraqi Mujahadeen poised to assist their Palestinian brethren in the coming conflict. Intelligence reports indicate that Saddam Hussein is rapidly rebuilding his chemical and biological weapons arsenals and he uses a number of terrorist organizations like Usama bin Laden's al-Qaeda (the base) as his surrogates. His "mother of all battles," as he called the opening stages of the last Gulf War, continues. The impatient Western mind would like to brush off his declaration, as a mother of all overstatements. The Near East breeds patient minds. The Gulf War of 1991 was the first skirmish of a war that will be carried on like a family feud from generation to generation. The sons of Saddam and his grandsons will continue this confrontation with the West and Israel. Shortly after the terrorist attack on America, Debka.com reported that Iraqi Intelligence agents, under the command of Saddam's son, Uday, provided information and training for the use of weapons of mass destruction to hundreds of soldiers of terrorist organizations connected to Usama bin Laden's network in camps in Northern Iraq. Not long after 5,300 victims were reduced to ashes in the funeral pyre of the World Trade Center's debris, Debka reported that 60 operatives from Uday Hussein's camp infiltrated the Balkans via Albania with the presumed intention to launch bin Laden's "secondfront" of terrorist attacks on America and her

Saddam Hussein

European allies. Another 100 returned to their terrorist bases in Afghanistan to face the Americans.

By the time you read this after the publication of this book in early 2002, you will most certainly see the focus of U.S. and Allied attacks move from Afghanistan to Saddam Hussein's Iraq. If in the coming conflict missiles should find their mark in one of Saddam Hussein's bunkers, he too could be made a martyr for a 27-year war of terrorism.

One cannot rule out the likelihood that Nostradamus intended "Mabus" to be a thing as well as a person. There is possibly one of Nostradamus' complicated double entendres working in this enigmatic codename. Mabus the "thing" then is Saddam the "person's" weapon of mass destruction, hurled at Israel. One of the Iraqi leader's hidden "al-Abbas" (Mabus) scud missiles could be the payload for a future chemical, biological, or even nuclear attack on Tel Aviv. In such a scenario the famous "Mabus" prophecy could describe the launch of an al-"Mabus" missile that "soon dies" in the flames of its own successful explosion after its seven minute supersonic journey. If the target is Israel, she may reply with one of her own 200 nuclear weapons. The last Gulf War clearly demonstrated how scuds or other intermediate-range missiles are perfectly designed for surprise in the compact theater of the Middle East. The chemical or nuclear extermination of just one of the region's cities would set alight "all at once" the Holy Land's ancient vengeances in an "undoing of men and animals" in a region-wide Armageddon. Mabus the missile and/or the person would be instantly consumed in a third world war in miniature that erases the land where Moses wandered, Jesus walked, and Muhammad drove his camels.

183

❋

*Throughout Asia Minor
(Turkey – Kurdestan) there will
be a great prohibiting of outlaws.
Even in Turkey, Iran and Iraq,
blood will flow because of absolving
a young dark man filled with evil doing.*

C3 Q60

The Saudi terrorist Usama bin Laden, is considered by the West to be the mastermind of the September 2001 attacks on the U.S. Pentagon and the World Trade Center buildings in New York. He often has Western reporters phonetically misspell the Arabic pronunciation of his first name with an "O." It is "Usama." Thus a true phonetic spelling makes his name a classic fit for Mabus if one follows Nostradamus' rules of wordplay. "Usama" = maaus b(IN) LADEN. Drop the redundant "a" and replace it with a single letter allowed by the rule and move the solitary letter "b" = Mabus.

It is not beyond imagining that Nostradamus has mistaken more than one man to be his fearsome Mabus. Where Usama bin Laden plays his public role as terrorist number one, the real perpetrators, and the real "Mabus," such as a Saddam Hussein, wait in the wings of the world stage of terrorism. What is clear is that whoever he is there will be a mass roundup of his operatives in Turkey and the Middle East. It is expected that greater bloodshed awaits Iran and Iraq from his deeds.

"TWENTY-SEVEN YEARS HIS BLOODY WAR WILL LAST"

Those of you who have read my books since 1987 know that I believe Nostradamus pointed to a third world war of international terrorism slated to begin around, or a few years after, July of 1999. New York was the prime target, or better, the target for a second Pearl Harbor. My understanding of the prophecies led me to believe that the terrorist leader responsible for masterminding the attack would be one of the first to fall in this war. I believe this man will be Nostradamus' "Third Antichrist."

This terrible figure emerging at the onset of the 21st century is introduced by Nostradamus in a prophecy that closely parallels the themes of his famous Mabus prediction.

I have long interpreted the appearance of the comet Hale-Bopp in 1997 as the clue to Mabus surfacing in our near future. I believed that Nostradamus points to him (at least in part) in a related Quatrain 72 of Century 10 as the "King of Terror" coming from the skies

184
✳

Mabus will soon die, then will come,
A horrible undoing of people and animals,
At once one will see vengeance,
One-hundred powers (Nations), thirst,
famine, when the comet will pass.

C2 Q62

the following prediction
continues the theme

The Third Antichrist very soon annihilated,
Twenty-seven years his bloody war will last.
The heretics are dead, captives exiled,
Blood-soaked human bodies, and a reddened,
icy hail covering the earth.

C8 Q77

either in "1999 and seven months" (July 1999) or "1999 plus seven months" (July 2000). Few could ignore the apt comparison of civilian jets crashing into the Pentagon and the World Trade Center towers as a terror descending from the skies.

There are many in the Nostradamus field who felt let down that no significant terrorist attacks came either in July of 1999 or 2000. Did Nostradamus get it wrong?

I believe the advent of "Mabus" has arrived, if slightly later than expected by Nostradamus. I for one, do not fault a man predicting events 450 years in the future who misses his written date by two years and four months or 14 months, depending on which "July" Nostradamus intended.

If you examine closely the Mabus and Third Antichrist prophecies, they reveal a rich assortment of parallel clues to what may happen as a consequence of the terrorist attacks on America on 11 September, 2001. Both prophecies clearly promise the rapid destruction of the Third Antichrist at the onset of his war. For instance the first prediction says "Mabus will soon die..." matches the second prediction's phrase that the Third Antichrist is "very soon annihilated."

Once he dies the first prophecy adds, "Then will come a horrible undoing of people and animals." The second continues the same apocalyptic vision but adds specific and horrific descriptions about the dead and dying. They are soaked and stained red by icy hail showers. These awful images bring to mind the result of a war bringing climatic catastrophe to the earth; one where "a reddened, icy hail covering the earth" is a watered down version of a nuclear winter – or what I have called a nuclear autumn. Could dust and fire clouds cool the climate after a sustained nuclear attack by the Anti-Terrorist Alliance against cities and countries that harbor terrorists in the Near East?

ASH-COVERED SURVIVORS FLEE THE SITE OF THE WORLD TRADE CENTER, 11 SEPTEMBER 2001

185

Is there another interpretation? Did Nostradamus – a man of the Renaissance period – find it hard to explain a future plague raining from biological and chemical agents? His nightmare visions of a "terrible undoing of people and animals" and "blood-soaked human bodies...a reddened, icy hail..." etc., could be his attempt to describe the "rain" from clouds of reddish and milky white biological or chemical agents falling upon the dead. Thus a rain that kills both human beings and animals alike in our future can come from a hail shower, if you will, of radioactive isotopes, Serin pesticide, or anthrax bacteria.

The "Third Antichrist" prophecy of Century 8 Quatrain 77 may augur condemnation, labeling the shadowy minions of Mabus as "heretics." Perhaps Nostradamus means they do not follow the teachings of their religion. "Islam" means "peace."[1] Moreover, they are "captives exiled," indicating that many terrorist operatives will soon be arrested and find their way into prisons far from their homelands.

The closing words of the Mabus prophecy of Century 2 Quatrain 62 imply an overwhelming counterattack: "At once one will see vengence" from "one hundred powers..."

The current U.S. coalition against terrorism numbers around one-hundred nations.

The mention of "thirst" and "famine" are common in what one could call Nostradamus' numerous third world war prophecies, which we will examine in more detail in the next chapter. These perhaps are the future results of today's growing stresses on food and water demands coming from overpopulation. Dozens of other prophecies in Nostradamus imply that our growing numbers could eventually overtax civilization and become a far more powerful factor than terrorism in dragging the world down into a third world war. If my reading of Nostradamus' numerous astrological dates for such a war and ecological disasters is correct, then we still have around 20 years in which to avoid this worldwide "free-for-all" over dwindling resources.

---

[1] Actually, "peace" is a secondary definition. "Islam" in Arabic means "to submit (to God);" from the root *asalama*, he surrendered, he resigned himself, from *salama*, he was safe.

THE PLAGUE OF FALSE DUST

Much of what I wrote in the following segment for the first and second editions of this book in 1986 and 1994 is essentially still controversial and includes potentially dangerous interpretations that today's uncertain world may see fulfilled. True, Abu Nidal has not been the firebrand I foresaw, but that does not mean another terrorist codenamed "Abu," may not fulfill the actions if not the decoding of the name Mabus. America finally felt the wrath of international terrorism to a degree of destruction and loss of life unknown in the world up to 11 September, 2001. A much worse attack may be coming to her allies in Europe; one that uses any number of possibilities hidden in Nostradamus' cryptic label for a catastrophic plague of the "false dust." Are these the spores of anthrax or some ebolalike plague? Is this the "dust" of chemical agents, or the "false dust" of stolen Soviet weapons-grade plutonium spread across Southwestern Europe, via a terrorist attack on Italy? Fortunately the time windows for terror mentioned in earlier editions decoding astrological conjunctions mentioned in the following prophecies have come and quietly passed. Now we must look to new figures and new time windows of terrible opportunity hiding in the cryptic words of his prophecies. Nostradamus may see a man of evil coming out from an "iron fish" off the shores of Italy to make war on the world.

THE VAST DOME THAT DOMINATES
VATICAN CITY, ROME, ITALY, ANOTHER
LIKELY TARGET OF A TERRORIST ATTACK

EUROPE AND THE MIDDLE EAST ARE CLOSE NEIGHBORS WHEN SEEN FROM THE SKIES

One who the infernal Gods of Hannibal
(Baal Hammon–Ma[b]us) will cause to be
born. Terror to all mankind! Never more
horror nor the newspapers tell of worse in
the past then will come to the Italians
through Babylon.

C2 Q30

Babylon (modern-day Baghdad) has been the haven for more radical terrorist leaders. Iraq has been a training camp for their operatives to learn how to wage a surrogate war of terrorism for Saddam Hussein, using weapons of mass destruction. Any terrorist currently being trained by the Iraq Secret Service could eventually make their way into Europe to commit unimaginable horrors through the doorway of Italy. In another terrorist prediction, Nostradamus says "Roman power will be quite put down." (C3 Q63) In World War II Italy did not turn out to be, as Winston Churchill predicted, the "soft underbelly of Europe," easy for the taking. British and American forces faced some of their hardest battles against the Nazi armies there. But what of the next war? These and other quatrains imply that Italy's lax security and long coastlines could present a soft underbelly for the man who might unleash World War III!

Through lightning in the box (ark) gold and silver are melded. The two captives will devour each other. The greatest one of the city stretched when the fleet travels under water.

C3 Q13

The first few lines might describe an alchemical process or are they a 16th-century man's attempt to describe the function of a modern submarine's atomic engines? The third line may represent the pope and the city of Rome as we shall see...

When weapons and plans are enclosed in a fish (submarine). (Or the line can read): When Mars and Mercury are in conjunction with Pisces. Out will come a man who will then make war. His fleet will have traveled far across the sea to appear at the Italian shore.

C2 Q5

In other predictions Nostradamus makes it clear that there is a Libyan (Barbary) connection to a future (terrorist) invasion of Southern Europe. Muammar Qaddafi, an admitted protector and supporter of Abu Nidal and other terrorist organizations, possesses five diesel-powered Soviet-made Foxtrot Class attack submarines in his fleet. Algeria, Syria and Egypt also possess a similar number of Soviet era submarines. Whoever the man is who has plans and special weapons to "make war," a date for his underwater journey to destiny may hide in the first line. The conjunctions of Mercury and Mars in Pisces take place frequently. The next conjunctions are April 2007, March 2009, February – March 2011, February 2013 and so on. The events foreseen here may come as late as the conjunction scheduled for March – April of 2026 and March of 2028, when the planet Neptune's transit through the sign of Aries (God of war) is at its highest malefic aspect for sparking a third world war.

THE CALM WATERS OF THEIR MOORING DO NOT DISGUISE THE POTENTIAL THREAT POSED BY THESE SOVIET-BUILT SUBMARINES

From the useless enterprise of honor and undue complaint, the ships are tossed upon the sea off the Italian coast. Not far from the Tiber river where the land is stained with blood. There will be several plagues upon mankind.

C5 Q63

One nuclear power plant exists less than 40 miles down the coast from the mouth of the Tiber river at Latina. Another is under construction at Montalto di Castro, nearly 50 miles up the coast. Currently they are off-line. Nothing in this quatrain directly hints to any reactors being seized by terrorists but one can infer that some bloody calamity may happen near or in Rome; a catastrophe that comes from the appearance of some man-made plague. As we will see in the following prophecies it may be connected to an evacuation of Southern Europe. The "ships" tossed or sunk may be the submarine fleet already mentioned. Perhaps they are detected and attacked? The first line hints that the "enterprise of honor" is another gesture in the legacy of stupid reasons that man slaughters his fellow man; or perhaps it could be Nostradamus naming the ship that will discover the submarines and sink them, the U.S. air-craft carrier *Enterprise*.

The quatrain numbers "62" and "63" often punctuate prophecies related to the Third Antichrist. Perhaps they stand for the date of a catalytic act launching the rise of Islamic fundamentalism. Ayatollah Khomeini captured world attention in 1963, when his Iranian followers started their Islamic revolution against the Shah. To this day, many of the prime candidates for the captain of the submarine fleet seek Iran as their haven and staging ground for international terrorism. Iran itself has received delivery of five Kirov-class attack submarines from Russia.

During the appearance of the bearded star (Halley's Comet in 1986, or a new comet?) The three great princes will be made enemies. The shaky peace on earth shall be struck from the skies: the Po, the winding Tiber, a serpent placed on the shore.

C2 Q4

The "three" could metaphorically stand for the First, Second or Third Worlds or, as we will examine in the following chapter, an alliance of three terrorist-sanctioning nations destined to fight amongst themselves. Peace being "struck from the skies" could link the "King of Terror" from C10 Q72 with the man of evil intent commanding the submarine fleet. The future may see a Libyan or Egyptian submarine under cover of darkness deposit a band of terrorist commandos and their metaphorical "serpent" – a metaphor for a stolen nuclear device or homemade atom bomb – off the Italian coast at the mouth of the Tiber River. Even a nuclear plant in Northern Italy's Po river region could be the scene of a terrorist attack. One of Italy's two Nuclear power plants is at Caorso, a town two miles south of the Po river near Cremona. At the moment the reactor is not in use.

The third Antichrist very soon annihilated.

C8 Q77

Mabus will soon die, then will come a horrible undoing of people and animals.

C2 Q62

The heretics are dead, captives exiled.

C8 Q77

Instead of some well-known leader of a state, the Antichrist may be a shadowy, almost mythical figure. His army may be no more than a dozen commandos with a nuclear device. His failed gamble at taking the world hostage could trigger World War III or...

189

...The detonation of the "serpent" atomizes the Antichrist, destroys a nuclear power plant and creates a reactor meltdown. Certainly little less than a nuclear or chemical weapon attack or nuclear disaster would force the evacuation of Southern Europe as a lethal radiation or chemical cloud spreads. Nostradamus tries only once to describe what dreaded pestilence causes the complete evacuation of South Eastern Europe: "a plague of false dust." The usual weather and wind patterns for March or April of any year give credence to there being some kind of nuclear disaster as the cause of Southern Europe's evacuation. Indeed croplands would be wiped out (hunger) from the "plague" (fallout) and the "war" of one nuclear terrorist.

Naples, Palerma and all of Sicily will be uninhabited through North African (Libyan) hands. Corsica, Salerno the island of Sardinia – hunger, plague, war...
C7 Q6

From Monaco as far as Sicily, all the coast will remain deserted...
C2 Q4

Paterno, will hear the cry from Sicily... Flee, oh flee... the dreaded pestilence!
C8 Q84

In the Southern Balkans and all of Greece, a very great famine and plague through false dust (fallout/anthrax/smallpox?). It will last nine months through the whole peninsula (Italy) as of Peleponnesus. (Greece)
C5 Q90

CHAPTER THIRTEEN
ARMAGEDDON

Throughout Nostradamus' forewarnings of the sequence of apocalyptic events before the world's renewal, runs a recurring litany of "plague, famine and war." We may be able to soften the effect of these disasters but we cannot avoid them.

Prophets down through history have maintained that the greatest cycle of centuries, the precession of the Equinoxes[1], will be renewed around the year 2001.

When a great cycle of centuries dies, everything that civilization has valued and held dear must also die in order that a new morality, religiousness and science can be born. Interpreters of prophecy generally date the first contractions of this re-birth to have appeared around 1984. On 19 January, 1991 some North American shamans of the Hopi Indian tribe claimed to see the doubling in intensity of what we might call the psycho-spiritual contractions of the birth to come. From now on these contractions will come in faster and faster waves until they reach a peak by the year 2012 and rage at maximum energy through the 2020s and 30s.

In this and the next three chapters we will examine the three kinds of birth pains through which the world must pass. They are Nostradamus' prophecies on Armageddon, ecological disaster, and our potential to counter-balance the doom in doomsday with a "blooms" day. This is a spiritual flowering; a revolution in consciousness.

---

[1] Every year the sun's gravitational pull on earth causes the zodiac star group behind the sun at the time of the spring Equinox to appear to make a minute backward slide. Thus, for the last 2,000 years or so, the star group at Equinox was Pisces. By the year 2001 it will be Aquarius.

THE ROAD TO ARMAGEDDON

The sword of death is approaching us now in the shape of plague and war
more horrid than has been seen in the life of three generations.

The Preface to Caesar

The Holy City of Jerusalem, scene of
desperate fighting during the Six-Day
War predicted in Quatrain 3
Century 22.

After a great misery for mankind
an even greater approaches.
The great cycle of the centuries is renewed:
It will rain blood, milk, famine, war
and disease.
In the sky will be seen a fire, dragging a
trail of sparks.

C2 Q46

Sooner and later you will see great
changes made,
Extreme horrors and vengeances.
For as the moon (of Islam) is thus led
by its angel
The heavens draw near to the Balance.

C1 Q56

Gabreel (Gabriel), is the avenging angel of the Christian and the Islamic Apocalypse. Nostradamus often uses the scales of justice as a symbol for democracy. As already hinted, the terror of the Middle Eastern Antichrist comes from the skies (the heavens). Therefore this could mean that nuclear "fires from the skies" will descend on the Western democratic powers, after July of 1999. The quatrain indexing may target the year 1956, the year of the Suez Canal crises.[1]

...Plague, famine, death from
military hands.
The century and the age approaches
its renewal.

C1 Q16

The first "great misery" for mankind is World War II. The next is World War III, expected to take place around the time the "great cycle of centuries" is renewed, at the millennium. Contrary to the hopeful signs for a new world order of peace with the end of the Cold War, collective prophecy down through history remains adamant that there will be three world wars in or shortly after man's 20th century after Christ. The fact that most casualties of a global nuclear war will come from starvation instead of blast and radiation effects has not been overlooked in Nostradamus' nightmare scenario of Armageddon, the final battle. The rain of blood could stand for rain choked with radioactive dust. Survivors of an attack by chemical or biological weapons sometimes describe the detonation of warheads as a "milky rain." The fire "dragging a trail of sparks" could be a double pun on Halley's Comet (1986) or Hale-Bopp (1997) and nuclear missiles (used after July 1999). If Halley's Comet is intended then the potential time window for World War III is either after 1986 or before the year 2060 when the comet returns.

---

[1] Suez Canal crisis. In 1956 Egyptian President Gamal Abdel Nasser nationalized the Suez Canal and forced French and British forces to withdraw.

Rain, famine and war will not cease
in Persia (Iran). Religious fanaticism
– and too great a faith in his allies –
will betray the Shah, whose end
was planned
and conceived in France.
A secret sign for one to be more moderate.

C1 Q70

In 1963, followers of Ayatollah Khomeini staged a series of demonstrations against the secular Iranian government of the Shah. After being removed from Iraq in 1978 he directed the Iranian revolution from Paris (so its beginnings were in France). So far the Iranian people have suffered continued deprivation, natural disasters and revolutions.

Six days the assault is made in front
of the city. Freedom is attained
in a strong and bitter fight:
Three will hand it over
(Egypt, Syria and Jordan),
and to them pardon (peace agreements?)
To the rest (Libya, Iraq and Iran?) fire,
and bloody slashing and slaughter.

C3 Q22

Throughout the Six-Day War,[1] fierce fighting took place around the Old City quarters of Jerusalem. Finally the Israelis retook the ancient platform where the Temple of Solomon once stood and where one of Islam's holiest shrines, the Dome on the Rock, stands today. With this prophetically significant victory came the prophetically horrifying consequences. War did not come by 1999 but it could come afterwards because that year did bring the core stumbling block to peace to the surface. Whose "holy" temple will dominate Jerusalem, the Islamic Dome on the Rock, or a Third Temple of the Jews to be built in the Dome's place?

The populated lands will become
uninhabitable
Great disagreement and discord in order
to obtain lands.
Nations given to men incapable of
prudence...
Then for the great brothers death
and dissension.

C2 Q95 (1995?)

In the previous edition I said the following: "The ancient blood feud between the descendants of Abraham (the Arabs and Jews) may see their wars over territory come to a head by the year 1995." October 1995 saw the peace process dealt perhaps a mortal blow when Israeli Prime Minister, Yitzhak Rabin, was assassinated. In other quatrains the "great brothers" seem to be the former superpowers who fought the Cold War (Russia and America). They begin fighting the final battle of Armageddon as allies but soon fall into dissension. Nostradamus does not give a good prophetic report card on today's latter-day world leaders such as America's George W. Bush and Russia's Vladimir Putin.

A new law will occupy a new land
Around Syria, Judea and Palestine.
The great empire of the (Arab or Libyan)
barbarian will crumble before the Century
of the Sun is finished (20th Century).

C3 Q97

The play on *barbare* represents Nostradamus' pro-Christian bias against the Arab "barbarians." It further hints that Islamic fundamentalist factions currently living in the regions once controlled by the Barbary Pirates (Algeria, Tunisia [PLO headquarters] and Libya) are catalysts for Armageddon. So far the dating for crumbling empires has missed the mark, unless Nostradamus mistook the Soviet Empire for its Arab allies.

---

[1] Six-Day War. Lightning attack by Israel on the Arab States in 1967. Israel extended its frontiers.

The fatal and eternal order will turn and turn

The chains of Phocen (i.e.,

Phoenicia = Lebanon) will be broken.

The city (Beirut) taken and the enemy at

the same time.

C3 Q79 (1979)

CONFLICT IN BEIRUT

The quatrain number may try to pinpoint the future-historical time of heightened attacks between Lebanese Moslems and Christian Phalangists in Beirut. Perhaps the more recent incursions of Israel into Lebanon in 1982 (the city taken) to destroy the PLO (and the enemy at the same time) are also implied. Usually Phocen is thought to be an ancient moniker for the French city of Marseilles, which in ancient times was originally colonized by the Ionians from the city of Phocæa in Asia Minor. The quatrain indexing and the poetic reference to the eternal cycle of fatality is at least metaphorically more appropriate for the Phoenician homeland of modern Lebanon. The Bekaa Valley remains a hotbed of terrorist bases run by Iranian surrogates, such as Imad Mugniyeh, who, until the rise of Usama bin Laden, was considered by the U.S. as terrorist number one. He planned a number of successful suicide bombings and hijackings and was responsible for the slaughter of hundreds of U.S. Marines sleeping in their barracks in Lebanon in 1982. A new direction in the prophecy would see Mugniyeh (who trained bin Laden) as the real logistical mastermind behind the World Trade Center attack. Once the ruin that was once Afghanistan is thoroughly bombed the next lightning storms of U.S. cruise missiles and carpet bombing will break over the terrorist camps of the Bekaa Valley. A new invasion of Lebanon by Western forces is at hand.

The city of Geneva stands here as a general synecdoche for the peaceful or destructive uses of the atom. In August of 1955, representatives of 72 countries gathered in the city for a first meeting on sharing information on the peaceful uses of atomic power. Some countries misused the knowledge and became today's Third World nuclear powers. In the following decades the name Geneva became synonymous with efforts by Russia, America and the United Nations to negotiate nuclear arms control and stem the tide of ethnic wars.

The quatrain clearly implies that the diplomats of Geneva have something to fear from this Nostradamian riddle. Deciphering the right meaning for the enigmatic word, RAYPOZ, could help forestall Armageddon.

One translation decodes RAYPOZ as a biblical anagram for "Zopyre," who betrayed ancient Babylon to Darius of Persia. Give this interpretation a modern parallel and it reveals Saddam Hussein of Iraq (Babylon) betrayed by the Reagan and Bush (Sr.) administrations (actively involved in diplomatic missions to Geneva). Although Reagan and Bush (Sr.) tacitly supported his war against the Ayatollahs of Iran, turned on him in August 1990 when he invaded Kuwait. There are some indications that the Bush administration used their U.S. ambassador to Iraq, April Glaspie, as a Zopyre-like patsy in a sting operation. Conspiracy theorists believe the U.S. Ambassador was duped into giving the dictator mixed messages. This led Saddam Hussein

to believe his U.S. handlers would look the other way if he invaded Kuwait, to settle his long border and oil field disputes with the little sheikdom. If there is any truth to this story then the CIA – and Bush (Sr.), its former chief, the then chief of state – used the resulting Gulf War as a sting operation to isolate and debilitate yet another U.S. supported dictator who had outlived his usefulness. Thus the betrayed tyrant will unleash RAYPOZ as his revenge.

Rescrambling the letters of RAYPOZ, while following the Nostradamian rules for decoding anagrams, supports this interpretation. RAYPOZ not only represents Zopyre but also an actual location called OSIRAK outside of Baghdad. If we spell RAYPOZ phonetically as "RAIPOS" and scramble the letters we get OSIRAP; following the rule of replacing a letter "P" with a "K" we get "OSIRAK." This was the name of the place not far from the ancient city of Babylon, where the French built an experimental reactor.

If we are following the correct path in this interpretation then RAYPOZ stands as an anagram for weapons of mass destruction which Saddam Hussein or his heirs will somehow use to take future revenge on America, her Western allies and on Israel. Despite the devastation of his country's infrastructure and the dismembering of his conventional armies in the Gulf War, large stockpiles of chemical warheads with hundreds of scud missiles to carry them aloft are still unaccounted for. The flow of weapons-grade plutonium smuggled out of the former states of the Soviet Union finds its way to Baghdad.

The final line encourages us to examine some of the major astrological "signs" that date an invasion of RAYPOZ in our near future. Wars often erupt when Mars (God of war) is in either the fire signs of Aries or Leo (Mars

PROPAGANDA POSTER OF SADDAM HUSSEIN

Leave, leave Geneva everyone!
The grim reaper (Saturn) will change gold to
iron (wealth to weapons)
Those against RAYPOZ (Israel, the EU, the
UNO and the USA)
will be exterminated.
Before the invasion the heavens will show signs.

C9 Q44

in Leo in negative aspect representing fiery egomania). The period is even more dangerous if Saturn enters the mix either in the same or another fire sign.

In the 21st century I would expect the highest potential for war when Mars enters Aries at the same time Saturn enters its two-year transit of Leo (2005-2007) and again when Mars is in Leo in June-July 2006, and in Aries again at the end of the Saturn transit of Leo in May-June 2007. The next time Mars aspects Aries and Leo several times during a Saturn-Leo transit (August 2034-October 2036) is also during the final degrees of Neptune's transit through Aries. In my opinion, this is the most dangerous time for a third world war in the next century because this would come when the planet's ecology, food and water sustainability reached a critical stress point due to pollution and overpopulation.

195

OPERATION DESERT STORM

He will enter, wicked, unpleasant, infamous,
Tyrannizing over Mesopotamia.
All friends made by the adulterous lady,
The land dreadful and black in aspect.

C8 Q70

In Century 8 Quatrain 70 the overriding question is just who is entering Mesopotamia (modern-day Kuwait and Iraq)? It cannot be ruled out that the prophet is labeling former U.S. President George Bush, his successor President Clinton, or even his son, President George W. Bush as the invading tyrant. Then again, the Shi'ite Iraqis would see this prophecy apply first to Saddam Hussein who brutally crushed their rebellion in Southern Iraq shortly after the Gulf War. The senior President Bush would come in second in many a Shi'ite Iraqi's view, as the man who publicly intimated America's support for their rebellion, but in the end, left them to be massacred by Saddam Hussein's Republican Guards. Perhaps Nostradamus judges Bush the elder and Saddam Hussein equally as wicked, unpleasant and infamous.

From a traditional Christian standpoint, the biblical metaphor of Babylon as the "adulterous lady" always stands for an all-powerful, depraved and markedly un-Christian empire destined for destruction. In a modern sense Babylon stands for Iraq. But it could equally be one of the royalist prophet's anti-republican metaphors for an all-powerful Western nation fallen into corruption and decadence, which uses the statue of French republican "Lady Liberty" as its now-adulterous label, i.e. America. Lady Liberty could symbolize New York, which was attacked.

In the new millennium, most Iraqis might soon point a damning finger at the push-button terror of stealth planes and "smart bombs" launched by President Bush, the junior.

The Second Gulf War left Kuwait shrouded in oil ash ("the land dreadful and black in aspect"). Massive coalition bombing effectively wiped out the water purification system. As a result, approximately 500,000 Iraqi children may have died from gastrointestinal diseases and malnutrition in a decade following the war. The economic sanctions righteously upheld by "Lady Liberty" have only made life more dreadful in aspect for the people of Iraq. The infamous, unpleasant and wicked Saddam Hussein has succeeded in exploiting U.S. and coalition sanctions to tighten his grip on power over modern Mesopotamia.

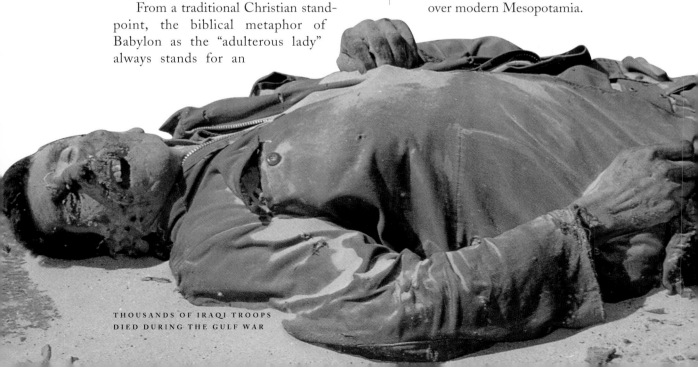

THOUSANDS OF IRAQI TROOPS
DIED DURING THE GULF WAR

BLOODY ALUS

His hand (or power) finally through the
bloody Alus, (Mabus?)
He will be unable to protect himself by sea.
Between two rivers (Tigris and Euphrates)
he will fear the military hand,
The black and angry one will make him
repent of it.

C6 Q33

This "Alus" quatrain gives us yet another prophetic riddle which could apply to the future of the Middle East and its political reversals and intrigues. It implies that Saddam Hussein may not be Nostradamus' fearsome "Mabus."

The original Renaissance French word for "hand" is *main* which can be taken literally as "hand," or as the Latin root "manus" which can have a variety of interpretations, including hand, strength, authority, power, force etc. or a "dealing hand" as in a wager.

For now I will make an interpretive "wager" that the "hand" belongs to Saddam Hussein. In other words, his hand is strengthened in the future by a terrorist leader or organization. Their fates are intertwined. Their weakness comes from vulnerability at sea. Saddam Hussein cannot defend himself from sea-borne cruise missile attacks, nor can the real Mabus – possibly Usama bin Laden – be safe from missile or commando attacks launched from the sea. The third line implies that Saddam Hussein fears a new coalition invasion through the Mesopotamian delta in a third Gulf War, or a renewed war with Iran.

The black and angry one could describe either a black-robed usurper of Ayatollah Khomeini's legacy, or he is the black-bearded, cold and dark eyed leader of the al-Qaeda terrorist network, Usama bin Laden. One finds clear evidence from American and Israeli sources that Al-Qaeda terrorists receive money, intelligence and training in the use of weapons of mass destruction from Iraqi secret services. The Western war machine will make Saddam repent this association from the sea-borne attack that brings his end.

A burning torch will be seen in the night sky
Near the source of the Rhône.
Famine and war will come, and help
will be too late,
When Iran mobilizes to invade Macedonia.

C2 Q96

The reference to comets in Nostradamus could also be the way a 16th-century man describes a falling intercontinental ballistic missile; in this case one aimed at a target near the mouth of the Rhône river in southern France. The war waged in the northwestern hill towns of Macedonia in early 2001 between Albanian separatists and the Macedonian army could indicate worse wars to come in the Balkans through surrogate extremists blessed and financed by Islamic fundamentalists from Iran. Imad Mughniyeh, head of the special overseas operations for the Iranian backed Lebanese terrorist organization, Hizbullah, has hundreds of operatives working in tandem with hundreds of al-Qaeda soldiers smuggled by ship into the Balkans via the Albanian mafia. Israeli intelligence believe they where put there after the September 2001 attack on America to widen the terrorist war to the Balkans and Western Europe. Perhaps "Bloody Alus" and/or "Mabus" are actually implicating Mugniyeh and not bin Laden, the West's most popular poster boy of terror.

197

ATTACK ON THE
"HOLLOW MOUNTAINS"

Fire approaches the great new city
Immediately a huge, scattered flame leaps up.

In the path of the hollow mountain.
It will be seized and plunged into a boiling cauldron.

I have issued many warnings based on my understanding of Nostradamus over the past 16 years, and many of you have heard them on television and radio or read them in my nine published books. Now a number of these observations take on the magic of prescience. They fall from the delicate sky of a September morn, arriving with the thunderclap of falling skyscrapers. This is some of what I understand is in the prophecies of Nostradamus concerning present and near future events. He spoke of a new type of world war to come; one using surprise and ambush. A rogue leader from the Middle East will trigger it. He is a terrorist, code named in the prophecies as "Mabus" or the "Third Antichrist." This man will be one of the first to fall in his war. He could become a symbolic martyr for terrorists who will soak the world with blood for 27 years.

On the same day terrorist attacks hurled jet airliners as missiles at America, the news and internet services spread a terror of another kind – a fraudulent prophecy attributed to Nostradamus issued by Reuters News Agency! Apparently the journalists at Reuters have forgotten the basic rule of good journalism: verify your facts! Clearly no one at that news agency checked the accuracy of the prophecy. It seems that Reuters shot first, and asked questions "never." Not a single Nostradamus scholar was contacted before they tossed a fraud to world media for sensational public consumption.

THE "HOAX-TRADAMUS" PROPHECY

In the year of the new century
and nine months,
From the sky will come a great
King of Terror...
The sky will burn at forty-five degrees.
Fire approaches the great new city...
In the city of York there will be
a great collapse,
2 twin brothers torn apart by chaos
While the fortress falls the
great leader will succumb
Third big war will begin when the
big city is burning.

Nostradamus: written in 1564

Let me advise you all, and the press at large, that you can always smell a rat in Nostradamus prophecy when the prediction has no indexed volume and quatrain number. Even in his own day, Nostradamus had to counter the publication of false books of prophecy attributed to his name. He protected himself and us by indexing every prediction for verification. The first two lines of this clever fraud mangle real lines of Nostradamus coming from Century 10 Quatrain 72. Then it steals the next two lines outright and out of context from the real lines of Century 6 Quatrain 97. Finally, there are no documented prophecies that even come close to what Reuters spread all over the planet as words written by Nostradamus from the year 1564.

THE AUTHENTIC PREDICTIONS

At forty-five degrees latitude,
the sky will burn.
Fire approaches the great new city.
Immediately a huge, scattered flame leaps up,
When they want verification
from the Normans (the French).

C6 Q97

In their long battle to enlighten the press not to fawn and frighten people with a fraud, Nostradamus scholars such as myself have spent decades bringing the following two AUTHENTIC prophecies to the world's attention, in the hope that their dire warnings can be softened or completely avoided. Here are the real and indexed predictions translated directly from the earliest editions of Nostradamus' original French texts (first printed in serialized form between 1555 and 1568). In C6 Q97, the "new city" is New York. It is relatively young as cities go and there are no cities exactly on or near latitude 45 that one could call "new" and significant enough to alert Nostradamus' attention. Lines 2 and 3 could describe the flaming engines of two jet airliners approaching the great new city. They crash into the World Trade Center towers. Huge fireballs of "scattered flame" erupt while intelligence sources in the U.S. seek verification from their French opposites about rumors of an imminent attack on America.

Indeed there were warnings coming from France the day before the attack! In her article of 13 October, Associated Press reporter, Jocelyn Noveck, documents clear evidence that a day before the attack on New York, on 10 September, French intelligence began looking into troubling indications that al-Qaeda operatives were about to attack American assets in Europe, primarily the American Embassy in Paris. French officials contacted their American counterparts who waited for verification. However, it was too late to stop the fire falling out of the skies over New York with the roar of jet engines. A month later France's top anti-terrorist judge, 'Jean-Louis Bruguière,' reportedly uncovered terrorist cells of al-Qaeda, using French computer terminals in suburban Paris apartments to transmit messages to Usama bin Laden's terrorist camps in Afghanistan.

If one can enlarge Nostradamus' theme then more huge and scattered flames are coming. We see them initially in the green glow of night scopes on cameras propped on mountains overlooking Kabul, Afghanistan under U.S. and British air attack. There no doubt will be a huge scattered array of terrorist targets blazing around the world in other locales beyond Afghanistan.

A HUGE FLAME OF DESTRUCTION

The second "real" prophecy (C10 Q49) narrows the focus on New York as Nostradamus' intended "new city" under attack. If you were to stand on the Western shore of the Hudson River, in New Jersey (also known as the "Garden State"), and look across to Manhattan Island, you would see the man-made "mountains" of New York. Even New Yorkers describe their boulevards as "canyons" among the mountainous skyscrapers. If you have ever flown into New York, or stood upon the shores of the Hudson, you might use Nostradamus' 16th-century metaphor of "hollow mountains" to describe the once Everest-like monuments of human architecture that until recently cast a giant shadow over the southern tip of Manhattan.

"In the path" of those "hollow" mountains raced terrorists in hijacked jet liners ready to unleash their mortal blows. The hollow mountains are "seized and plunged" into the boiling "vat" or *cuue* as Nostradamus describes it in Renaissance French. The *cuue* is a fermenting cauldron wherein Nostradamus, a

Garden of the world near the new city,
in the path of the hollow mountains:
It will be seized and plunged
into a boiling cauldron,
drinking by force the waters
poisoned by sulfur.

C10 Q49

physician and cosmetics manufacturer, would plunge materials for the mixing of his medicines and cosmetics. The cauldron would summon boiling clouds as objects were seized and thrown into it. I believe his use of *cuue* is a poetic attempt to capture the vision of vast, mountainous buildings being pushed down by gravity. It describes the hollow mountains crumbling and melting away in the ferment of boiling clouds made of their own pulverized debris.

201
✳

THE WORLD TRADE CENTER OVERSHADOWED BY ITS NEMESIS

The final line of Century 10 Quatrain 49 could also augur a future and far more catastrophic attack on New York. Starting all the way back in 1986, I began warning my readers that this prophecy may describe a terrorist attack on New York's financial district. I thought the attacker would use a small nuclear weapon or other weapons of mass destruction. The prediction that says, "It will be seized and plunged into a boiling cauldron, drinking by force the waters poisoned by sulfur," may describe yet another terrorist attack on New York. The next attack could come from terrorists hiding a crude nuclear device hidden in the belly of a cargo ship anchored off south Manhattan island.

Back in 1994, in *Millennium Book of Prophecy,* I warned of attacks on New York and other cities by something as seemingly incongruous and harmless as a small plane loaded with plutonium or anthrax dust. The plane could pass over the towers of the hollow mountains sprinkling their noisome loads on unsuspecting civilians. Reuters received news from the well-regarded Jiji News Agency in Japan that terrorists plan such an attack by small private planes and crop dusters.

I pray that such a future will be prevented by the vigilance of the American people. I also pray that my interpretation of prophecies of mass terrorism are only terrible, because they are terribly wrong.

TERROR IN NEW YORK CITY

AMERICA'S CALAMITOUS WAR AGAINST TERRORISM

If my interpretations from June 2001 are accurate then you will see the perpetrator of the attack on America this September of 2001 banished and annihilated[1] no later than early July of 2002. That conclusion can be derived from an understanding of Quatrain 24 of Century 6. The JPL American Ephemeris sets the next conjunction of Mars and Jupiter for 29 June through 8 July, 2002. I would not rule out the drift of predicted events to kick in, as early as April through the summer of 2002.

America is ruled by the sign of Cancer in astrology. Cancer also rules the month of July wherein Mars and Jupiter will be conjoined with such furious intensity in 2002. The current American president, George W. Bush, is also born under the sign of Cancer. Thus one could decode the second line of the prophecy above to read "a calamitous war under America and its leader." If this is a correct decoding of the line, then America's war waged by President Bush against terrorism will be a calamity for his country, the American economy, and perhaps bring catastrophe even to himself.

The reason for this interpretation goes beyond the prophecies of Nostradamus. Predictive astrology warns us that the U.S. presidential campaign of 2000 was once again under the shadow of the malefic planetary conjunction of the planets Jupiter and Saturn. This conjunction takes place once every 20 years. Since 1840, every president who has campaigned under this conjunction in a year ending with a zero has faced near-fatal harm or death through illness during their presidency. President Bush must weather this dire destiny, with its threat of sudden health crises or assassination, just like Presidents Reagan and before him, John F. Kennedy, Roosevelt, Harding, McKinnley, Garfield, Lincoln and Harrison. In my own presidential predictions logged

Mars and the sceptre (of Jupiter)
will meet in conjunction,
A calamitous war under Cancer:
A short time afterward a new king
will be anointed,
Who will bring peace to the earth
for a long time.

C6 Q24

U.S. PRESIDENT, GEORGE W. BUSH

over the years I have stated clearly that the current president – whether it would be Gore or Bush – is in danger of dying in office before finishing his first or definitely his second term. I have been publicly stating this danger since 1998. At that time I declared that we may lose the next president in a crash of Airforce One, or see him die from a sudden and unexpected heart attack.

203

---

[1] From the essay "Who Will be Mabus," posted 4 June, 2001 on my website's HogueProphecy Archive Page. (See www.hogueprophecy.com.)

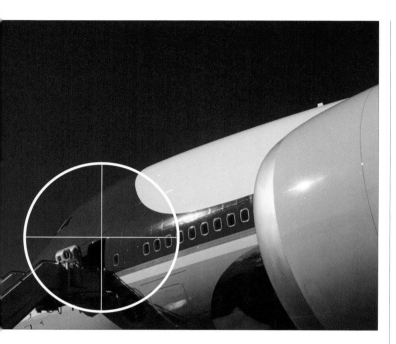

THE NEW VULNERABILITY

*The king will want to enter the new city
(New York?),
Through its (his) enemies
they will come to subdue it (him):
Captives liberated to speak and act falsely
King to be outside, he will keep far from the
enemy.*

C9 Q92

The syntax of line 2 is open to switching *its* with *his* so it can read, "Through its enemies they will come to subdue" him. One could apply this prophecy to the events of 11 September, 2001. On that terrible morning, Airforce One was on course to land President G. W. Bush in a "new city." In this case another city that didn't exist in Nostradamus' time, Washington DC. A third hijacked plane had just plowed into the Pentagon building and reports of a fourth abducted plane heading for Washington warranted an emergency rerouting of Airforce One out of harm's way. Thus the "king" or president "to be outside" and kept "far from the enemy." The liberated "captives" may stand for the many hundreds of bonafide Arab terrorists released from Israeli jail during the 1990s as a gesture of reconciliation to the Palestinian Authority during peace negotiations. Perhaps some of these "captives" have returned to their Hamas, Hizbullah and al-Qaeda terrorist networks to speak falsely in the name of Islam and do evil to others, including the American people and their president.

Let us return to Nostradamus, and Century 6 Quatrain 24. Perhaps by April, June or early July of next year, President Bush will be a casualty in this war as well as the fearsome Mabus. The perceived threat to Airforce One and the President from terrorist attack on 11 September – and the continued trouble Vice-President Cheney has with heart disease – unfortunately plays into this prophecy. I still hold a hope that my predictions are wrong about both men, but I fear that Nostradamus in Century 6 Quatrain 24 points to more tragedy visiting America. Still, there is some hope for a positive outcome and soon. Shortly after July of 2002 a new leader is elected. Perhaps this is a vice-president taking office or even a new president elected in 2004. Time will only tell. The line in Nostradamus' prophecy that says, "he will bring peace to the earth for a long time" may give us hope for a rapid resolution of what could have been a war lasting 27 years. There is always the possibility that a new "king" or leader could be a new European head of state or even a new French president for whom Nostradamus has taken a fancy. One cannot even rule out the "anointing" of a new pope by, or shortly after, July of 2002 who will bring the olive branch of peace on earth. The prophecies attributed to the Irish St. Malachy points to the next pope after John Paul II being known by the motto "Gloria Olivae." (Glory of the Olive.)

PEACE ON EARTH FOR A LONG TIME?

The astrological key word "Cancer" and phrase "calamitous war" in Century 6 Quatrain 24 links the prophecy to the notorious "King of Terror/July 1999" prophecy of Century 10 Quatrain 72. Cancer in astrology rules the month of July. I have always believed that this prophecy about a calamitous war under Cancer ending in July of 2002 is an alternative future outcome to a war started by a "King of Terror" descending from the skies around or after July of 1999.

Here is the full text of the 1999 prediction, line-by-line, with my inserted notes:

In 1999 and seven months...

(In other words, in the month ruled by Cancer.)

...the great king of terror will come from the skies.

(That terror descended in hijacked civilian jet airliners crashing into the Pentagon and the "hollow mountains" of the World Trade Center.)

...He will resurrect the king of the Mongols...

(I believe this statement shows a 16th-century man recognizing the assent of China as a superpower to rival its influence in world history to that of its Mongol overlords of the past. If "he" infers the Third Antichrist, then a future conflict between China and America could be over the horizon because of his terrorism.)

...Before and after Mars rules happily.

Most interpreters and amateur Nostradamus scholars overlook the occult significance of the use of Mars in the last line of C10 Q72. They usually translate this to mean "war" because conventional wisdom in occult circles says Mars rules war. Those interpreters are wrong. A more thorough understanding of the symbolic potentials of Mars in predictive astrology could see the final line of this dark and terrifying prediction translated with a silver lining.

205

✳

THE CRAB, SYMBOL OF CANCER

THE LOWER AND HIGHER
ASPECT OF MARS

In its lower mystical potentials, Mars does stand for war, droughts, famines, the release of suppressed and explosive anger, self-righteous cruelty, heated words, and perhaps in an abstract sense the heating up of the climate from global warming. If you translate the phrase "before and after, Mars rules happily" by inserting the planet's higher symbolic aspect then "Mars" represents the god of magic and spiritual transformation. Thus if we combine the two prophecies of C10 Q72 and C6 Q24 together, the new millennium may start with a calamitous war against terrorism fought under those of the sign of Cancer (America). In other words "before" we have Mars representing war. Then America could shift the vision of Mars towards its higher aspect sometime after July of 2002. In other words, "after" that time Mars "rules happily" in peace and a political climate of fresh and inspired beginnings.

If this interpretation is correct then we will see a new leader rise to take the reins of America either in mid-term of the current presidency or "shortly afterwards" by 2004. Look to him to bring on the potential of a future ruled by the higher aspect of Mars – long and sustained peace. In this positive translation of Mars the resurrected Mongol who is a metaphor for the rise of China as a superpower is not the murderous Genghis Khan, but his grandson, the more civilized and peace loving Kublai Khan. Rather than China going to war with America as a competitor, as superpowers they find a balance in power that increases prosperity and peace on earth.

I believe what I wrote back in 1997 can yet apply to a hopeful outcome of today's terrible events. At that time I wrote, "The rise of China as a superpower to match the United States could bring balance and stability to the world. The quality of effort, courage, and skill that leaders of both great nations employ to effect the change from nationalist to internationalist government before and 27 years after

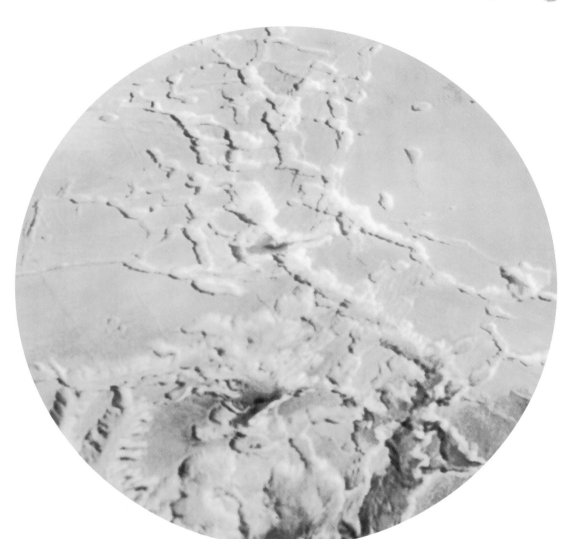

207
✴

MARS – BLOODY OR BENIGN?

1999 will determine which aspect of 'Mars' will 'rule' – bloody war or benign enlightenment." (*Nostradamus: The Complete Prophecies*, page 800.)

We cannot fulfill both these destinies of War or Peace together. The current leader of America may die in the coming struggle, but perhaps a new leader will take his place. Under a new administration, America may back away from its own historic part in its dysfunctional and self-righteous relationship with the Middle and Near East. May America's current and future leaders rule with the understanding that all people and all things are divine, and deserve our tolerance and love.

We stand at a crossroads on the Cusp of time. One destiny leads to sustained terror and war, the other to understanding and peace. The actions of history's power players around July of 2002 can create a new world war or set us on a course for a spiritual awakening that brings a millennium of peace.

I pray for peace for all, and a life lived beyond those conditioned habits of history that have doomed each generation up to the present time to be so predictable.

THE WAR OF THE GREAT MONGOL

In the year 1999 and seven months (July),
The great King of Terror will come
from the sky.
He will bring back Genghis Khan.
Before and after Mars rules happily.

C10 Q72

From the kingdom of Fez (North Africa)
they will reach out to those of Europe
(European Union)
The city (Paris) blazes, the sword will slash:
The Great man of Asia (the new Genghis
Khan) by land and sea with a great troop
So that blues (UN forces?), perse (Persians?
Iranians),
he will drive out the cross (Western
coalition) to death
(Or the last line reads:)
So that the Iranians, the cross drives out to
death.

C6 Q80

Nostradamus' most famous doomsday prediction warns future generations of a "King of Terror" falling out of the skies in July 1999. This holy terror could be linked to the Third Antichrist who may be the fearsome Mabus of C2 Q62 or the North African terrorist from C2 Q30 who is from the land of the infernal Hannibal's God. Hannibal's God or "Baal" was called "Hammon," the patron deity of Carthage – and a name that can mean

"Lord of the Sky." When Baal Hammon is angered he is described as a real reigning terror from the skies. As we have noted earlier the ruins of Carthage are quite close to the former headquarters of the Palestinian Liberation Organization during its most radical period, implying that a candidate for the Third Antichrist may have been trained there in his formative years. By 1999, or some time shortly after that year, this terrorist from the land of "Baal" might wage war on Israel or its Western allies from the sky. He will use a stolen nuclear missile or detonate a civilian jet loaded with plutonium dust or chemical weapons over a city.

Many interpreters have tried to understand the prophetic significance of Nostradamus bringing back to life the *Roi d'Angolmois* (the great king of the Mongols) by the last July of this millennium. Genghis Khan united the Mongolians of the Central Asian steppes into an all-conquering army that forged the largest

GENGHIS KHAN

THE RUINS OF THE SILENT CITY IN THE BAMIAN VALLEY

land empire in history. By 1279 the empire stretched from the east coast of Asia to the Danube River in Europe, and from the Siberian steppes to the Arabian Sea. Sixteen years later the Mongol Empire became the world's first Sino-Islamic superpower. The vast Islamic western wing of his empire included modern-day Iraq, Iran, Pakistan and the Central Asian republics of the former Soviet Union.

Genghis Khan was one of history's greatest kings of terror. Tens of millions died in the bloody conquests initiated by the warlord and his successors, and his record of destruction, devastation and genocide is appaling. According to the prophet, Genghis Khan and his empire are now returning: the warlord has been brought back to life.

In 1990, in a major propaganda campaign designed to uphold the virtues of totalitarian role models and condemn democratic dissidents, the leaders of the People's Republic of China restored Genghis Khan to his "rightful" place in Chinese history.

Our First Antichrist, Napoleon Bonaparte, who appears to have had some prophetic powers, is said to have coined the famous warning: "China? There lies a sleeping giant. Let him sleep! For when he wakes he will move the world."

The recent rehabilitation of the Mongol warlord responsible for China's greatest imperial glory corresponds with a new awakening of Chinese world influence. It is forecast by many prophetic traditions that China will awaken from her long, slumbering isolation to assume a position of great influence in human history and culture, or she will be the prime mover in unleashing the mayhem and violence of Armageddon. For either destiny, the die will be cast in the final years of the 20th century. The good or evil consequences of China's rise to superpower stature will, however, depend largely on how other nations help or hinder her great destiny. China will become either the spokesman or the armoury for the non-aligned nations of the Third World.

At the present time (written in 1994 and updated in October 2001) the aging communist leadership remains in power, and the Chinese economy continues to grow. The ever mounting stresses of food sustainability and employment for the world's most populous nation continue to stretch her ability to maintain social and political stability. The possibility exists that China may become more reactionary and militant by the century's end (this statement from 1994 was fulfilled). Although America remains the world's foremost arms dealer, China supplies the highest volume of regional ballistic missile delivery systems, plus the reactors, know-how, and fissionable materials for the nuclear arms programs of North Korea, Iran, Libya, Pakistan and India. United States Intelligence believes China is Iran's principal source for their secret nuclear weapons project.

The possibilities flowing from the present moment, tempt me to believe that 1999 is not the end of the "27-year war of the Third Antichrist" (C8 Q77) but its beginning. Between 1999 and 2026, if the United Nations cannot become the unquestioned world parliament and if international law does not have greater weight and fairness than national law, peace will not be restored to the Middle East, and the Arab and Islamic nations will look to China, the new superpower, as their defender against American domination.

By the 2020s, oil and food will be the new weapons of geopolitics. By that time China will require all the world's stock of exportable grains from 1996 levels to survive. America will import two-thirds of its oil from the Arabs. China may be forced to counter America's politics of food with a Sino-Islamic alliance that allows her to curb America through the politics of oil. If a new Sino-American Cold War takes place, China will become the new safe haven and training camp for the jihad of terrorism. In a worse-case scenario China – whether communist or not – may find herself under the dictatorship of a future Genghis Khan. She fulfils a biblical and Nostradamian nightmare as the linchpin to a new regional Sino-Pan-Islamic alliance against Europe, Russia, and America in a nuclear third world war by the mid-2020s.

The final line, as mentioned earlier, makes a cryptic reference to Mars. A consideration of the occult meaning of this planet which, in conventional wisdom, represents the god of war and mayhem, opens up the possibility of a positive outcome in the future. Another hopeful future may be derived from the quatrain's indexing perhaps standing for a date. Quatrain "72" could be a near-miss for the year 1973. Count back 27 years from 1999 and you get the beginning of Nostradamus' 27-year war of the Antichrist. If we move safely past July of 1999, perhaps the destiny of the Third Antichrist will have been effectively neutralized.

The result of ethnic strife and the growing plague of wars fought over dwindling food and water resources indicates a balkanization of the world as early as the 2020s. Ethnic cleansing is a plague that could infect continents with the pustulous boils of war. The continued effectiveness with which the Western and Russian leaders handled growing crises in the Balkans and Trans-Caucasia during 1994–1996 period is even more crucial in the coming 2005–2008 time window in Nostradamus' prophecies. Depending on this unsteady marriage of Russia and America in their post-Cold War political and military alliance, they could either cauterize the ethnic plague at its source in the Balkans and Chechnya, or let it spread worldwide via the Balkans down into Turkey and Greece, and via Chechnya, down through the Near and Central East.

THE GREAT ETHNIC WORLD WAR

ETHNIC STRIFE IN THE BALKANS

What a great oppression shall be made upon the princes and governors of kingdoms and especially those that shall live eastward and near the sea [the Near East]... *And in the last era all the kingdoms of Christianity* [the Western coalition] *and also of the unbelievers shall quake for the space of 25 years* [perhaps related to the 27-year war of the Third Antichrist]. *There shall be more grievous wars and battles. Towns, cities and other castles* [fortresses] *and other buildings all shall be burnt, desolated and destroyed with a great effusion of virgin blood, married women, and the widows ravished, suckling children dashed against the walls of towns. So many evils shall be committed by the means of the infernal Prince, Satan, that almost the entire world shall be undone and desolate.*

Epistle to Henry II

"THE BROTHERS WHO ARE NOT YET BROTHERS"

And when shall the lords be two in number, victorious in the north against the Eastern ones, there shall be a great noise and warlike tumult that all the East shall quake for fear of those two brothers of the North who are not yet brothers... they will be victorious against the Easterners.

Epistle to Henry II

The two will not remain allied for long: within 13 years they will give in to Barbary [Libyan–Arab] power. There will be such a loss on both sides, that one [perhaps America in this case] will bless the bark of Peter and the cape of the pope.

C5 Q78

...Great disagreement and discord in order to obtain lands [i.e., the Balkans, Central Asian and Arab oil fields, and Israeli–Palestinian disputes over the Holy Land]. Kingdoms given to men incapable of prudence. Then for the great brothers [US & Russia] death and dissention.

C2 Q94

Nostradamus never supported the apocalyptic theme of Cold War adversaries pushing a button and blowing up the world. The quatrains strongly suggest that such a war comes only after Russia abandons communism. But Nostradamus seems to support the idea of them becoming unsteady friends first (halved or split). Later they could push the nuclear button, as a result of their shaky alliance falling victim within either three or thirteen years to a former Near Eastern ally's support of terrorist behavior. The question remains: what event defines the solidification of this new friendship? When do we start counting down three or thirteen years to a potential confrontation with Russia and America? I believe this countdown date is still in our future. I predict that the terrorist attack on America in September of 2001 will see Russia forge a secret alliance with America in the next few years to fight Near Eastern terrorism. Signs already indicate that America will give the Russians carte blanche in their war against Usama bin Laden-trained Chechen terrorists, if Russia allows America to attack Afghanistan or other Near Eastern countries from bases in the newly independent (and former Soviet) Central Asian republics. In short, you will see the forces of the "northern kings," Russia and America, fighting side-by-side in a new Crusader alliance against perceived Islamic terrorism between 2002 and 2008. This alliance, like other Crusader "brotherhoods" before it, will stand on clay feet. My sense is the breakdown will come in the 2020s when China brings pressure against the Russo-American alliance over the management of Central Asian oil fields.

THE KINGS OF THE NORTH

One day the two great leaders will become friends [the Latin/French blended word Nostradamus uses for "friend" (demis) can also mean, "halved" or "split."] their great power will be seen to increase. The new land [America] will be at the height of its power.

C2 Q89

The rule left to two [Russian and America]. They will hold it for a very short time. Three years and seven months having passed, they will go to war. Their two vassals rebel against them. The victor is born on American soil.

C4 Q95

The indexing of Quatrain 89 of Century 2 dates the year 1989 as the beginning of the end of the Cold War and the turn toward Russo-American friendship. Three years and seven months after formalizing their friendship they will go to war over actions of rebellious regional allies. Clearly America as the sole surviving superpower is at the height of its power. Israel, the American vassal, could pick a fight with any number of former Arab allies to the defunct Soviet Union (such as Iraq, Libya or Syria) and undermine the friendship between Russia and America. They then go to war within three years and seven months. When does one begin the countdown to this apocalypse? Obviously not 1989. There must be an important milestone in US-Russian relations coming in the near future.

NUCLEAR WAR "AFTER" THE COLD WAR IS OVER?

At sunrise one will see a great fire. Noise and light extending towards the North. Within the earth death and cries are heard. Death awaiting them through weapons, fire and famine.

C2 Q91

There will be let loose living fire and hidden death. Horror inside dreadful globes. By night the city will be reduced to dust...

C5 Q8

The world will be so diminished, and its people will be so so few that no one will be willing or in enough numbers to till the fields...

The Epistle

According to Nostradamus and the warnings of many other proven forecasters of future disasters, we could not be living in more dangerous times than these. The fulfillment of Armageddon is assisted by the ignorance or collective denial of some basic facts. A reduction of nuclear arms in the early 21st century of even 75 percent of the Russian and American Cold War nuclear arsenals will still leave enough nuclear bang in their "peace" agreement to annihilate the planet. There is enough destructive force to match the arsenals both countries had in the early 1970s at the height of the Cold War. Just one misstep, or crisis between Russia and America and the missiles of the Cold War can be retargeted within hours. The Northern Hemisphere could be consumed by the thermo-nuclear war everyone wanted to believe was no longer possible. Awareness of the continuing danger is our best defense in voiding the Nostradamus prophecies above as well as a prophecy from the 17th century German prophet named Stormberger, who left the following warning about the third and final conflagration: "With open eyes will the nations of the Earth enter into these catastrophes."

CHAPTER FOURTEEN

THE APOCALYPSE OF GAIA

A YOUNG AFRICAN CHILD SUFFERS DURING DROUGHT

214
✳

Early man was forced to view the world and its creatures as adversaries to be tamed. The prehistoric taming instinct has resulted in terrible abuse, both of the beautiful planet itself and of its resources.

According to the Gaia[1] theory of British pioneer, inventor and biochemist James Lovelock, the Earth is a vast organism which unconsciously maintains itself through systems of checks and balances. These include, for example, the photosynthesis of plant life, which produces clean, fresh air, the ocean currents and volcanic movements. The combined effect of all these systems working together results in an equilibrium of health.

Man's determined destruction and neglect of his natural world has been criticized by famous prophets, including Nostradamus. The collective prophetic voice warns us that, if it continues, we will, someday very soon, see appalling natural catastrophes occurring all around the world.

Every 60 seconds, 50 acres of the tropical rain forest, which enrich and purify earth's atmosphere, are cleared for use as grazing land. In just one year an area approximately the size of the British Isles is cleared. By the 2020s, a major part of the rain forests will be gone, taking with them earth's most efficient air-purifying mechanism.

---

[1] Gaia, the ancient Greek name for the Goddess of Earth.

Through the process of photosynthesis, trees absorb carbon dioxide and give out oxygen. Deforestation through slash and burning dumps billions of tons of carbon into the atmosphere every year. This atmospheric pollution, plus the tons of chemical pollution produced by industry and road transport, traps the sun's heat within the atmosphere, creating a global greenhouse. With no moisture returning to the atmosphere from the deforested wastelands and the barren soil reflecting the sun's heat back into the air, the greenhouse effect is further aggravated, altering ocean and weather patterns and setting the scene for drought and famine on a worldwide scale.

The plagues, famines and droughts predicted by Nostradamus have already begun, and continue to be right on astrological schedule, as I correctly forecast in the first edition of this book in 1986.[1]

The growing world drought and the spread of famine and hunger, especially in early 1990s Africa, continues to remind a foot-dragging new world order that the "greenhouse effect" cannot be ignored. Yet in a second Bush presidency, the millennium dawns with the U.S. delaying ecologically sound policies to avert the disasters coming from global warming. The Bush presidency came to power over just four percent of the world's human population, but the U.S. consumes 35 percent of the world's energy and resources, leaving behind 25 percent of the world's waste and pollution. Rather than being scandalized, the new administration encourages even more energy use. This is not so surprising when you consider that most of the Bush team consists of former leaders in fossil fuel production. It takes no prophet to tell you that global warming will rapidly increase.

Nostradamus' predictions indicate that – following the spread of worldwide drought and famine – the developed nations' stockpiles of grain would eclipse oil as a primary political weapon. "In the year when Saturn and Mars are equally fiery, the air is very dry, a long comet (a missile?). From hidden fires a great place burns with heat. Little rain, hot winds, wars and raids. (C4 Q67) Bushels of wheat will rise so high that man will devour his fellow man." (C2 Q75) His astrological clues point to the time when Mars and Saturn are in conjunction in fire signs and wars of terrorism are fought across a hot and desiccated world. The conjunction of these two planets happens a number of times but the stated equality in fire of the two by Nostradamus indicates we should look more closely at the conjunctions of Mars and Saturn in the same fire sign in our near future. Watch for drought, wars and raids for June/July of 2006 (in Leo), September/October of 2016 (in Sagittarius), and especially in October/November of 2026 (in Aries). The latter conjunction takes place around the time Worldwatch Institute estimates that China will not be able to feed itself, and Indian demographers believe India will run out of potable water. Both are nuclear powers that could, as Nostradamus may imply, launch their "long comet" or arrays of nuclear missiles in a war over food and water.

In Century 6 Quatrain 35, Nostradamus states: "Near the bear (Canis Major constellation) and near the white wool (the Milky Way), Aries, Taurus, Cancer, Leo, Virgo (perhaps for a period of five months), Mars, Jupiter and the Sun will burn the great plain, woods and cities."

Mars, Jupiter and the Sun passed through these constellations, sometimes in conjunction, from April through August, 1987, and April through August, 1991. The summer of 1987 hosted unprecedented drought and brush fires in Provence and the French and Spanish Riviera regions. The summer of 1991 saw a major drought across the savanna of central

215

✳

Brazil. Temperature records were broken from the Rocky Mountains to New England as much of the United States sweltered under the hottest weather of the summer. In Southern Europe, a record-breaking August heat wave was responsible for the deaths of at least 70 people in Spain and central Italy. The great Russian grain belts across the Volga, the Urals and Black Soils regions saw temperatures often exceeding three digits during the summer, destroying an estimated 30 million tons of expected grain yields.

The comet Hale-Bopp transited the northern skies in spring of 1997 near the "bear" constellations of Canis Major and Minor and through part of the Milky Way. A conjunction of Mars, Jupiter and the Sun did occur in March 1998, which saw severe droughts around the world from the lingering effects of the strongest El Niño heat-up of the Eastern Pacific in recorded history. The planets will be together again in Aries in April, 2011. We could expect a major drought from March through September of the year, which Mayan prophecies from Ancient Meso-America believe marks the final year before a great revolution of the centuries.

Back in the first editions of this book I interpreted Quatrain 3 of Century 3 as an astrological dating for a major quake "reported in the bottom of Asia" – in other words, India – for October of 1993 when Mercury, Mars and Saturn are in Aquarius. Indeed the last day of September, 1993 did see the massive Killari-Latur earthquake strike central India and kill 10,000 people. The prophecy also said the quake in India would take place when Turkey and Greece are in a "troubled state." At the time of the Killari-Latur quake both countries nearly went to war over disputed islands in the Aegean Sea.

The Gujarati quake in northwestern India of 26 January, 2001 nearly saw the same astro-

Mars, Mercury and the Moon in conjunction. Towards the south there will be a great drought. An earthquake will be reported from the bottom of Asia (India) Corinth (Greece) and Ephesus (Asia Minor) in an unstable and troubled state.

C3 Q3

logical conjunction. Around the time when one out of every ten high rise apartments from Bhuj to Ahmedabad collapsed into dust heaps of unreinforced rubble, the planet Mercury and the Moon were in conjunction in Aquarius. Mars was in Scorpio this time, though, putting it nearly 90 degrees from the other conjoined two – this "square" of Mars to other major planets often appears around great quakes. Although Mars was not in conjunction, two of the three planets were again in the sign of Aquarius as before in the Killari-Latur quake! Perhaps this is another example of Nostradamus overlapping more than one of tomorrow's events seen from the far-off 1550s. Except for Mars not being in Aquarius there were certainly other parallels. Greece and Turkey are still in a troubled, adversarial state. The "unstable and troubled state" mentioned by Nostradamus could also stand for the series of catastrophic earthquakes unleashed on Greece and especially Western Turkey in August of 1999. This is close enough in time for the Gujarat quake to be a part of the prophecy. The mention of great Indian quakes at the time of great drought in and south of France applies itself well to temors 1993 and 2001 and to the ongoing desertification of sub-Saharan Africa.

THE GREAT GREENHOUSE DROUGHT

In the summer of 1996, and six years before the first summer solstice of the new millennium ended in June, 2001 in what climatologists around the world have declared as the hottest spring in known history, I wrote the following:

"Scientists have traced the regularity of sunspot activity over the last billion years and related it to 11-year cycles that coincide with periods of drought such as the one that created the famous Dust Bowl in the American farming belt during the 1930s. Sunspot activity is now entering a new phase that will continue up to the year 2000. The great planetary alignment in May of that year is expected to generate some of the greatest sunspot activity ever recorded.

"Nostradamus warns us against creating a future drought of biblical proportions that will burn a swath across latitude 48 in the Northern Hemisphere. Drawing a line across that latitude on a map, we touch on nearly all the world's chief grain belts. Today's amber oceans of wheat stretching across North America and the Ukraine revert to prairies and inhospitable steppes in the [21st] century.

"[I added] In my last Nostradamus book [*Nostradamus: The New Revelations* published in 1994], after pointing out that the quatrain's index number '98' = 1998, I correctly interpreted the increase in global warming after the mid-1990s when dust from the eruption of Mt. Pinatubo [in 1992] that slightly cooled the world had cleared the skies. With this interpretation in mind we can expect a wave of global droughts and heat waves by July 1998. From that time onward, global warming steadily kicks in, disrupting weather patterns, and the climatic conditions needed to grow grain start to shift hundreds of miles north of where they are now."[1]

At a latitude of the forty-eight degrees at the end of Cancer (late July) ; so great is the drought that fish in the sea, river and lake are boiled hectically. Southwest France in distress from fire in the sky.

C5 Q98

(Quatrain '98' may stand for 1998)

Six years later, my interpretation seems to have hit the mark. The summer of 1998 did see the beginning of significant droughts in the North American grain belts. The year marked the beginning of the mainstream news media's acknowledgement that global warming was not a fluke, but that its hot breath was upon us. The following summer of 1999 saw the drought in the Midwest deepen. Already, in 2000 through 2001, we have endured the greatest spate of solar flares on record and the heat desiccating our fields of food stuffs has come earlier than climatologists ever imagined. The early spring of 2000 experienced late-summer-style fires raging in Minnesota. By May, wild fires plagued Florida and the early onset of drought in the sunshine state was so intense that many farmers there decided not to even plant for the season. When high summer came five hundred wildfires spread across Western America. A deadly heat wave did not beset Southwest France but a relentless heat did seize Southeastern Europe, prompting officials in Greece and Bulgaria to declare states of emergency because of hundreds of wildfires and scores of heat-related deaths.

217

---

[1] *Nostradamus: The Complete Prophecies*, p. 437

THE REAL "KING OF TERROR" IS GLOBAL WARMING

In July of 1999, the dramatic intensification of hot and violent weather inspired me to declare that Nostradamus' long awaited "King of Terror" expected to descend from the skies in July of 1999 was not a person, but a phenomenon. It is Global Warming. Furthermore, this "king" and his "terror" of superstorms, global droughts and subsequent global famines is with us for the coming 30 years.

The events of the spring of 2000 [when I wrote these observations[1]] only add to the efficacy of Nostradamus' famous warning: "In 1999 and seven months, the great King of Terror will descend from the skies..." (Century 10 Quatrain 72)

The obscurity of Nostradamus' Old French syntax allows the prophecy to also cover July [2000] by adding "seven months" from the end of 1999 and getting July 2000. This could tie into the first prophecy's warning of a terrible drought in latitude 48 in "Cancer." By the end of July (a month represented by "Cancer" in astrology), we could witness more dramatic climatic upheavals. There may be powerful level 5 hurricanes, and a boiling of field and stream from unprecedented heat waves spanning across the American Midwest and Southeast all the way to Southwest France.

(Update: The summer of 2000 saw a half-dozen typhoons flood China, Taiwan, the Philippines, Japan and Vietnam. The United Nations announced that at least 60 million people in central and southern Asia had been affected by a severe drought. By August, India was beset by monsoon downpours flooding along the Brahmaputra and Ganges rivers leaving more than 51 million people homeless. The American Midwest and Southeast endured a third year of the worst drought since the Dust Bowl years of the 1930s. In July, visitors returning from the North Pole reported that the polar ice cap had melted for the first time in recorded history. There was open ocean at the top of the world where one used to tread upon thick ice.)

In a world where the polluted atmosphere traps the sun's heat, extreme weather is the norm. Many prophecies I have recorded in my books forewarn of areas flooded and whipped by dreadful storms, while other regions suffer droughts of biblical proportions. Add to this the dwindling supply of fresh water to sustain a billion new people appearing on the earth in the first eleven years of the new millennium [and a billion more twelve years after that] and [my new and controversial interpretation of this famous prophecy] will perhaps find [its] fulfillment.

If the end of July 2000 marks the onset of these unpleasant events they may yet again warn us in time to change. Killer droughts and storms could galvanize the public and leaders alike to create a long-term policy to prevent a runaway weather catastrophe before it is too late.

(Update: Since the summer of 2000, the developed nations of Europe have moved to initiate an emission-limiting regimen delineated by the Kyoto Accords, but the United States has backed away from any official reductions. The new Bush administration, which is clearly pro-fossil fuel in its energy policies, will not support the reduction of emissions and is doing its utmost to roll back twenty years of ecological and energy saving policies to produce more greenhouse gas emissions to feed its sagging consumer economy. Indeed, the new leadership scoffs at the overwhelming scientific evidence that an increased use of fossil fuel will only bring on greater fever and convulsions in future climatic weather. Thus at the time of this writing, the greatest polluter and energy-using developed nation continues to feed the King of Terror called Global Warming.)

---

[1] Taken from the HogueProphecy Bulletin: "It's Too Darn Hot!," 20 June 2000. See HogueProphecy.com/archive.htm. The updated inserts are from October 2000.

THE GREAT ECLIPSE OF 11 AUGUST 1999

Then the great empire of the Antichrist will begin – where [once] Attila['s empire] and Xerxes descended [Central Asia and Persia] – in numbers great and countless, so many that the coming of the Holy Ghost, proceeding from the 48th degree [of latitude], will make a transmigration, driving out the abomination of the Antichrist [who is] making war against the Royal [Pope] who will be the great Vicar of Jesus Christ, and against his Church, and his reign for a time and to the end of time.

And [the events listed above] will be preceded by a solar eclipse more obscure and more dark [and mysterious], than any since the creation of the world except for the death and passion of Jesus Christ, from that time till now, and there shall be in the month of October some great movement and transference and it will be such

that one will think that the Earth has lost its natural movement, and that it will be plunged into the abyss of perpetual darkness; there will be initial omens in the spring, and extraordinary changes in rapid succession thereafter, reversals of kingdoms and mighty earthquakes, with the increase of the new Babylon [modern Iraq], the miserable daughter [who as we saw earlier could either stand for a hypocritical Lady Liberty of America or a more biblical allusion to Babylon/Bagdhad, or both], augmented by the abomination of the first Holocaust, and it will last no less than 73 years and 7 months... and then great peace will be established.

**Epistle
To Henry II**

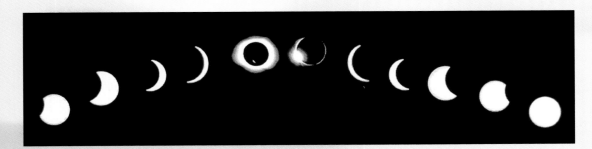

The last total eclipse to obscure Flanders and Europe was on 11 August, 1999. The sun's shadow cut a path through England, Belgium, France, Eastern Europe, Turkey, Israel, Iraq, Iran, Afghanistan, Pakistan and Western India. It must be remembered that July of 1999 is slotted by the prophet for a significantly apocalyptic terror to descend on humanity from the skies (see C10 Q72). Nostradamus accurately plots the passing of the shadow of that eclipse over Flanders eleven days after July of 1999 ended. He believes this eclipse will be remembered as the most significant since the same moon's shadow darkened the same skies over Jerusalem during the crucifixion of Christ 2,000 years before.

I am inclined not to take much of this disturbing passage of catastrophic earth changes from his Epistle literally, but at the very least I wouldn't rule out that Nostradamus, admittedly exaggerating, may be getting some grasp of the sudden climatic, natural, economic and social disruptions we can expect for the first half of the new 21st century beyond the eclipse at the end of the previous millennium.

I cannot rule out Nostradamus clouding his own vision with millennial terrors and expectations. Certainly no shift of the earth's axis took place after 11 August, nor were the foundations of civilization toppled after the shadow of a solar eclipse darkened Europe. Yet there were significant earthquakes in areas over which the moon's shadow passed that August: Greece and Turkey suffered catastrophic and frequent earthquakes a few days after the celestial event. In August, 1999, the people of Gujarat enjoyed the passing of the Moon's shadow over their Western Indian state, but by early 2001 that similarly beshadowed land suffered one of the most devastating earthquakes in modern history.

Nostradamus, in his letter to King Henry II of France, pitches events taking place sometime after the great eclipse on 11 August, 1999 in a prequel stream of visions. We see the war of the Third Antichrist. He makes classical allusions to a new "empire," or Pan-Islamic superstate, that includes the newly independent states of former Soviet Central Asia (Empire of Attila), united with modern day Afghanistan, Syria, Iran, Iraq, Pakistan, Trans-Caucasia and Turkey (the Empire of Xerxes). The eastern potentates of Attila and Xerxes were notorious for their attempts to invade and conquer Western Civilization; the same allusion therefore is applied to a future Asian or Middle Eastern potentate of an Islamic superstate who has designs to do the same. It must be noted that U.S. intelligence sources date the first infiltration of nineteen al-Qaeda's operatives into America who would eventually attack America on 11 September around the summer of 1999. In other words, the first members of bin Laden's suicide terror squad began flying out of the skies that summer from overseas to mingle with an unsuspecting American public. While the sun was obscured on 11 August, 1999 they had already begun preparations that would eventually lead to the hijacking of four planes and the destruction of the World Trade Center towers two years later.

Efforts to unite the Islamic world into one state are not new. The unity of language, culture and religion makes this theoretically more feasible than uniting the various religions, cultures and language groups of Europe into a European Union. Fear and prejudice of Christendom against Islam has seen the West do its utmost to keep the Islamic world divided. These efforts will eventually fail in the first few decades of the 21st century, if our Islamaphobe prophet is correctly foreseeing a new Islamic federation, or, as he says with prejudice, the "Empire of the Antichrist."

The *Epistle to Henry II* then waxes biblical and paints a picture of a vast Asian horde assembled to do battle with the Christian West sometime after the great eclipse of August, 1999. They are routed by a transmigrating "Holy Ghost," who issues from some place at latitude 48 degrees. The references to latitudes 45 and 48 appear in quatrains for what some believe are either the bombing of New York (C6 Q97) or a catastrophic drought in the 21st-century grain belts of the world on latitude 48, bringing on a global famine (C5 Q98).

A more abstract reading of the descent of the Holy Ghost could suggest that the holy spirit of love and consciousness awakens in the hearts of human beings to such an extent that the forces of unconsciousness that fuel the "Antichrist" – or better, "anti-consciousness," in humanity – are driven out of our hearts. The Antichrist – whether he is literally an Islamic potentate or a force of human

FATIMA-GATE

Mount Aventine will be seen
to burn at night,
The heavens obscured very
suddenly in Flanders:
When the monarch will chase his nephew,
Then Church people
will commit the scandals.

C3 Q17

Aventine Hill is one of the seven hills of Rome. This could be another "Destruction of the Vatican" scenario (see Chapter 10) in which St. Peter's Basilica and the papal enclave are destroyed by fire and tidal waves. In several prophecies Nostradamus speaks about a great solar eclipse that occurs just prior to the Apocalypse. A total eclipse did obscure Flanders and Europe on 11 August, 1999. It must be remembered that July of 1999 is slotted by the prophet for a significantly apocalyptic "terror" to descend on humanity "from the skies" (see C10 Q72). Indeed this "terror" has descended out of the skies in a number of ways: first as global warming, then a few years later as the terror of hijacked planes crash-ing into the tallest skyscrapers in New York, and later still as U.S. stealth planes sending terror down from Afghani skies in retaliation. It may be a stretch but the "monarch" could be President G. W. Bush. He is "chasing" the "nephew" – in this case the strange political bedfellow, Usama bin Laden – who was trained to be a terrorist by the CIA during the Soviet-Afghanistan conflict of the 1980s only later to turn on his American teachers.

It seems that "Church" officials are committing "scandals" after the eclipse. Less than a year after the moon's shadow obscured the Dome of St. Peter's Basilica, the Vatican's chief theologian, Cardinal Joseph Ratzinger, presented what was purported to be the handwritten *Third Secret of Fatima* to the world. This prophecy is said to be a message from the Virgin Mary given to the Portuguese shepherdess, Lucia dos Santos, when she was a child in 1917. The revealed prophecy was immediately met with suspicion by Catholic prophecy watch-ers who quickly pointed to signs of a forgery in the hand-writing. Moreover, many of the apocalyptic themes alluded to for decades by the now aged authoress and "Sister" Lucia of the Carmelite Order were not to be found in the unsealed letter presented by Ratzinger. Even the opening line of the prophecy that she herself publicly revealed decades ago was omitted in Ratzinger's "authentic" letter revealed to the world. These and other disturbing discrepancies are viewed by many Catholics as the first signs of the long dreaded apostasy of the Church that will herald the apocalypse.

unconsciousness – is attacking a future pope in the 21st century. Other references in Nostra-damus' writings to this attack of the Antichrist make a spiritual battle within the Church itself equally possible. In more down-to-earth inter-pretations the future pope and the Roman Catholic Church are victorious against the Eastern, pan-Islamic fundamentalist invasion. But one must be careful here and note how difficult it is for even the finest, most self-observant prophets not to project their hope that their religion is victorious over all others.

Many prophetic traditions share the Epistle's theme of Mother Nature's ultimate revenge for the abuse of this planet by mankind. Nostradamus' account is one of the most terrifying. It seems that he dates the slow apoc-alyptic rock or roll starting in October 1999 and continuing through May 2000. If he was not dreadfully wrong then Nostradamus did not mean October 1999 and May 2000 (which were remarkably uneventful months for seismic activity), but a future October to May sequence of seismic hammer blows across the world in some future year. The only possible hint to the year in the prophecies is in C10 Q57 concern-ing a vast hailstorm in far off AD 3755.

I personally lean towards the interpretation that the upheaval that will undermine civiliza-tion as we know it will be caused by a spiritual shift in consciousness rather than a physical jolt. Revelations of a cosmic kind could shift human consciousness overnight as well. The discovery of intelligent life on other planets might tip the axis of our religious and political moralities on their ears, would it not? The existence of "others" out there would end nation-ism overnight (reversals of kingdoms). When faced with an unknown intelligence lurking in the cosmos, our world would make "extraordinary changes" and unite as one at least out of necessity if not through enlightenment.

The excerpt of a passage Nostradamus wrote to his king about eclipses and upheavals ends with the prophet stepping back in time through the gates of Auschwitz to the "first Holocaust" of the Jews in the 1940s. A second holocaust spawned by the machinations of a "new Babylon" (in modern terms, Saddam Hussein's Iraq) is waiting in our near future. The threat from new Babylon will last for "73 years and seven months," but as usual Nostradamus does not tell us when to start our countdown, unless "seven months" is a clue to C10 Q72's, "In the year 1999 and seven months." For all we know Nostradamus could be talking about the length of the Babylonian-Iraqi threat to the state of Israel. In that case the number "73" suggests we start counting 27 years from 1973 to 1999. Perhaps we can count 73 years and seven months from the inception of the Israeli state − from 1948 through 2021 − which gets us close to the best astrological time window for the Third World War in the 2020s. Finally, one might even say that "73" stands for July of 2073 when a great spiritual master − a Magus rather than a Mabus − is the catalyst for changing the direction of human consciousness and spiritual evolution. Anyway, depending on what course we plot in the present, the jet stream of things to come can either blow us towards terrible tribulations of ecological, geological, and social catastrophes, accompanied by the rise of religious intolerance and the Third Antichrist; or, steer us towards a counterbalancing fate. On course for doomsday or a bloom's day: an end of days or a spiritual rebirth that will arise again from a mysterious source of human enlightenment, bringing humanity out of childishness and into maturity for a golden age of peace.

THE DIVINE "MONSTER" OMEN

When the eclipse of the Sun
then will be (11 August 1999?)
The Monster (divine omen) will be seen
in the plain daylight:
Quite otherwise will one interpret it,
High price unguarded,
none will have provided for it.

C3 Q34

One cannot rule out that Nostradamus' use of the word *monstre* (monster) stands for some kind of extraterrestrial omen or alien contact coming sometime after the eclipse that conclusively signals doomsday for many of our spiritual dogmas and nationalistic ideas. The final line could stand for a misinterpretation of this divine omen bringing about a future economic collapse. The collapse could also come from the dog days of an endless greenhouse-effected summer. We may have a future date hidden in the quatrain's indexing: Century 3 (March of) Q34 (the year 2034). Another total eclipse is expected on 20 March 2034, just prior to the sun's transit from Pisces to Aries (the sign of wars, droughts, heat or magical transformation).

GAIA'S COSMIC SHOCK SYNDROME

Sunrise in the afternoon. That is how the citizens of Athens in the next millennium might have described what happened if they had survived the following event.

At three o'clock the eastern horizon glowed brighter than daylight, flash-burning the retinas of those living along the Aegean coast. Minutes later, Athenian ear drums would be perforated by an explosion as loud as 2,000 one-megaton hydrogen bombs. Next, the deafened citizens of Athens would behold a new mountain range rising into the sky and falling as sea water over the eastern hills.

The day the asteroid fell, the ocean drowned Athens from the sky!

This is what Nostradamus may be implying will happen if a "mountain" or asteroid from space hammered the Aegean sea off the island of Evvoia (known by the Italians as Negrepont). On that future day, an asteroid one square mile in size will cause the Mediterranean to drown the countries skirting its shoreline.

The initial splash sent the sea over Mount Olympus. Proud Monaco was scoured down to its sandstone foundations by seven tidal waves hundreds of feet high. The citizens of Fiesole, Italy, perched high above the Arno Valley, watched helplessly as neighboring Florence was consumed by the Arno river. Florence, the

The great mountain, one mile in circumference, After peace, war, famine, flooding.
It will spread far, drowning great countries. Even antiquities and their mighty foundations.

C1 Q69

Other versions either have them taking place before the year 1999 or date this event for early in the next century.

At the place where Jason has his ship built, there will be such a great sudden flood that one will not have a place or a land to fall on. The waters mount the Olympic Festulan.

C8 Q16

Erika Cheetham interprets "Olympic Festulan" to mean Mt. Olympus, just under 10,000 feet high and/or the city of Fiesole in Tuscany just under 1,000 feet above sea level. This may describe what the initial splash of impact would do: throw a wall of sea water over 10,000 feet, unleashing tsunamis large enough to run 75 miles up Italy's Arno Valley and crest at 900 feet above sea level.

city of art, is finally engulfed not, as in previous floods by runoff coming from the Apennines, but by a new and terrible retrograde flood of sea water.

This scenario hidden in the cryptic lines of Nostradamus' quatrains could be waiting for us. Not in some distant future but perhaps as a clear and present danger every 13 months for the next 30 years. The danger will come in the shape of a shadow-mountain from space, a chunk of refuse labeled by author Jane Blosveld in *Omni* magazine as "rocky placenta left over from the solar system's birth" which, each year orbiting ever closer to our earth, might eventually collide with either the earth or the moon.

In March 1989 retired geologist-turned-asteroid hunter Dr Henry Holt studied photographs taken by the 18-inch Schmidt telescope at Palomar Observatory in California and discovered an asteroid between 500 and 1,000 feet in diameter, which he labeled 1989FC. The asteroid hurtled past the earth at a distance of 450,000 miles – a very close shave in cosmic terms. Dr Holt estimates that, "sooner or later," it will hit something.

223

✳

*Because of heat like that of the sun upon
the sea, the fish around Negrepont
(modern-day Evvoia) will become
half cooked...*

C2 Q3

*With blood and famine (perhaps again
hinting the coming apocalypse) even greater
calamity: seven times it approaches the sea
shore. Monaco...*

C3 Q10

224

According to Clark Chapman, a researcher at the Planetary Science Institute in Tucson, Arizona, "this asteroid passed closer to the earth than any asteroid or comet ever observed." Fortunately, a rock as big as 1989FC has only a one in 20,000 chance of making this interpretation of Nostradamus correct in this year or any other. But many scientists still believe that asteroid 1989FC or a cosmic fragment of similar proportions will eventually score a hit. If it does, Bevan French, a program scientist at NASA's Solar System Exploration Division, says its 2,000 megaton impact would unleash blast waves and firestorms flattening everything within a 50 mile radius.

If the cosmic shock of Gaia follows the Nostradamus scenario (above) and an asteroid spears the Aegean, the waters off Evvoia would flash-boil all marine life, sending a plume of steam higher than earth's mountains "because of the sun upon the sea." The scientist Bevan French inadvertently sides with the esoteric prophet Nostradamus in his expectations that such an ocean impact would immediately conjure "a great sudden flood," or what French describes as "tidal waves hundreds of feet high, probably wiping out most cities on the nearest coast."

The world orbits in the 1989FC's shadow of death. If it does smash into Gaia, no nuclear wars will be needed to snuff out continents with flames, no axis shifts required to engulf them in waves or set off rings of volcanic fires and convulsions in unraveling tectonic plates. Mother Earth might see the abuses wrought on her by mankind controlled by a greater hand of chance, an ancient and powerful mechanism dispensing catastrophe and calm that will exist long after we have played out our scene in the evolutionary drama.

Mother Gaia may yet again receive cosmic shocks. She will reel, shake and, in the process, extinguish a number of life forms; in time she will exert again her unconscious checks and balances, returning to equanimity and her eternal evolutionary play.

*The city is almost burned down by fire from
the sky, water again threatens Deucalion
(the Greek name for Noah).*

C2 Q81

*Very near the Tiber (Rome) hurries the
Goddess of Death. A short while before
a great flood.*

C2 Q93

NOSTRADAMUS (1555-1557)

CHAPTER FIFTEEN

A NEW RELIGIOUSNESS

FOUNDER OF UNIFICATION CHURCH, SUN MYUNG MOON

225

ALMOST ALL THE publications on Nostradamus' work which have appeared this century focus exclusively on the negative aspects of his predictions, making him, in the popular mind, a prophet solely of destruction and disaster.

But are we inevitably doomed to a future world of natural and ecological disaster, plague and nuclear war? Is our future destiny, as foreseen by Nostradamus, immutable, or will we be given an opportunity to improve our chances of survival?

Throughout the prophet's visions of apocalypse the theme of a new religious consciousness occurs again and again. It will flourish, he says, before the end of the 20th century.

Nostradamus' positive predictions, of which the new religious consciousness is a central theme, may stem partly from his own strong sense of the need for "spiritual" growth and from his 16th-century conditioning. This explanation, however, in no way diminishes the importance of his message, since it is clear that 20th-century man is growing conscious of a need to develop his awareness beyond technological and scientific development.

In their present state the established religions show little sign of an ability to bring peace to the earth. On the contrary, most of the wars of history have been fought over differences of faith and different definitions of the nature of "truth." By clearly predicting the flowering of a new religion, Nostradamus discounts all the familiar established faiths. What is the nature of this new religion? Is it already developing, or yet to be born?

DANGEROUS MEN OF VISION

*Many people will want to
come to terms
With the great world leaders who will
bring war upon them:
The political leaders will not want to
hear anything of their message,
Alas! If God does not send peace
to the Earth*

C8 Q4 *Duplicate*

Radical attempts to lift human conscious-ness always meet with violent opposition, particularly from those with vested interests in retaining the status quo. Throughout history men of vision have been subject to persecution. Ironically, many of the political and religious groups, the "authorities," which silenced them, later capitalized on their deaths, presumably in an effort to consolidate both their power and their influence.

An example is the way the pagan Roman Empire crucified Jesus, then later established Christianity as a state religion. The history of the Roman Catholic church and of its Vatican, built over the bones of a crucified Peter, stems from these beginnings.

Can we be open to the possibility that there may be spiritual teachers among us now who have new insights into how we can all live happily on our planet? Such a fresh look at our mystic contemporaries may require us to set aside our accepted beliefs and preconceptions. By branding modern visionaries as eccentric, or dangerous enough to outlaw, as our society often does, we may be repeating the mistakes made by the God-fearing citizens of Jerusalem 2,000 years ago when they branded Jesus Christ as a guru of a mad cult.

ZOROASTER
6th century B.C.

Persian mystic and founder of Zoroastianism. Stabbed to death.

SOCRATES
470?–399 B.C.

Greek philosopher charged with corrupting the minds of the young. Convicted of heresy against the state and condemned to death by poisoning.

GAUTAMA SIDDHARTA, THE BUDDHA
563?–483? B.C.

One of the world's most eloquent and enlightened masters. Many attempts were made on his life by fundamentalist Hindus. It is very possible that he did not die from dysentery, as is popularly assumed, but was assassinated by premeditated food poisoning.

POINTERS TO
A NEW SPIRITUALITY

Y'SHUA BAR ABBAS
(Later called Jesus Christ)
A.D. 0–33

An eccentric healer preaching "God is Love." A common murderer named Barrabas was spared by the righteous citizens of Jerusalem so that Jesus should be crucified.

MOHAMMED
A.D. 570–632

Founder of Islam. An assassination attempt by poisoning resulted in stomach damage which wracked his final years with pain.

AL-HILLAJ
MANSOOR
10th-century Sufi Mystic

Executed for shouting "ana'l Haq!" – "I am the truth." The method of his execution was unusually cruel - he was condemned to die through being slowly cut to pieces but laughed throughout this terrible torture.

Some 60 quatrains of Nostradamus' prophecies seem to chronicle today's new spiritual teachers and their movements. The pattern of these prophecies indicates the unique historical phenomenon which we call the "Human Potential" or "New Age" movement.

Within this movement there are currently many groups (both fraudulent and genuine) which experiment with alternative life-styles, philosophies and religions, often Eastern in origin, and practice new psychological and physical therapies. These groups, although not always in agreement over details, are all concerned with discovering new paths to world peace and ecological balance. All strive to awaken humankind to their potential for higher consciousness.

These 60 quatrains contain eight major clues to the character of the new religion and its teachings, and to the identification of its visionaries.

In the section below I have set out the clues in quatrain form with explanations and guides to their meaning. I have then listed the potential candidates who may, according to indications in the quatrains, be the visionaries who will act as the spiritual catalysts of a new religiousness. This arrangement aims to help the reader form an opinion of the veracity of each qualification.

227

1. THE MAN FROM THE
EAST AT HOME IN THE WEST

*He will appear in Asia (and be) at
home in Europe...*
C10 Q75

*The man from the East will come
out of his seat
Passing across the Apennines to see France
He will fly through the sky...*
C2 Q29

*The Caduceus Wand
entwined with two snakes,
which symbolize Hermes
and medicine.*

228
✳

During Osho's world tour in early 1986 he was expelled from Greece through pressure from the Greek Orthodox Church and the American Embassy. It may be no more than interesting coincidence that his flight plan closely matches the path of Nostradamus' escape route four centuries before. Osho crosses the Apennine mountains of Italy to indeed "see France." His Lear jet landed in Nice and was immediately surrounded by police with automatic weapons. After refueling, it was forced to take off at gunpoint to travel over the "rains" and "snows" of the Alps to Sweden.

Juliet Forman[1], relates that once the harried guru left Nice, his attendant, Swami Dhyan John, tells how Osho contemplated over the snow-covered Alps bathed in sunlight rolling beneath his jet. After a few minutes he turned to Dhyan John and said, "Maybe if the world ended existence would be better off, and we could start again."

Dhyan John relates that Osho's statement "reverberated in me – it really went into my bone marrow, the way [Osho] said that."

[1]See *Bhagwan Shree Rajneesh: One Man Against the Whole Ugly Past of Humanity* (Rebel Publishing House), by Juliet Forman.

2. GREAT HERMES' ROD

In two major quatrains about a man from the East there are allusions to the iron rod of Hermes. This rod is often interpreted in terms of a nuclear missile, a reading which makes the man an agent of the Antichrist. But interpreters should also remember the occult significance of Nostradamus' choice of vocubulary. The Hermes reference links the rod to the caduceus wand, the Western mystical symbol for enlightenment. The rod has the power to transform, liberating the individual to the truth. This man from the east wields the rod like a Zen stick to jolt the world into waking from its illusions. From this, we can infer that Nostradamus is describing an Eastern teacher who strikes out at the world and would, therefore, be unpopular. He might use unusual and unorthodox devices to stir people up, disturbing the status "codes" of social and religious behavior in our materialistic times.

...He will fly through the sky, the rains and the snows
And strike everyone with his rod.

C2 Q29

...He will appear in Asia, at home in Europe.
One who is issued from great Hermes...

10 Q75

229

3. THE OUTLAW TEACHER

The idea that old religion is a fantasy or a shadow of its living teaching is a recurring theme. The man mentioned in Century 1, Quatrain 96 will strike out against traditional rock-like dogmas, earning the unified wrath of the world's organized religions.

A man will be charged with destroying the temples and religions altered by fantasy.
He will harm the rocks rather than the living.
Ears filled with ornate speeches.

C1 Q96

"He will be charged with destroying the temples and religions altered by fantasy." (Cl Q96) The Indian mystic Osho was put in chains in America in 1985. Unification Church leader, Sun Myung Moon was vilified. Bahai mystic 'Abdu'l-Bahá and his father before him (Bahá'u'lláh) spent much of their lives in exile or in prison for their beliefs and teachings.

4. THE MYSTIC ROSE

Against the red ones religions will unite...
C9 Q51
The rose (color) upon the middle of the world scene...
To speak the truth they will have closed mouths.
Then at the time of need the awaited one will come late.
C5 Q96

Most interpreters of Nostradamus believe that his references to the color red relate to revolutionaries. But perhaps these revolutionaries are not those from Russia or France which spring most readily to mind. Red or shades of "rose" are colors used symbolically by Eastern mystics and seekers to represent the fire of awareness, the sunset of the old world and the dawning of the inner enlightenment, described by spiritual traditions as "The Mystic Rose." A riddle "to speak with closed mouths" is almost a Zen *koan*, and may very well describe the 1990's worldwide interest in Eastern meditation techniques. In fact, there is more mainstream interest in meditation in these latter-days of the 20th century than there was during the revolutionary 1960s.

The final line may be poetic suggestion that, since spiritual truth is always ahead of its times, people "come late" to recognize their mystics. The indexing may date the year 1996 as a time of great political and theological struggle between the vested interests of orthodox religions and the new religiousness of the next millennium. In 1996 we will see the right-wing Fundamentalist Christian movement in the US Republican party embark upon its ultimate crusade to take back the American presidency before the millennium. I predict the election will be a landslide for the president Bill Clinton and Vice-President Gore. Both are advocates for many of the therapy techniques and earth-friendly philosophies of the Human Potential Movement.

THE DALAI LAMA OF TIBET

5. MARS AND THE FLAME

A Buddhist monk meditating in his traditional orange flame colored robe.

...at the eve of another desolation when the perverted church is atop her most high and sublime dignity... there will proceed one born from a branch long barren, who will deliver the people of the world from a meek and voluntary slavery and place them under the protection of Mars. ...the flame of a sect shall spread the world over...

Epistle to Henry II

231

❋

Here Nostradamus attempts to describe what is the cornerstone of all major religions - the concept of complete surrender to belief. His poetic references to liberating individuals from the "voluntary slavery" of belief, a tenet of faith historically abused by religious leaders to keep people obedient, becomes less clear in the last line of the quoted section from Nostradamus' *Epistle to Henry II*: "...place them under the protection of Mars."

But, if we look at the occult connection between Mars in its higher form and Hermes, the bearer of the enlightened rod, the meaning is less obscure. Mars rules the astrological sign, Aries, a fire sign, and both are represented by the color red. Eastern mystics wear red or orange, for similar symbolic reasons, as described in clue four. Higher Mars is represented by the Hermes the Magician holding the caduceus rod of enlightenment. The philosophical similarities between Hermetic teachings and Eastern Tantra, the main essence of Eastern philosophies, seem to imply that this new religion is not like the old, judgemental faiths, but perhaps teaches a new acceptance of life. This reading would certainly be in tune with modern developments toward change through the "Human Potential" movement – a kind of magic used as a launchpad to an experience of the divine.

6. DIANA (THE MOON) AND DHYAN

Sooner and later you will see great changes
Extreme horrors and vengeances,
For the moon is led by its angel,
The heavens approach the Balance.
(Astrological — Pluto transit of
Libra 1972–1984)

C1 Q56

Second to the last of the prophet's name
Will take Diana's day (the moon's
day) as his day of silent rest...

C2 Q28

The great amount of silver of Diana
(moon) and Mercury (Hermes).
The images will be seen in the lake
(the mind of meditation)
The sculptor looking for new clay.
He and his followers will be soaked in gold.

C9 Q12

(a Hermetic reference to the attainment
of enlightenment).

The Moon in the middle of the night...
The young sage alone with his mind
has seen it.
His disciples invite him to become immortal...
His body in the fire.

C4 Q31

THE BUDDHA

The allusions to "silent rest," "images...seen" and "alone with his mind" imply the silence and distance from thought experienced by the individual who, in a state of meditation, observes the changeability of life, the mind, and the emotions. Buddha called meditation Dhyana or Dhyan, a name which corresponds to the French pronunciation of "Diana" used by Nostradamus. Here again, therefore, fire and Hermes are linked. The references in the first line of Quatrain 28 Century 2 also seem to infer that the new spiritual leader has a name related to the moon.

Gautama the Buddha proclaimed that the "Wheel of Dharma" — the dynamo for human spiritual evolution — would be turned once every twenty-five centuries by a world teacher to generate man's rise to new states of consciousness. A new turn comes at the end of this millennium.

7. THE INFURIATING TRAVELER

lue 5 also refers to a "people" linked to Hermes, the moon and meditation and the coming to the West of an Eastern teacher. Perhaps the teacher travels, or will travel, around the world? Maybe the controversial message of his "drive to infuriate" orthodox belief will keep the teacher on the move. Nostradamus implies that he will only rest on Diana's day, which would be Monday, the moon's day.

...(he) will take Diana's day as his day of silent rest.
He will travel far and wide in his drive to infuriate, delivering a great people from subjection.
C2 Q28

THE MAHARISHI MAHESH YOGI

233

8. THE RARE BIRD CRIES "NOW!"

Birds are free to live in the "now" forever.

...the Antichrist returns for the last time...All the Christian and infidel nations will tremble...for the space of twenty-five years. Wars and battles will be more grievous than ever. Towns, cities, citadels and all other structures will be destroyed...So many evils by Satan's prince will be committed that almost the entire world will find itself undone and desolated. Before these events many rare birds will cry in the air. "Now!" "Now!" and sometime later will vanish.

Epistle to Henry II

Nostradamus is fond of using riddles about animal life, such as the swarms of bees and the eagle used to describe Napoleon's crest of arms. The birds in this part of the *Epistle to Henry II* may be another riddle, perhaps a symbol relating to some aspect of the religious visionary who will help ward off the dire apocalyptic events described in the rest of this passage. The message may be anti-prophetic in that the key to avert disaster may come from abandoning both the past and our obsession with tomorrow. Instead, we should focus all our intelligence and energy on "NOW!" The rod or the Zen stick only "strikes" in this present moment. According to Eastern mystics, enlightenment is ever "now."

VISIONARIES OF THE NEW AGE

Twelve men have been in the forefront of a spiritual revolution during the 20th century. In this section we will consider these personalities in the light of the prophet's quatrains.

Yogananda was one of the first successful pilgrims from the East to spread the concept of spiritual union (yoga) with God through ancient meditation techniques of India. The year 1993 saw the Self-Realization Fellowship's largest convocation in its history with more than 6,000 people from 52 countries gathered in attendance at the Fellowship's ashram in Los Angeles.

235

SWAMI PARAMAHANSA YOGANANDA
1893-1952
Indian mystic, founder of the Self Realization Fellowship

Yogananda, who introduced Kriya Yoga to the West, taught that the mind and heart could be raised from a limited moral consciousness into union (yoga) with the consciousness of God. Yogananda and his disciples sometimes wore orange robes in the Eastern tradition of the seeker.

Nostradamus' references to "teaching flowers," Eastern origins, intensive travel and new ways of teaching can all be applied to this teacher. However, Yogananda's desire to synthesize the beliefs of the established religions of the world make him unlikely to be the one against whom "religions will unite." So far, Yogananda's followers have not been universally rejected by the mainstream religions.

MEHER BABA
1894-1969
Indian Sufi mystic

Meher Baba, a master of the devotional path of Sufism, taught through silence. "To speak the truth they will have closed mouths." He had come, he told the world, to sow the seeds of love in all hearts. He was opposed to of religious hierarchy, ritual and ceremony, and his motto was, "Don't worry, be happy." His followers set up "Baba Lover" centers all over the world and, in America alone, Baba's teaching attracted an estimated 6,000 disciples.

But he was a peaceful rebel: his teaching was neither inflammatory nor designed to unsettle the established religions – he was no infuriating traveler! Although his philosophy did include the concept of living in the "Now," it contains no bird symbolism, no moon aspect (symbolic or actual) and no mention of the color red, nor flames.

L. RON HUBBARD

SWAMI PRABHUPADA

1896-1978

Founder of the Hare Krishna movement

This Indian mystic came to the West to spread
the message of Krishna Consciousness. One
symbol of the consciousness is flame, represented by the shades of red. His followers, the
orange-robed Hare Krishna now familiar on
Western streets, have angered and puzzled but,
more often, amused mainstream society.

Prabhupada's teachings, although "new"
for people in the West, are based on ancient
Hindu-Vedic scriptures and he encourages his
western disciples to adopt the lifestyles prescribed by those traditional texts. Moreover,
the movement has not significantly grown in
size since the mid-1980s and, as a movement,
seems to have passed its peak.

L. RON HUBBARD

1916-1986

Author of Dianetics™, *Founder of the Church
of Scientology*

Scientology aims to help people recover spiritual health after psychic and mental traumas,
guiding them on the path towards re-estab-
lishing a "clear" mental and spiritual state. The
creator of Scientology, and his "new" religion
itself, have encountered opposition around the
world and fought many legal and political battles. His Church has an estimated five million
adherents and is considered dangerous by
many established religions. One of its symbols
is a flaming volcano (fire, red).

The ideas of the Scientology movement,
which Hubbard drew mainly from Hinamaya
Buddhism and mainstream psychology, are
basically traditional. Although his teaching is
essentially Eastern in its source, Hubbard does
not come "from the East," was not born under
Mars, has no moon connection and does not
follow an Hermetic tradition.

SWAMI PRABHUPADA

236
✳

J. KRISHNAMURTI
1891-1986
Indian philosopher and meditator

Theosophists claimed Krishnamurti to be the incarnation of Maitreya – the returned Buddha – but he publicly denied this title and dismantled the organization which had been created to spread his Messianic message. He then traveled and lectured widely in America, England, Switzerland and India for over 70 years. His concept of meditation was related to "witnessing," which he taught could offer each individual complete and absolute freedom.

Krishnamurti was opposed to any "guru" concept and any religion created in his name. As a consequence, his insights were never directed or challenging to the status quo. Since his death there has been no upsurge in proponents of his teaching.

237

KRISHNAMURTI WITH ANNIE BESANT

Krishnamurti was born in Madras but educated in England by the theosophist Annie Besant. In 1925, she proclaimed him the new Messiah.

"ABDU'L-BAHA"
1844-1921
Leader of the Bahá'í faith

The eldest son and successor of Bahá'u'lláh. Upon the death of his father, he assumed full authority for the Bahá'í movement, interpreting teachings which pave the way for a synthesis of all religions in a spiritual global village. Throughout much of his adult life, he spread the faith from its new religious seat on Mt. Carmel in Israel. Like his father, he had a prodigious correspondence with believers and inquirers around the globe, and endured long years of prison life.

He made extensive tours to Europe and America and was a prophetic advocate for a League of Nations.

Despite the fact that the Bahá'í movement and its founding masters are Eastern (Iranian), have provoked controversy and been the catalyst for the 20th-century's new openness to the interrelation of different faiths, the movement is not universally rejected as a cult by orthodox faiths, except fundamentalist Islam. There are millions of Bahá'í's the world over, and their message of peaceful rebellion through diplomacy has great merit, but the movement does not conform to all Nostradamus' eight clues.

G.I. GURDJIEFF
1877-1949
Sufi master

There could be many labels pinned on this modern mystic: enlightened one, Sufi master, devil. Gurdjieff's favorite was simply, "a teacher of dance." He was born in Alexandropol in Russian Armenia. For some 20 years, his obsession to understand life's strange and mysterious phenomena drove him to travel throughout the remotest regions of Tibet, Central Asia and the Middle East. Leaving Russia after the Bolshevik take-over, he established a communal spiritual campus outside of Paris in 1922, and later set up a Gurdjieff school in America. His teachings are a revolutionary synthesis of Sufi, Central Asian and South Asian techniques of medita-

tion and awareness training. In 1924, he disbanded the Mystery School and devoted himself to recording his teachings in three volumes: *Beelzebub's Tales to his Grandson, Meetings with Remarkable Men*, and finally, *Life is real only then when "I am."* From 1933 onward he lived almost exclusively in Paris.

His written teachings are still steady sellers and Gurdjieff study groups exist all over the world. But the generally exclusive quality of his mystery schools, notwithstanding their great merit, do not indicate any significant worldwide spread of his brand of "religiousness" to the mainstream. Nor do the orthodox religions unanimously consider his teachings a particular threat.

SWAMI SATYA SAI BABA
Born 1925
Siddi yogi

This man proclaims himself to be the reincarnation of the Moslem mystic Sai Baba (1856-1916). He is a noted miracle worker, with millions of disciples in India and a more modest following in the West. In the Hindu tradition of *sannyas* (seeker and follower) he wears orange robes and, while he currently shows little interest in traveling to the West, this may change in the future. His teachings, primarily Hindu-fundamentalist, are not highly controversial in nature. There is no Hermetic aspect to his work.

Of the living masters, Satya Sai Baba has one of the largest followings but it is mainly confined to India. Though his teachings do not constitute any threat to international authorities, an assassination attempt was made on his life in June 1993 by former disciples with connections to Hindu fundamentalists. Since 1986 no significant change in his status has taken place and there are signs that, outside India, his movement is gradually running out of momentum.

G.I. GURDJIEFF

SUN MYUNG MOON

SUN MYUNG MOON

Born 1920

Founder of Unification Church

Sun Myung Moon's Church has come into conflict with the authorities on numerous occasions and, as a result, Moon has spent a period in jail. His claim is that he is the personification of Jesus Christ in the foretold Second Coming and his last name phonetically coincides with Nostradamus' prediction that the leader will be associated with the moon.

Moon has antagonized many people with his determinations regarding links with Jesus Christ. He has also angered families and members of the general public by the apparent disruption adherence to his Church causes in the family lives of his followers. He has traveled extensively and his symbol is red. He is an arch anti-communist ("delivering a great people from subjection"). There are, however, no connections with Hermes.

Sun Myung Moon (center) with some of America's chief Christian leaders of the 1980s.

Since my last report in 1986 Moon, now released from jail, has gone significantly mainstream in the right-wing Christian fundamentalist movement in the American Republican Party. He has been embraced by mainstream evangelist leaders like Jerry Falwell. Evidence supports Moon's Unification Church as a major supporter of the Reaganites and former president George Bush. Though Moon resembles more Nostradamian clues than any other teacher examined thus far, he appears to be ever more a politically correct religious insider rather than a spiritual rebel. Also, to claim himself as the messianic successor to the founder of one of the major orthodox religions does not make him the foretold catalyst of a new religious sect.

240

OSHO

OSHO (Rajneesh Chandra Mohan)
1931-1990
Indian philosopher

A former philosophy professor from India, this man and his following have been front page news all over the world in the last few years. His red-clad followers, called *sannyasins*, have taken part in his experimental communes in India and in the United States, and political, local and religious controversy surrounds him. Osho's spontaneous daily discourses on love and meditation embrace a wide range of subjects, from sex to superconsciousness. His merciless, humor-filled insights into man's unconscious and conditioned behavior, and his uncompromisingly critical view of political and religious institutions, has earned him unanimous rejection by all orthodox religions.

In the mid-80s Osho was jailed and deported from the United States. After his departure, his attempt to go on a world religious tour met with strong political and theological pressure and he was expelled or denied entry to 21 countries in the space of only five short months.

Following his deportation from the United States, his followers allege that pressure from the Christian fundamentalist controlled Reagan government used threats to pressure other governments to keep their borders closed to the mystic. One example of this is explained in investigative reporter Max Brecher's book *A Passage to America*.

Osho was one step away from being granted permanent residency in Uruguay when, according to Brecher's highly-placed sources, the Uruguayan president Sanguinetti received a phone call from the American Ambassador Malcolm Wilkey who said, "You are a free country. You can do what you want. But you owe the United States 6 billion dollars. And this is the year for re-negotiating a new loan. If you do not make your payments on time, we will raise the interest rates."

Sanguinetti discovered that the thinly-veiled threat hinged on Uruguay granting Osho permanent residency. The Uruguayan government decided not to grant permanent residency to the mystic and he was very pressingly "invited to leave." Not long afterward Sanguinetti was invited to the Reagan White House where it was announced that Uruguay's loan would be, after all, extended, and that his country would be the location for the next round of GATT[1].

Osho's teachings lean towards Tantra, the Eastern religion related, as we have seen, to Hermetic teachings. They also contain the meditative concept of living in the present – the "Now." The Osho movement was symbolized in the 1980s by two flying birds; its current symbol is a lone swan.

And, bringing this man very close to Nostradamus' quatrain messages, the name Rajneesh means "Lord of the Full Moon," and his middle or "second to the last" name, Chandra, in his full legal name – Rajneesh Chandra Mohan – means "Moon."

Since my last entry in 1986, the movement has re-established itself in Poona, India. Osho died of heart failure in 1991. Although his followers have now ceased to wear their red colors in public, their Indian ashram teems with tens of thousands of people wearing robes in shades of maroon. Despite his death, Osho's movement continues to flourish: Erich Folath of "Stern" magazine reported in 1993 that attendance to Osho's commune is up by 40 percent from the previous year.

Osho's links to Nostradamus' eight provided clues seem to match extremely well although we do not know, of course, that the prophet intended his quatrains to imply one religious leader – there could be several.

"Many rare birds will cry in the air, 'Now! Now!'"

DA AVABHASA
Born 1939
American mystic

Da Avabhasa (previously known as "Bubba," "Da Free John" or Da Love Ananda), continues to draw a growing following. Currently resident in the Fiji Islands, this unpredictable American mystic calls himself a Master of the Heart. He teaches self-transcendence or union with God, otherwise known as Divine Consciousness. This is a Hermetic teaching which works through self-observation of each moment – "now." Da Avabhasa has suffered considerable persecution from organized religions and governments.

He is not from the East although his teachings have Eastern origins. He does, however, claim to be the reincarnation of Swami Vivekananda, an early Eastern mystic catalyst (1863-1902), who visited Europe and America in the 19th century. Da Avabhasa has traveled extensively and lived in India as a disciple prior to his self-realization. His teachings are unquestionably related to the Eastern "flame" and the symbolic Martian "red" of Eastern self-observation. There seems to be no significant relationship to "birds": the Free Diast movement uses as its symbol the Dawn Horse, a prehistoric variant of Kalki, the White Horse of Hindu prophetic tradition.

The early 90s have seen a transformation in Avabhasa's style of teaching, but its spread is limited by comparison with the burgeoning increase in the following of Maharishi Mahesh Yogi or Osho. That situation could change.

241

---

[1]GATT. General Agreements on Tariffs and Trade.

SWAMI MAHARISHI MAHESH YOGI

Born 1911

Founder of the Transcendental Meditation Movement

A former physicist, born in northern India, this leader founded the highly successful Transcendental Meditation Movement, now practiced by millions in the West as a technique for personal stress reduction and the attainment of inner tranquillity. He has also traveled widely and provoked considerable controversy, especially during the 1960s.

"TM" has tap roots in the ancient Hindu Vedic Scriptures and seems now to have been largely accepted by orthodox religions as representative of the "New Age" movements. It was taught in Western colleges until 1977.

Since 1986, the Maharishi and the TM movement continues to hold its own as a likely candidate. But the Maharishi's generally diplomatic integration with the religious mainstream does not bode well for fulfilling Nostradamus' forecast of the new Messiah being one who will shake down the dogmas of fossilized religious thought.

Swami Maharishi Yogi in London in 1961.

242

THE COMING OF MAITREYA

A VISIONARY LEAGUE TABLE								
THE CLUES	EAST	HERMES	OUTLAWED	ROSE	MARS	MOON	TRAVELS	BIRD
VISIONARIES:								
YOGANANDA	*			*			*	
MEHER BABA	*						*	
PRABHUPADA	*		*	*			*	
HUBBARD			*	*	*	*	*	
KRISHNAMURTI	*	*			*		*	
'ABDU'L-BAHA'	*	*	*				*	
GURDJIEFF	*	*	*		*		*	
SAI BABA	*			*				
MOON	*		*	*		*	*	
OSHO	*	*	*	*	*	*	*	*
DA AVABHASA		*	*	*	*		*	
MAHARISHI	*	*	*	*			*	

243

Gautama, the Buddha, taught that the Wheel of Dharma - the teaching of truth, is like a great wheel which, 2,500 years from its first revolution, runs out of momentum. The next great world teacher, who is given the name "Maitreya" meaning "friend," would appear around the year A.D. 2000 and will restore momentum and power to all those seeking after religious truth.

Nostradamus corresponds to this prophecy with the Quatrain 24 Century 4.

This quatrain predicts that organized religion will be destroyed by words of truth spoken by the "friend" through the "human flame" of a new religion. In the original French the word "sacred" is represented by the word "saint" written in the archaic form with an "ƒ" written for "s," thereby implying that the "saint" is "ƒaint" or false.

The soft voice of the sacred friend is
heard under holy ground.
The human flame shines for the
divine voice.
It will cause the earth to be stained
with the blood of the celibate monks,
And to destroy the sacred (or false)
temples of the impure ones.
C4 Q24

THE PYRAMID PROPHECIES
Constructed to be a prophecy in stone, the Great Pyramid of Cheops[1] measures the complete Adamic Age, beginning around 4000 B.C. and covering 6,000 years. Every inch of the inner passages that lead towards the king's chamber represents one year.

[1]Cheops or Khufu, second king of the fourth dynasty (c. 2650 B.C.) builder of the Great Pyramid at Gizeh, Egypt.

A measurement of the distance between the entrance and the opposing wall of the chamber sets the final period of the Adamic Age at between 1953 and 2001 - the time prophets tell us that civilization will end or the human race be transformed into a higher consciousness. It may be only an interesting coincidence that the early 1950s are an important period for several of our candidates for the new world teacher. It is said that Krishnamurti obtained his full enlightenment at that time. Osho achieved self-realisation in 1953. Meher Baba experienced one of his most intense periods of seclusion in that year, as he prepared for a new direction in his teaching.

Nostradamus dates the appearance of a new sect to correspond with the discovery of Peter's tomb.

The founding of a new sect
The bones of the great Roman will
be found...
C6 Q66

The "Roman" is St Peter whose bones, Nostradamus tells us, will be found beneath the Vatican at the time of a cataclysm. We cannot rule out the interpretation of another future trend, expressed in previous chapters, that the tomb was dated to be found in 1978, a year that saw a dramatic influx of interest in the teachings of Osho, Hubbard, Moon, and Da Avabhasa. It can be assumed, therefore, that a "new" religious sect has already appeared. The indexing of C6 Q66 could, on closer inspection, hide the biblically symbolic number 666, representing man and the Antichrist. If this is a correct interpretation Nostradamus does not make it clear whether the number stands for the new sect or is

intended as a jibe at the Roman Catholic church as un-*Christ*-tian. Certainly, all the candidates examined are, to varying degrees, considered threats to the orthodox Christian view of the universe.

MADAME BLAVATSKY
1831-1891
Psychic and prophet

Madame Blavatsky, one of the leading psychic seers of the 19th century, predicted that the Maitreya would appear in Asia around the year 1950. "We are at the close of the cycle of five thousand years of the present Aryan Kali Yuga, or Dark Age. This will be succeeded by an age of light...A new messenger of the spirit will be sent to the western nations. He is appearing in 1975." In that year the teachings of Osho were spread westwards from the subcontinent in a stream of publications. Interest in the leaders and teachings of the New Age/Human Potential Movement also accelerated suddenly from 1975 throughout the late seventies. And interest in the teachings of both Da Avabhasa and Moon, although to a more limited degree, also expanded in that period.

Nostradamus' equivalent to Blavatsky's prophecy occurs in Century 4, Quatrain 50.

Libra will see the western lands
(America) to govern,
holding the rule over the skies and the earth
No one will see the forces of Asia destroyed
Until seven hold the hierarchy in succession.
C4 Q50

The quatrain number may imply 1950 and the superpower America, represented by Libra's scales of democracy. Here again is the reference to Middle and/or far Eastern alliances being destroyed, clearly placing this event in our near future. America is portrayed in many prophetic traditions as the most fertile ground for the new religious teachings. The "seven" are the seven millennia in Nostradamus' calculations which end in A.D. 2000, which also links this quatrain to the quatrain below:

The year the great seventh number
is accomplished
Appearing at the time of the games
of slaughter,
Not far from the age of the great
millennium (2000)
when the dead will come out of their graves.
C10 Q74 *1974?*

If, before the year 2000, man can reject political power games in favor of a new awakening, the world may survive into the next millenium. Note that the indexing of the quatrains shown above and below parallels Blavatsky's predicted year for a "messenger to come to the west in 1975." For our last quotation in this chapter it thus seems appropriate to remind ourselves of the following quatrain describing the new spiritual teacher from the East, the man we are in danger of missing.

An image of calm beauty
reflects the possibility that
the Millenium may bring
blissful tranquillity rather
than terrible destruction.
It depends on us.

Long awaited he will never return.
he will appear in Asia (and be) at
home in Europe,
One who is issued from great Hermes...
C10 Q75 *1975?*

We are still not far enough down the line to draw precise conclusions as to the identity of the man or men whom Nostradamus and many other prophets saw as the instruments of the birth of the new religion. As the prophecies unfold into reality, it remains to be seen just what we can hope to enjoy or suffer in the coming "New Age."

CHAPTER SIXTEEN

BEYOND THE MILLENNIUM

THE MYSTERY AND CHALLENGE OF OUTER SPACE

The year the great seventh number accomplished,
(A.D. 2000)
It will appear at the time of the games
of slaughter,
Not far from the age of the great millennium,
When the dead will come out of their graves.

C10 Q74

During the Second Gulf War, US pilots talked about airstrikes as if they were plays in a football match. In a quatrain set for a future time, when people treat the ultimate human tragedy of war with new lows of banality, there comes a promise of hope that mankind will transcend its ancient tomb of fossilized traditions which has sustained endless cycles of war and rape and be reborn through a new millennium of peace.

246

THE MILLENNIUM OF PEACE

Nostradamus sketches out two possible future scenarios for mankind. The first is total nuclear war by 1999, the second a golden age of enlightened peace by the end of this millennium.

A global nuclear war would so devastate the earth that all life could be extinguished for ever. It is hard to see how it could lead to a golden age. In this brief chapter we will examine the prophet's predictions for generations to come after our own, the time in which our children may or may not survive. These last predictions of Nostradamus take us into the science fiction world of tomorrow.

As we saw in the last chapter, many of the world's great seers have viewed this age as a crossroads at which we need to take a leap away from our established traditional habits. Since these prophets have given us little in the way of a foundation for life in the next millen-nium, we can either take this as a warning that there will be no next millennium or, more posi-tively, as an assertion that future humans are unpredictable creatures.

George Gurdjieff, one of the 20th centu-ry's greatest mystics, said that true spiritual growth cannot begin unless each individual becomes aware that each moment could be his last. Nostradamus, warning us that we face the possibility of apocalypse, understood this well. But this fearsome concept also carries within it the idea that facing disaster is one of the best ways to learn to live in the moment. Somehow man may have presented himself with this expectation of ultimate horror in order to give himself the push needed to propel him through to a better existence.

Nostradamus states clearly that if we sur-vive our next generation we may look forward to thousands of years of earth-related history.

247
✳

GLOBAL WAR MUST NOT DESTROY OUR INHERITANCE

AGE OF AQUARIUS
A.D. 2000–4000

In astrological reckoning "The Great Year" contains 12 astrological months, each about 2,000 years long. Each astrological "month" is a human epoch and is guided by the positive and negative potentials of the sign by which it is governed. The beginnings and endings of these ages overlap by several centuries and the

Mars and the scepter will be in conjunction,
(June 21st, 2002)
A calamitous war under Cancer.
(July 1999)
A short time afterward a new king
will be anointed
Who will bring peace to the earth for
a long time.
C6 Q24

There will be peace, union and change,
Estates and offices (that were) low, (are) high
those high, (made) very low.
To prepare for a journey torments
the first (child).
War to cease, civil processes, debates.
C9 Q66

The first quatrain may be a promise of redemption for the world after the terrible natural disaster or war that brings terror down from the skies in July of 1999 (calamitous war in Cancer). The next time Jupiter (scepter) conjuncts Mars will be on 21 June 2002. The new king could be the long awaited Christian Messiah, or the Messiah of a half-a-dozen other religious traditions, who triggers Nostradamus' promised millennium of peace on earth. The second quatrain could represent any post-cataclysmic or post war period. An occult interpretation of the third lines identifies the "first" as the children of a new mankind who are about to embark on a new era of exploration of space and the inner exploration of the soul.

change-over which is now occurringn between Pisces and Aquarius, both dominated by water or the fish. The Piscean age heralded the Christian epoch. The Aquarian age, the epoch of science and humanity, began in the 18th century with the American Revolution, the industrial age and the rapid advances in science and technology. The year 2000 marks the point in the age at which both Pisces and Aquarius have equality.

Aquarius' air element, forcing mankind's imagination towards the sky and new frontiers of space, may produce radical human reform through a wider and more objective view of our planet, creating the opportunity for effective world government and a celebration of the sanctity of the individual.

In this age we may make contact with other civilizations and begin to live as members of a galactic community. Nostradamus therefore predicts a millennium of peace and wisdom, but his insights also take him further. He is able to look past this era and warns us that this Aquarian humanity, although achieving an equilibrium between the opposites of science and religion, could easily turn in on itself and become selfish. If we do not stay alert and self-aware we could, in a world of no boundaries, become intoxicated with our new freedom and sense of our own strength.

If we could see them, the future generations of the year A.D. 3000 would appear to us as gods, holding the power to create life and travel freely through the cosmos. From Nostradamus' *Epistle to King Henry II* we can interpret that, by the dawn of the Fourth Millenium after Christ, even the power of Satan could be unleashed by our inability to maintain awareness of ourselves and our essence. The definition of the word "sin" is to forget and the Aquarian motto "free from all boundaries." Without the exercise of some wisdom, this could lead us into megalomania.

AGE OF CAPRICORN
A.D. 4000–6000

*Before the moon has finished her
entire cycle (1889–2250), the Sun
(20th century) and then Saturn
(Aquarius Age) will come.
According to the Celestial signs the
reign of Saturn will come a second
time (Capricorn Age), so that all is
calculated, the world draws near to its
final death dealing cycle.*

Preface

Saturn co-rules Aquarius and rules Capricorn. The Capricorn epoch will see man either destroyed or transcending the material (earth) plane. The 38th century after Christ will see this theme influencing the dying Aquarian Age. The key words for Capricorn are "utilize" or "restrict." The human race will need to utilize all its hard-earned lessons from the past or be destroyed by its near god-like power over mind and matter. The Capricorn Age will be heralded by the physical destruction of the Earth from a cosmic source. In his preface to his son, he tells us that the world will end in A.D. 3797.

HOW THE WORLD WILL END
A.D. 3797

*A very mighty quake in the month of May,
Saturn in Capricorn. Jupiter and
Mercury in Taurus.
Venus also in Cancer, Mars in Virgo:
(At that time) hail will fall greater
than an egg.*

C10 Q67

This rare astrological configuration takes place 42 years before Nostradamus' predicted end of the world in A.D. 3797. When the sun expands into a red giant the earth will experience tremendous gravitational and climatic stresses. The reference to May could tie this quatrain in with those speaking of great earthquakes in California or the shift of the earth's axis. Rather than scaring Californians every May with prophetic cries of "Wolf!" for the next seven years interpreters might consider "the Big One" hitting LA or San Francisco not next May or May of 2000 but on some "May" over 1,800 years hence in the spring of A.D. 3755.

*For eleven more times the Moon will
not want the Sun.
Both raised and lessened in degree.
And put so low that one will sew little gold:
That after famine and plague (AIDS?) the
secret will be revealed.*

C4 Q30

This occult quatrain may be dating the number of Grand Astrological Lunar Cycles to the end of the world. If we begin counting the cycles from the life of Christ we reach the year 3894, a little over a century past the projected destruction of the earth in 3797.

In his *Preface* to his son César, the prophet gives us a detailed account of what modern astronomers believe will happen to the earth billions of years from now, when the sun exhausts its nuclear fuel and swells into a red giant, eventually devouring our planet. Nostradamus believed that Mars would continue its orbit after the death of earth. He may find grudging agreement among astronomers who believe the earth's orbit could see it devoured by the expanding sun since our dying star would not have the mass to expand further. Nostradamus believed that this would occur in 1,800 years from now.

...before the universal conflagration the world will be deluged by many floods to such heights that there will remain scarcely any land not covered by water, and this will last for so long that everything will perish except the earth itself and the races which inhabit it. Furthermore, before and after these floods many nations shall see no rains and there will fall from the sky such a great amount of fire and meteors that nothing will remain unconsumed. All this will happen a short time before the final conflagration.

Preface

250

AGE OF SAGITTARIUS
A.D. 6000-8000

The world will be approaching a great conflagration, although, according to my calculations in my prophecies, the course of time runs much further.

Epistle

Nostradamus also tells us that the human race will yet survive even this last conflagration – indicating that, by that time, we will have colonized space.

Some will assemble in Aquarius for several years, others in Cancer for a longer time.

Preface

Perhaps this is an indication of where we shall be living - orbiting the stars of the constellations of Aquarius and Cancer.

THE MYTH & THE MILLENNIUM

DEATH ERODES a man's legacy, like the waves at sunset washing over an abandoned sand castle. Time's wave destroys man's mortal monuments, returning the materials of their construction to a beach of infinite potentials, to lie at the mercy of other sand castle makers to come.

I believe Michel de Nostredame, even as he shaped his sand castle dreams, understood this and, like most men, wished to protect his memory with something lasting, constant and indestructible.

Few have succeeded so well.

By the end of his life Michel de Nostradame had established a fortress of reputation that would be the envy of any astrologer/physician-cum-heretic of those intolerant times and perfected a "sand castle" which could survive the waves of time because it could be dissolved and reformed by others.

When he dared to write a history of the future, he consciously chose to mortar his legacy with peculiar pebbles of opaque poetry and occult obscurity. The waves could not help but deposit traces of his sandy magic onto the laps of future debunkers and wanna-be prophets. The sand in his castle was gritty with myth and provocation. It has a strange hypnotic color, and possesses a continually alluring subjective gravel to pave the path of a true believer's interpretation - and to feed the abrasiveness of skeptics. If all other monuments of the man who was once Michel de Nostredame should be washed away by time, the sandy dream (or grit) of his prophecies will remain eternally enigmatic. For enigmas never die. They are fed and nurtured by our constant bewilderment, obsessive fascination, and hesitant doubt.

The enigma of prophecy attracts our romantic imaginations and we are constantly drawn to maps of our future.

The prophet Nostradamus instructed infinity's beachcombers in the proper use of "his" sandy treasure map, when he said:

"The one who is reasonable can learn from my prophecies how to find the right path to take as if he would have found footprints in the sand from someone who has gone before."

Trying to make reason of this Renaissance poet's prophetic rhymes has seen his interpreters glorified, killed, laughed off history's map, or tacked on history's footnote for pinning the donkey's tail, as it were, on an interpretation of Nostradamus that was fulfilled – whether or not the interpretation was Nostradamus' intended message.

If you try to fabricate a science from Nostradamus' quatrains, or employ objective thinking to exorcise mankind's enduring fascination and superstition about his predictions, you miss the essential legacy propagated by the prophet himself.

There is little that is scientific about Nostradamus: he is a mystic. To make reason of his rhyme is like trying to use trigonometry to compute the silent meaning between the words of Walt Whitman's poetry.

For five hundred years more they
will take notice of him.
Who was the ornament of his time.
Then suddenly a great revelation will be made
which will make people of that century
well pleased.

C3 Q94

The obscurity of the grammar makes this quatrain as much a prophecy as it could be a grammatical trap laid to expose the delusions of grandeur of most interpreters of Nostradamus to date. Nearly all scholars of the seer attribute this quatrain as some kind of edification for their particular interpretation. The key to unlocking this quatrain's message is in how one deciphers which "people" of which "century" will be "well pleased" by their finest interpreter's commentary. On the other hand, all overt or covert self-delusion aside the answer may be too obvious for the self-focused Nostradamian scholar to divine. The people and century could be that of Nostradamus' contemporaries. Counting five hundred years from the publication of *The Centuries* gives us until A.D. 2055 to ponder on whose occult understanding of Nostradamus is right.

When twenty years of the Moon's
reign have passed
Another will take up its reign for 7,000 years.
When the exhausted Sun takes up its cycle and
gathers up its days
Then my prophecy and threats will
be accomplished

C1 Q48

The Nostradamus controversy is approaching 450 years-in-running. The quatrains above give us two future time-tracks for the length of the prophet's legacy. Roussat believes the astrological lunar cycle mentioned above is that of 1535 to 1889. Twenty years after 1535 gives us *The Centuries* publication date, 1555. This could extend his chronicle of human history beyond the ninth millennium.

THE BEAUTY OF THE "CELESTIAL ROUND"

The poetry of prophecy is not objective. But we do not live solely by objectivity, as anyone who has not lost their innocence or their wonder at the moment-to-moment mystery of being, or of non-being, in a Universe understands.

What is clearly objective is the fact that Nostradamus makes a conscious effort to fashion his own obscurity. For centuries to come we may continue to ask why his meaning is so nebulous; by so doing, we continue to satisfy the only man, long departed, who knows the objective answer.

The prophet's science of obscurity compels this interpreter, like all interpreters before and after him, to offer his own theory about the prophet's essential motivation for writing his history of the future: I believe Nostradamus wished to keep alive a dialogue about tomorrow and destiny.

As long as human beings are provoked into thinking about their tomorrow, they may find the courage to change it "today."

ACKNOWLEDGEMENTS

ABBREVIATIONS: R = RIGHT; L = LEFT; AB = ABOVE; B = BELOW; C = CENTER

Pictures were reproduced by kind permission of:

ASSOCIATED PRESS: ABC NEWS/AP, page 9
AP/GULNARA SAMOILOVA, page 185
AP/CHAO SOI CHEONG, page 202

THE BRIDGEMAN ART LIBRARY /FORBES MAGAZINE, NEW YORK: page 86
THE BRIDGEMAN ART LIBRARY, LONDON/CHATEAU DE VERSAILLES: pages 80, 85

CORBIS: pages 152, 175, 186, 188, 190, 191, 203, 206, 207, 209, 211, 218, 220

CORBIS/STOCKMARKET: page 201

E.T. ARCHIVE: pages 26, 66, 72-3, 76, 87, 97, 133
E.T. ARCHIVE/CORRER MUSEUM, Venice: page 53
E.T. ARCHIVE/GALLERIA ESTENSE, Modena: page 14
E.T. ARCHIVE/LOUVRE: page 94
E.T. ARCHIVE/MUSEE MALMAISON: page 81
E.T. ARCHIVE/MUSEE DE VERSAILLES: page 90
E.T. ARCHIVE/NATIONAL MARITIME MUSEUM: page 54
E.T. ARCHIVE/TATE GALLERY: pages 82-3
E.T. ARCHIVE/TURKISH & ISLAMIC ART MUSEUM, Istanbul: page 54

MARY EVANS PICTURE LIBRARY: pages 17, 21(L), 21(R), 24, 33, 45, 47, 50, 52, 57, 58, 59(T), 59(B), 59(R), 61(TL), 61(TR), 61(C), 61(BL), 63, 68, 69, 71, 78, 79, 84(TL), 84(BR), 89, 95, 111, 144, 170

HULTON DEUTSCH COLLECTION LTD: pages 11, 23, 30, 47, 61, 64, 74, 75, 81(BR), 84(BL), 98, 99, 100, 103(T), 103(B), 104, 108, 109, 110, 111, 114, 115, 116, 118-19, 120(L), 120(R), 121(T), 121(B), 122, 123, 127, 131, 132, 133, 135(T), 135(B), 138, 139, 141, 144, 148, 157, 160, 166, 167, 169, 170, 232, 236, 237, 238, 242

IMAGES COLOUR LIBRARY: pages 192, 234, 245, 246, 247, 252

MICHAEL JENNER: page 155

NASA: pages 129, 142

POPPERFOTO: pages 29, 102;
SERGIEI KARPUKHIN/REUTER/POPPERFOTO: page 213

REX FEATURES: pages 6, 10, 55, 102(L), 105, 107, 117, 126, 128, 130, 134, 136, 145, 146, 147, 149, 150, 151, 152, 153, 156, 158, 159, 161, 162-3, 164, 165, 168, 172, 175, 179, 181, 182, 194, 195, 196, 202, 214, 219, 222, 225, 233, 236, 239

SYNDICATION INTERNATIONAL: page 234

ROGER-VIOLLET, PARIS: pages 2-3, 13, 22-3, 29(C), 29(R), 49, 51, 67, 77, 92, 93, 96, 106, 112, 132

OSHO INTERNATIONAL FOUNDATION: page 240

253

INDEX